Crossroads

In this ambitious study, Anna K. Boucher and Justin Gest present a unique analysis of immigration governance across thirty countries. Relying on a database of immigration demographics in the world's most important destinations, they present a novel taxonomy and an analysis of what drives different approaches to immigration policy over space and time. In an era defined by inequality, populism, and fears of international terrorism, they find that governments are converging toward a "Market Model" that seeks immigrants for short-term labor with fewer outlets to citizenship – an approach that resembles the increasingly contingent nature of labor markets worldwide.

Anna K. Boucher is Senior Lecturer in Public Policy and Political Science at the University of Sydney. She is the author of *Gender, Migration, and the Global Race for Talent* and numerous peer-reviewed articles. She is the holder of major research grants, including from the Australian Research Council. She frequently reports to governmental reviews on immigration matters and comments in the media on migration topics, including for the BBC, *The Guardian*, *Die Zeit*, *The Australian Financial Review*, and the Australian Broadcasting Corporation. In 2007, she co-founded the Migration Studies Unit at the London School of Economics.

Justin Gest is Assistant Professor of Public Policy at George Mason University's Schar School of Policy and Government. He is the author of *The New Minority: White Working Class Politics in an Age of Immigration and Inequality* and *Apart: Alienated and Engaged Muslims in the West*. He has authored many peer-reviewed articles appearing in journals including *Comparative Political Studies*, *Ethnic and Racial Studies*, and the *International Migration Review*, and has provided analysis for numerous news organizations including the BBC, CNN, *The Guardian*, NPR, Politico, Reuters, and *The Washington Post*. In 2007, he co-founded the Migration Studies Unit at the London School of Economics.

Crossroads

Comparative Immigration Regimes in a World of Demographic Change

ANNA K. BOUCHER
University of Sydney

JUSTIN GEST
George Mason University

CAMBRIDGE
UNIVERSITY PRESS

CAMBRIDGE
UNIVERSITY PRESS

University Printing House, Cambridge CB2 8BS, United Kingdom

One Liberty Plaza, 20th Floor, New York, NY 10006, USA

477 Williamstown Road, Port Melbourne, VIC 3207, Australia

314–321, 3rd Floor, Plot 3, Splendor Forum, Jasola District Centre, New Delhi – 110025, India

79 Anson Road, #06-04/06, Singapore 079906

Cambridge University Press is part of the University of Cambridge.

It furthers the University's mission by disseminating knowledge in the pursuit of education, learning, and research at the highest international levels of excellence.

www.cambridge.org
Information on this title: www.cambridge.org/9781107129597
DOI: 10.1017/9781316416631

© Anna K. Boucher and Justin Gest 2018

First published 2018

Printed in the United States of America by Sheridan Books, Inc.

A catalogue record for this publication is available from the British Library.

ISBN 978-1-107-12959-7 Hardback
ISBN 978-1-107-57005-4 Paperback

Contents

Figures

Tables

Preface

The Start of a Conversation

This book starts a conversation.

It is a conversation about how countries around the world vary in their migration demographic outcomes. It is a conversation about which countries' profiles are similar and which are exceptional. It is a conversation about what drives immigration regimes and demographic trends across these different countries. And ultimately, it is a conversation that we – as immigration researchers – wanted to have with each other, but found impossible given the current state of the field.

We asked ourselves, "What information would we need in order to pursue such a conversation?" And ultimately, we needed concepts and data that simply did not exist or which existed but had not been adequately collated and compiled. We needed a comprehensive conceptualization of an immigration regime. We needed an enumeration of the different dimensions of an immigration regime. We needed a way to measure these dimensions in a systematic way across space and time. We needed a taxonomy that grouped different regimes according to their similarities.

These are substantial goals. And after initially wrestling with the available concepts and data, we decided more needed to be developed. Accordingly, in this book we offer a number of contributions:

(1) We construct a new conceptualization of what constitutes an immigration regime and how one might measure its outcomes in a valid and reliable manner across countries and time.

(2) We build a database measuring these dimensions and their constitutive metrics for fifty countries around the world. After five years of data collection and assembly, this database brings together available data from international institutions and data from independent

reports, national statistics agencies, and newspaper reports, which
we standardize to United Nations and OECD measurements.

(3) Using this first-of-its-kind, standardized, statistical database, we
produce a taxonomy of thirty countries' immigration regimes for
which we have full data across all dimensions.

(4) Finally, we undertake an early analysis of this new demographic
data-derived taxonomy that seeks to understand what drives immigration regimes and governance.

By the end of this book, the conversation is far from over. Rather, it can
now get started – or resume – with access to greater information. Indeed,
with this book, we hope to provide the tools and data that will permit
others to carry on this conversation with newer data and with a broader
group of people. We make an initial attempt at analysis based on our conceptual development and data collection. However, in scope, this book
sets up others to expand the available data according to universal standards and definitions, and to undertake a more extensive analysis that
incorporates new variables and other phenomena related to the migration of people around the world.

Acknowledgments

A book with global scope relied upon a truly global network of support. Our colleagues, advisors, and research assistants spanned as many countries as we covered in our data collection. Indeed, our co-authoring partnership depended upon strong internet connections and stronger relationships that crossed the earth.

We conceived the book in 2010 when we were newly minted lecturers at the University of Sydney and Harvard University, respectively. Having concluded over multiple video calls that we would like to see a big-picture book on migration regimes worldwide, we embarked on what turned out to be a lengthy and, at times, challenging journey. Beyond our perseverance and partnership, it was made possible by countless pieces of guidance, feedback, and information from scores of colleagues, friends, and family members.

We are especially indebted to the volunteer attendees at two book workshops we held at George Mason University and the City University of New York in April 2016: Jeremy Ferwerda, Phil Kasinitz, Susan Martin, John Mollenkopf, Maggie Peters, Marty Schain, Audrey Singer, and Matt Wright.

We sincerely thank a number of colleagues in the interdisciplinary field of migration research. These include many members of the American Political Science Association (APSA) Migration and Citizenship Section: Irene Bloemraad, Katrina Burgess, Antje Ellerman, Gary Freeman, Terri Givens, Sara Wallace Goodman, Jim Hollifield, Rey Koslowski, Gallya Lahav, Willem Maas, Jeannette Money, Jill Stein, and

Maarten Vink. We have also received helpful feedback from Dovelyn Agunias, Alex Aleinikoff, Lora Berg, Hamutal Bernstein, Spencer Boyer, Lucie Cerna, Rafaela Dancygier, Sarah de Lange, Feline Freier, Aubrey Grant, Dominik Hangartner, David Held, Dan Hopkins, Konrad Kalicki, Gregory Maniatis, Henrietta Moore, Caglar Özden, Demetri Papademetriou, Dilip Ratha, Catherine Smith, Joo-Cheong Tham, Carlton Yearwood, Reymundo Zambrano, Yang-Yang Zhou, and the various discussants who offered feedback about our research at conferences over the years.

We learned an enormous amount from our colleagues as part of the International Migration Policy And Law Analysis (IMPALA) Database consortium: Michel Beine, Brian Burgoon, Mary Crock, Michael Hiscox, Pat McGovern, Hillel Rapoport, Joep Schaper, and Eiko Thielemann. In many ways, this book was in response to our work together.

We also want to thank our colleagues who are or were our contemporaries at our respective institutions, who offered generous advice on argument, structure, presentation, and method. At the University of Sydney: Stephen Castles, Ben Goldsmith, Ryan Griffiths, John Keane, Allan McConnell, Pippa Norris, Nicola Piper, Simon Tormey, Ariadne Vromen, Colin Wight, and Chris Wright. At Harvard University: Bart Bonikowsky, Amy Catalinac, Ryan Enos, Noah Feldman, Filiz Garip, Noam Gidron, Peter Hall, Ben Herzog, Jennifer Hochschild, Michèle Lamont, Steve Levitsky, Shawn Ling Ramirez, Noora Lori, Gwyneth McClendon, Rich Nielsen, Gerry Neuman, Hilary Rantisi, Jared Schachner, Shauna Shames, Arthur Spirling, Jessica Tollette, Sid Verba, Mary Waters, and Daniel Ziblatt. At George Mason University: Katrin Anacker, Terry Clower, Des Dinan, Jim Finkelstein, Jack Goldstone, Bassam Haddad, David Hart, Naoru Koizumi, Mariely López-Santana, Peter Mandaville, Jerry Mayer, Jim Pfiffner, Mark Rozell, Bill Schneider, Louise Shelley, Jen Victor, Janine Wedel, and Jim Witte.

Experts within international organizations have been very helpful in providing data and insights on interpretation, in particular the OECD's Migration Section former head, Georges Lemaître, Thomas Liebig, Cecile Thoreau and the United Nations' Hania Zlotnik and Bela Hovy. The GLLM provided important Gulf country data and we thank Francoise De Bel-Air for her assistance in interpreting this information. We are very grateful to Tom Janoski for sharing the cross-national naturalization data that he has collected since his 2010 book. In countries where we undertook original data collection the following government officials and external experts were very important. For the Russian Federation: Kirill Boychenko, Tim Colton, and Esther Tetruashvili. In Kuwait: Khalid

AlMuhailan, Weam Al Othman, and Hilary Rantisi. In South Africa, we would like to thank Mark Addleson and Loren Landau for their assistance. In interpreting the Singapore data, Leong Chang Hoong. In Chile, Rodolfo Honorato Torrealba. In China, Pang Lihua and in Singapore, Brenda Yeoh and Leong Chan Hoong.

We have benefited from the assistance of some very talented research assistants and country experts, who have gone on to do wonderful things in their own research and careers: Andrea Ortiz, Andrew Butters, Colin Brown, Sam Clark, Max Dikkers, Emma Franklin, Tarsha Gavan, Eda Gunaydin, Ting Luo, Nadica Pavlovska, Tyler Reny, Aaron Roper, Ari Rubin, Yang Shen, Maria Teresa Vanikiotis, Megan Eloise Vincent, Alexander Wang, Laila Parada Worby, and Jin Yunan.

We are grateful to our editors at Cambridge University Press, Lew Bateman and Robert Dreesen, for their support and shepherding of our manuscript. We also acknowledge the use of content from our 2015 article, "Migration Studies at a Crossroads: A Critique of Immigration Regime Typologies" in *Migration Studies*, 3(2) pages 182–198, published by Oxford University Press.

Our research has been generously supported by the following sources: the Kuwait Foundation for the Advancement of Science, through the Middle East Initiative and Belfer Center for Science and International Affairs at the Harvard Kennedy School; Harvard University's Institute for Quantitative Social Science; Harvard University's Center for European Studies; the Institute for Social Sciences and the School of Social and Political Sciences at the University of Sydney; and a Data Visualisation Grant from the Faculty of Arts and Social Sciences at the University of Sydney. We also appreciate the interest and assistance of Jeff Blossom, Giovanni Zambotti, Devika Kakkar, and Fei Carnes from Harvard University's Center for Geographic Analysis, who helped prepare the visualizations and maps on the book's website: crossroads.earth.

We thank our families for their backing: Robert Boucher for his unpaid proofreading and data-checking; Gail, Max, Darren, Rebecca, and Phillip Gest for their enthusiasm and for giving Anna refuge in Los Angeles during Hurricane Isaac. Most profoundly, we would like to thank our spouses, Kare and Monika, who have tolerated our weekly calls at ridiculously anti-social hours and our demands for work trips with complex stop-over arrangements. This book is dedicated to our new babies, now toddlers, who were both born over the period we wrote this book: Jasper and Valentina.

Finally, we would like to thank each other: Justin for his optimistic big-picture thinking and vision; and Anna for her exceptional diligence and attention to detail. We laughed, we clashed, we confided, we kvetched, but ultimately, we thoroughly enjoyed our time working together.

To view data maps, visualizations, and related content, please visit the book's companion website: crossroads.earth.

I

The Liberal Model and the Market Model

MIGRATION AT A CROSSROADS

For much of world history, human migration[1] was largely unregulated. Since antiquity, people have moved from place to place, crossing frontiers in search of resources, trade, or refuge. However, the obstacles to individual movement were historically social and logistic, rather than legal. When societies sought new sources of labor for expansion, colonization, or trade, they attained them through conquest or slavery. As territorial states developed over time, as transportation became faster and more accessible, and as resource disparities broadened, desirable destinations have each been confronted with the need to manage the growth and composition of their populations. This process continues into the present day, when societies that were once considered to be on the world's periphery now face far greater numbers of prospective voluntary and involuntary immigrants and a stronger impetus to govern their entry and settlement.

---

[1] In this book, we employ a demographic definition of an international migrant as employed by the United Nations and OECD: a person residing outside of the country of his or her birth. This includes temporary migrants, who hold visas permitting a period of residence, often allow renewals, and sometimes have pathways to permanent migration or citizenship. However, this does not include tourists and others who are not permitted to reside or work in the destination state for under three months (UNPD 2008: 1).

It is worth underscoring that this book is exclusively concerned with international migration, as opposed to internal migration. These are ultimately different phenomena that merit separate treatment, though they have been considered together by a collection of geographers and anthropologists in the past (see Skeldon 2006). Internal migrants only alter local and regional socio-political trends and, as most states do not monitor sub-national borders, movement is typically unregulated and difficult to measure.

The rise of international human rights norms around migration in the second half of the twentieth century has complicated the transactional nature of migration evident in earlier periods. Finland's Foreign Minister Erkki Tuomioja (2004) discussed the humanity of immigration when addressing his population's desire for "foreign labor" during Finland's economic boom:

It would not really be "labour" we would be bringing into the country, but human beings who want to move to Finland for a variety of reasons and for shorter or longer periods of time. And these human beings may well have children and spouses they wish to bring with them. People have a whole spectrum of expectations and needs, also outside the world of work. They should not be seen only as somebody who fills the slots in labor markets but also as somebody who enhances Finnish society as a whole.

The extent to which countries address these "expectations and needs" – as they pertain to migrants' duration of stay, reunification with family members, and citizenship – drive the differences between them. In this book, we catalogue these differences and identify various types of immigration regimes. And we see how, as migrants pursue opportunities in new destination societies with alternative forms of governance, the national regimes regulating admission and naturalization are evolving in different ways.

One prominent evolution took place amidst the liberal spirit that permeated the afterglow at the end of the Cold War. The collapse of old boundaries and the opening of new economies facilitated the global movement of people, goods, and money with new intensity and breadth during the 1990s. Throughout this period of globalization, there was a sense that immigration regimes would also liberalize. Outside of some areas of Eastern Europe, immigrant stocks rose across the European continent, Naturalization Rates spiked in the world's primary destinations, and the birth of the internet rendered a sense that all states and peoples would soon be connected and integrated. Scholars like Gary Freeman (1995) and Christian Joppke (1999; 2005a; 2005b) argued that the world was converging toward an increasingly open, liberal, and non-discriminatory immigration system, even if countries retained distinctive models. Over time, these observers implied, migration countries

---

International migration requires individuals to register and adapt to a new society and system. In a similar spirit, we choose not to examine sub-national forms of governance and their outcomes. In all states, sub-national bodies ultimately submit to the authority of the national government in controlling the admission and settlement of international immigrants, and while sub-national governments are competing with national authority and filling gaps in legislative control, this activity does not determine admissions.

would converge to a "Liberal" Model akin to those of settler states, characterized by permanent and equal incorporation of immigrants into national communities.

However, during the same period, an alternative reality was emerging – one that saw the facilitation of global movement as an economic opportunity to be exploited, and a risk to the security of national identity and sovereignty. Beginning in the 1960s but accelerating in the 1990s, the Gulf Arab states of Bahrain, Kuwait, Oman, Qatar, Saudi Arabia, and the United Arab Emirates responded with a vision of governance that views migrants as guests who are expected to quietly execute their work, quarantine themselves from society, and otherwise return to their country of origin. In many ways, this *kafala* system, under which migrants are treated as human capital controlled by their employer, is similar to the immigration regime of Singapore, which has issued temporary work permits since the 1970s. Under the terms of these permits, low-skilled immigrants to the Southeast Asian city-state must repatriate if their employment is terminated or should they become pregnant. If they wish to marry a Singaporean national, they must receive special government approval. Immigrants are subject to regular medical tests and their employers must post sizable bonds and purchase insurance policies in case of accidents or illness (Yeoh and Lin 2012). These low-skilled workers are, in sum, economic resources to be managed.

While this variation in immigration regimes is reflected in a growing range of social science analysis, it has not yet been adequately understood in a unified, systematic, and comprehensive typology of national immigration regimes. In short, researchers know little about how immigration regimes differ – a descriptive question – or why different countries govern human migration the ways they do – an explanatory question. International migration and its scientific examination have therefore reached a crossroads. A principal reason is that we lack a standardized means of measuring and classifying immigration regimes. In response to this gap, this book examines fifty countries' demographic immigration outcomes, derives a typology of immigration regimes for thirty countries for which complete data are available, and attempts to explain what drives the variation in outcomes across borders.

A NEW TAXONOMY OF IMMIGRATION REGIMES

We define an immigration regime as the migration policies and their outcomes that collectively reflect the admission and settlement of foreign-born people over time. This encompasses both the array of policies adopted by states and the outcomes of those policies (as implemented) that relate to the movement of people into and out of national territory. They are generated both by regulatory processes, but also by a range of powerful interests who enforce policies, contest policies, and sometimes evade policies.[2]

Across the chapters of this book, we develop a number of new concepts in the measurement of migration demographic outcomes, and then assemble these to create a multidimensional concept of immigration regimes that reflects the approaches that immigration destination states take to the governance of people's admission and citizenship. We do so across a much larger number of countries than earlier research, incorporating data from outside the Organisation for Economic Cooperation and Development (OECD) in light of the growing profiles of these countries as migrant destinations. Due to limitations on the availability of data across this exceptional variety of countries, we focus our analysis on a single year of data: 2011, as this is the year for which we have the most available data across the broadest array of countries. However, we also discuss trends across time when they are known, and our method of analysis is replicable across any number of years and countries, should new data be collected or released.

Based on these concepts, we create a taxonomy – a system of classification – that features seven types of immigration regimes across the primary destination states we examine for the thirty countries for which we have full data:

(1) **Neoliberal Regimes** (Australia, Canada, New Zealand, and the United Kingdom) – many of which began as settler states – feature high levels of temporary migration, a strong labor admissions focus, and elevated Naturalization Rates.

(2) **Humanitarian Regimes** (Finland, Sweden, and the United States) most reflect the legacy and influence of historic settler state models

---

[2] This definition applies earlier definitions of "regimes" related to other spheres of governance, largely in the international sphere. Krasner (1982: 185) defines regimes as sets of "principles, norms, rules, and decision-making procedures around which actor expectations converge in a given issue-area." More pertinent to this study, Kratochwil and Ruggie (1997: 32) focus on nation states and define regimes as "governing arrangements constructed by states to coordinate their expectations and organize aspects of international behavior in various issue areas." These authors clarify that regimes include "a normative element, state practice and organizational roles." We expand this definition beyond a focus on institutions by incorporating a consideration of migration demographic outcomes.

in North America and Oceania, which sustained significant flows under diverse visa types, with high rates of naturalization – even though only the United States is actually one of these historic settler states.

(3) **Extra-Union Regimes** (Belgium, France, Ireland, Italy, Portugal, and Spain) are characterized by moderate levels of free movement inside the European Union, a moderately diverse admissions program, and low levels of naturalization.

(4) **Intra-Union Regimes** (Austria, Denmark, Germany, the Netherlands, Norway, and Switzerland) have elevated levels of free movement from member states of supranational unions (e.g. the European Union), limiting flows under other visa types and suppressing demand for citizenship.

(5) **Kafala Regimes** (Bahrain, Kuwait, Oman, and Saudi Arabia) are characterized by exceptionally high migrant flows, and an exclusive focus on temporary labor admissions with few outlets to citizenship.

(6) **Quasi-Kafala Regimes** (China, Russia, and Singapore) follow the economic efficiency of Kafala Regimes but with significantly lower migrant flow levels.

(7) **Constrained Regimes** (Brazil, Japan, Mexico, and South Korea) feature lower flow levels, less economically focused admissions, and – with the exception of Brazil – low Naturalization Rates.

THE MARKET MODEL

Examining this taxonomy and its underpinning demographic data more critically, we see that the world's most prominent migration destinations no longer appear especially influenced by the policies of the settler states of yesteryear. Indeed, today, even some of the most liberal settler states like Australia and Canada no longer look much like settler states at all, with some of the highest rates of temporary immigration as a percentage of annual migrant flows among the world's democracies and dominant emphases on labor. Rather, the countries in this study quite generally exhibit elevated numbers of temporary migrants, a focus on labor migration via economic visas or, more commonly, free movement agreements, forms of tacitly ethnicity-based selection, and relatively low levels of naturalization. Relative to the openness and permanence of Freeman and Joppke's "Liberal" Model, this emerging approach resembles the increasingly contingent nature of labor markets worldwide.

This approach demonstrates states' countervailing acknowledgment of human capital needs and their reluctance to make permanent commitments to newcomers. It reflects new premiums placed on short-term, flexible hiring in a world economy of greater expedience and less concern with the rights and stability of people's lives. And it appeals to societies that have experienced nativist and xenophobic backlashes to the way that global migration dilutes demographic homogeneity and national heritage. In economically unstable times characterized by public concern over various threats to national security, the Market Model permits governments to have it both ways – effectively sanitizing globalization from its purported ills while enjoying the economic benefits that it brings.

This approach, which we call the Market Model, is characterized by a more market-oriented approach to immigration selection and regulation. As it relates to the distribution of entry visas, while economic migration selection does not predominate in all states, most countries rhetorically preference either economic immigration or a combination of economic and free-movement-based entry. At the same time, many regimes have attempted to reduce humanitarian and family-based immigration, which implies permanent settlement and is viewed as less economically robust than these other streams, although with mixed effectiveness. Simultaneously, we observe across most of the studied countries a focus on temporary labor and attempts by governments to reduce opportunities for economic migrants to remain on an indefinite basis. This reflects governments' desire to enjoy the economic benefits of immigration without open acceptance of the societal and demographic transformations that might result. This is particularly the case in non-democratic countries, where rates of temporary immigration are especially high. Finally, with regard to Naturalization Rates, we observe that Naturalization Rates of new migrants have trended downward over the last two decades. More restrictive or stringent integration policies also reinforce these changes in naturalization. Collectively, the effect of these policies is to shift immigration regimes toward a more transactional style of immigration governance.

It is this context that made Germany's generous response to the influx of over one million asylum seekers from Syria, Iraq, and Afghanistan since 2015 appear so counterintuitive. Historically, Germany had attempted to execute this Market Model even as other countries were liberalizing through the country's *gastarbeiter* (guest worker) program, in which immigrants, particularly Turks and Southern Europeans, were admitted on short-term labor visas. Germans have since focused their admissions on immigrants from within the European Union – which could be viewed as an implicit form of ethnicity-based selection (Favell 2008: 701). Discomfort and uproar in response to the Germans' unexpected accommodation of the largely Muslim asylum seekers has fueled the rise of xenophobic politics across other European states like Austria, France, Switzerland, and the United Kingdom, deepening their commitment to Market Model policies in the future and undermining their commitment to the European Union and free movement within it.

WHAT DRIVES IMMIGRATION REGIMES?

After presenting our new migration taxonomy in Chapter 7, in Chapter 8 we seek to understand the central reasons for this local variation and the overarching convergence toward the Market Model. We present a segmented theory of regime development, which demonstrates different explanatory pathways for different regime clusters. In short, we reject a single grand narrative for the variation in regime clusters, instead arguing that there are different pathways to migration outcomes that depend on the broader context of each regime's environment and history. We then argue that the subtle shift to a Market Model across these seven clusters is influenced by three main factors: first, the greater adoption of neoliberal economic models that has permeated labor standards, trade, financial markets, and now immigration governance globally; second, voting publics' increasing xenophobia and protectionism (Gest 2016); and third, politicians' rhetorical attempts to connect immigration with pervasive paranoia about international terrorism (Gest 2010).

BOOK OVERVIEW

Chapter 2 explains why it is important to develop a rigorous means of classifying immigration regimes. We then explore existing systems of classification and their limitations. We emphasize three primary limitations: first, a heavy focus on Western democracies that excludes prominent, new immigration destinations; second, the unclear indicators behind existing systems of classification; and third, these systems' inability to account for the relationship between admissions and citizenship policies. In response, we propose our approach, which examines a broader variety of countries, a variety of admissions and citizenship outcome dimensions, and is based on a set of demographic indicators that are replicable and more comprehensive. We outline each of these indicators and then conclude by explaining the basis of our case selection – a blend of convenience and consideration of immigrant stock levels.

Chapter 3 situates our focus on immigration regimes and their determinants within a historical context. While debates continue over the relative size of contemporary migration flows compared with those of the late nineteenth century (Hatton and Williamson 2008; cf. Castles and Miller 2009: 2), it is clear that there are several distinctive features to current migration trends, when compared with an earlier period. In this chapter, we sketch the comparative history of immigration regimes across countries and regions – tracing the move from a relatively laissez-faire approach to immigration in the late nineteenth century based mainly on economic factors, to the emergence of passports and visa categories, to the rise of race-based selection that sought to control the extent to which migrant origins are concentrated in certain regions or source countries. We elaborate about the regulation of migrant origins, and then discuss the modern shift toward organized family, economic, and free-movement-based categories. Linked to the empirical chapters that follow, we also consider the implications of rising centers of economic power – China, Brazil, and the Gulf states – on North–South migration dynamics and immigration regime variation more broadly. In so doing, we account for enduring explanations for the contemporary trends that we analyze.

We then begin a three-chapter examination of the three categories of outcomes that we argue comprise immigration regimes. Chapter 4 considers a dimension of immigration outcomes that is central to policymakers, but often overlooked within academic immigration scholarship: the "Visa Mix" – the relative contribution of economic, humanitarian, and family migration to immigration flows. As noted, in light of claims of a shift toward skilled immigration (Doomernik et al. 2009), it is important to consider the extent to which immigration regimes demonstrate an economic focus in their actual immigration outcomes. Why some states have more economically dominated immigration outcomes than others is of central relevance in an age of global competition for "the best and the brightest" (Boucher 2016). Before we can answer this explanatory question, it is necessary to map the variation in the Visa Mix across states. Non-democracies may be more able to tilt migration outcomes toward economic migration, in light of the democratic imperative to confer family reunification rights to accompanying family members. Given the central importance of family migration for women's migratory paths (Boyd and Pikkov 2004), the trends mapped in this chapter are essential for assessing the gender dimensions of immigration regimes. Finally, it is necessary to consider how well these patterns are influenced by rules around free movement of either a bilateral or a multilateral quality.

Chapter 5 considers the percentage of total immigration that is economic and temporary in nature, which we refer to as the "Temporary Ratio." For instance, in 2008, 2.3 million temporary migrant workers entered OECD countries, compared with 1.5 million permanent migrant workers (OECD 2010: 30). Temporary migration typically places conditions on the residency period and work rights of migrants. Given the increasing premium placed on flexible workforces, especially since the global financial crisis began in 2007, this ratio may grow more exaggerated as governments seek to satisfy employer demand for labor and assuage public xenophobia by rendering migrants' status more contingent. After setting out our approach to defining the Temporary Ratio, this chapter assesses the extent of temporary economic migration in our country cases.

Chapter 6 considers the Naturalization Rate of immigrants. Some states are comprised almost entirely of people of national birth (such as North Korea, Cuba, and Vietnam). Others are comprised largely of people who were foreign-born (such as Qatar, the United Arab Emirates, and Kuwait). Meanwhile, the rest of the cases we examine are somewhere in between these two extremes. Within this variation, there is also variation in how much states facilitate access to national citizenship. We ask what percentage of immigrants is naturalized and we consider the implications of different policy approaches to naturalization. This chapter also confronts confounding trends such as where states with high proportionate migrant stocks have low rates of naturalization, such as in the Gulf states.

Chapter 7 aggregates values from the three dimensions of immigration regimes: Visa Mix, Temporary Ratio, and Naturalization Rates. Using an unsupervised k-means clustering algorithm, this chapter identifies seven clusters in the universe of immigration regimes for our global selection of countries and five similar regimes in the selection of OECD countries we consider. This yields a taxonomy of immigration regimes, grounded in the demographic data we collect. We examine the attributes of each taxonomic group, and discuss the methods we use to corroborate its structure. Notwithstanding this variation, across all regimes, we observe a move toward a Market Model, characterized by either increased permanent economic or free movement migration, a focus on temporary economic visas and a gradual reduction in naturalization over time. The emergence of this model stands in contrast to early expectations of a movement toward a more open Liberal Model that draws upon the settler state experience.

Chapter 8 addresses the question of what explains the regime cluster variation that we outline in Chapter 7. We find that no single theory applies across all regime clusters. Rather, we propose a segmented theory to best address the trends that emerge. So while the Kafala Regimes are united by a high reliance on resource welfare and centrally controlled economics, in other clusters, the legacies of *Pax Britannica* or other colonial empires appear more important. In yet other regimes, a confluence of factors is important, and for both the Quasi-Kafala and Kafala Regimes, the autocratic status of the governments appears to be central.

A Methodological Appendix provides an overview of the key research methods employed in the monograph. We discuss and collate the sources of our data, and clarify any assumptions we make in our data collection and analysis.

2

The Classification of Immigration Regimes

It does not require a database such as ours for observers to appreciate
the diversity of migration outcomes and their migration policies around
the world. These differences are conditioned by historical legacies, cultural norms, institutional constraints, popular will, the character of sending states, and economic forces. Some earlier researchers contend that
the diversity of migration systems as well as methodological approaches
within migration studies militates against the development of grand typologies or theories of migration (e.g. Portes 1997; Freeman 2006; Messina
2007; Alba and Foner 2015). Clearly, any attempt to develop large-scale
cross-national comparisons will face the classic trade-off between parsimony and complexity.

Notwithstanding these challenges, in this chapter, we argue that there
are empirical, theoretical, and practical policy reasons for attempting to
describe and understand immigration regimes across a large number of
countries. We critically review attempts to classify immigration-related
policy regimes and note their limited geographic coverage, often unclear
indicators, and narrow focus on specific policy dimensions. Finally, we
outline an alternative approach based on the analysis of standardized
immigration demographic data, collected from a wide range of countries
across admission and naturalization outcomes. This approach forms the
foundation of our investigation.

WHY DO WE NEED TO CLASSIFY IMMIGRATION REGIMES?

Without a systematic, comprehensive classification of immigration
regimes, we simply cannot address a number of important questions and
topics in social science and migration studies:

*How do countries differ across key demographic dimensions of migra-
tion? Is there greater variation between classified types or within them?*
Understanding how, if at all, countries are clustered together across different dimensions of migration outcomes also assists in developing a more
generalized understanding of patterns in migration. It also provides a
more rigorous basis for case selection in future studies that examine specific cases, as analysts could more accurately identify "exemplar" cases of
particular types of countries (George and Bennett 2005: 251–64).

*What is the nature of the relationship between different aspects of the
immigration process, including immigrant selection and naturalization?*
Consideration of the interrelationship between these various stages of
the migration experience is underexplored. While some such as Tomas
Hammar (1985) have identified a clear bifurcation between admission
and integration, for others, the two are interconnected in important
ways and effectively amount to an immigration–integration "nexus" (see
Meyers 2004; Freeman 2006: 228). Bader (2007: 875–7) acknowledges
emerging demand for the "construction of patterns" that demonstrate
"some minimal internal coherence" within the "unstructured complexity" of public policies addressing these otherwise separate areas.

*Is there is a gap between government immigration policies and actual
policy outcomes?* This gap between outputs and migration demographic
outcomes (a term we employ to distinguish these outcomes from other
demographic outcomes related to fertility and aging) may arise either
through implementation shortcomings or the unintended consequences
of policy design (Cornelius and Tsuda 2004: 4–5; Messina 2007;
Hollifield, Martin, and Orrenius 2014: 3–5). The varieties of migration
demographic outcomes – the focus of the approach in this book – can
be compared against documentation of immigration laws and policies
in order to identify the relative capacity of states to manage migratory
flows. A clear mapping of migration outcomes is essential to undertake
this work.

*How do immigration regimes relate to other forms of governance or
social norms?* Immigration regime classifications create important input
data to test theoretical claims that may not be intrinsically related to
migration studies, but which are relevant to the broader social sciences.
As such, taxonomies are central in the development of a wide range of
"independent, intervening and dependent variables in explanations"
(Collier et al. 2012: 226). These include questions pertaining to partisanship and party politics, ethnic relations, trade, democratization, and
support for the welfare state. For instance, immigration regime type

could be a central explanatory variable behind the rise of the radical right (Arzheimer 2009).

What countries most effectively govern immigration? From a practical public policy perspective, there is also utility in developing classifications of demographic migration outcomes. Such classifications allow governments to more carefully benchmark themselves against other countries according to whatever criteria is desired. This assists countries in determining how they are performing compared with other countries deemed to be "most similar," and can provide aspirations for improvements in the future, as well as more knowledge about competing destinations for migrants.

WHAT IMMIGRATION REGIME CLASSIFICATIONS EXIST AND WHAT ARE THEIR LIMITATIONS?

A variety of immigration regime typologies have been developed covering both immigration selection as well as naturalization and settlement. Hammar (1985: 7) drew a distinction between (a) "immigration policy" or "the regulation of flows of immigration and control of aliens"; and (b) "immigrant policy." Following this original distinction, typologies can be loosely divided into those that deal with issues of admission and those that cover the treatment of immigrants once they settle in the destination society. This distinction governs the divisions we adopt in Table 2.1, which sets out the major typologies of both immigration and integration, covering both policy outputs and outcomes.

Looking first at the issue of immigration control, Table 2.1 indicates that most current typologies distinguish between "traditional" or "settler states" (United States, Canada, Australia, New Zealand), Northern European states that received large numbers of workers through guestworker programs in the period after World War II (Germany, United Kingdom, France), and the former sending states of Southern Europe that became immigrant-receiving nations (Spain, Italy, Greece) (see Freeman 1995: 893; Cornelius and Tsuda 2004; Janoski 2010: 9–16). Other studies follow these general distinctions but focus on a smaller number of countries (Joppke 1999; 2005b; Freeman 2006).

Moving to integration and naturalization, Table 2.1 makes clear that there are a number of well-developed typologies and taxonomies that classify regimes according to models situated in national history. Brubaker (1992) distinguishes between French republicanism and German ethno-nationalism and considers the implications for integration

TABLE 2.1. *Existing immigration and membership typologies and taxonomies*

Date	Author	Title of study	Countries considered	Aspects of immigration/ integration considered	Method and variables
		IMMIGRATION TYPOLOGIES AND TAXONOMIES			
1985	Tomas Hammar	*European Immigration Policy: A Comparative Case Study.*	Germany and Switzerland ("guest worker or rotation system"); Britain and Sweden ("permanent immigration"); and Britain, France and the Netherlands ("postcolonial immigration").	Immigration control and integration policies.	Qualitative, comparative chapters on different aspects and written by different authors. Some descriptive statistical analysis and some comparative analysis in final chapters but analysis is not uniformly comparative or assessed through key variables.
1995	Gary Freeman	"Modes of Immigration Policies in Liberal Democratic States."	United States, Australia and Canada ("English-speaking settler societies"); France, Britain, Germany, Switzerland, the Netherlands, Sweden and Belgium ("post-World War II immigration countries"); and Spain, Portugal, Italy and Greece ("former emigration countries").	Interest group relations; role of immigration in labor market; external pressures on immigration.	Qualitative and not clearly specified variable.

Year	Author	Title	Cases	Focus	Method
1999	Christian Joppke	*Immigration and the Nation-State: The United States, Germany and Great Britain.*	The United States, Germany, and Great Britain.	Immigration histories; cultural dimensions of immigration, including citizenship laws; modes of selection.	Qualitative and no clearly specified variables.
2005	Christian Joppke	*Selecting by Origin: Ethnic Migration in the Liberal State.*	United States and Australia ("settler states"); Northwest and Southwest Europe ("postcolonial constellations"); and Israel and Germany ("diaspora constellations").	Immigration selection and its relationship to ethnicity.	Qualitative approach.
2006	Gary Freeman	"National Models, Policy Types and the Politics of Immigration in Liberal Democracies."	Australia, Canada, the United States, and the European Union.	Division across immigration visas rather than countries.	Qualitative approach.
2009	Georg Menz	*The Political Economy of Managed Migration: Nonstate Actors, Europeanization, and the Politics of Designing Migration Policies.*	France, Germany and the United Kingdom ("established countries of immigration") and Ireland, Italy, Poland ("new countries of immigration").	Focuses on the labor union/industry relations that inform the political economy of labor immigration selection.	Largely qualitative, some reference to descriptive immigration statistics.

(continued)

TABLE 2.1 *(continued)*

Date	Author	Title of study	Countries considered	Aspects of immigration/integration considered	Method and variables
2010	Uma A. Segal et al.	*Immigration Worldwide: Policies, Practices and Trends.*	All available countries with large immigrant populations.	Differentiates between countries with large immigration populations, growing immigrant populations and low or declining immigration populations.	Quantitative, focusing on immigration stock.
2010	Alexander Caviedes	*Prying Open Fortress Europe: The Turn to Sectoral Labor Migration.*	Western Europe (the United Kingdom, Germany, Austria and the Netherlands).	Economic migration analyzed using a modified Varieties of Capitalism framework	Qualitative, using elite interviews and processing tracing of secondary sources.
2011	Camilla Devitt	"Varieties of Capitalism, Variation in Labour Immigration."	Uses the standard varieties of capitalism categorizations: Sweden, Denmark and Finland ("Nordic regimes"); Germany, Austria, the Netherlands and Belgium ("the Conservative-Continental model"); Italy, Greece, Spain, Portugal and France (the "Southern-Statist model"); and the United Kingdom and Ireland (the "Liberal model").	Focuses on labor immigration admissions and labor market regulation.	Flows of immigrants into Europe; type of work undertaken by immigrants. Combination of descriptive statistical analysis and qualitative analysis.

2014	James F. Hollifield et al.	*Controlling Immigration: A Global Perspective.*	United States, Canada and Australia ("nations of immigrants"); France, Germany, the Netherlands, Britain, Scandinavia, and Switzerland ("reluctant/de facto countries of immigration"); Italy, Spain, Japan, and South Korea ("latecomers to immigration"); and the European Union ("global governance of migration").	Variety of issues (immigration, public support for immigration, multiculturalism and integration policies, regional efforts at migration governance).	Qualitative approach. Variables include control-outcomes gap, immigration policies, and public support for immigration. Individual chapters on each of these countries and the EU written by different authors.

INTEGRATION/CITIZENSHIP TYPOLOGIES AND TAXONOMIES

1992	Rogers Brubaker	*Citizenship and Nationhood in France and Germany.*	France and Germany.	National path dependence and the resilience of national traditions of citizenship and national identity.	Historical institutional analysis of limited cases and indefinite indicators.
2006	Migration Policy Group	"Migration Integration Policy Index (MIPEX)."	All EU states plus Switzerland, Norway, Canada and the United States.	Focuses on integration policy indicators including labor market mobility, family reunion, education, political participation, long-term residence, access to nationality, and anti-discrimination laws.	Expert survey coding that separates integration from immigration policy and uses unclear aggregation methods.

(continued)

TABLE 2.1 (continued)

Date	Author	Title of study	Countries considered	Aspects of immigration/ integration considered	Method and variables
2006	Rainer Bauböck et al.	*Acquisition and Loss of Nationality: Policies and Trends in 15 European States.*	Fifteen European states.	Documents the diversity of legal regulations and policies concerning the acquisition and loss of nationality in the fifteen old member states of the EU. Inquires whether any trends toward greater similarity are emerging from international and European law or from parallel domestic developments in the member states.	Expert survey coding basic legal techniques, procedural characteristics and material conditions (residence requirements, integrity clauses, conditions of integration, reasons for loss of nationality, etc.) as well as major changes to procedural details and conditions since 1985 (without data on administrative practice).
2007	Costică Dumbravă	"Citizenship Regulation in Eastern Europe: Acquisition of Citizenship at Birth and Through Regular Naturalisation in Sixteen Postcommunist Countries."	Sixteen Eastern European states.	Applies Howard's (2006) model for cross-national analysis of citizenship policy on Eastern	Original policy analysis and coding of limited but clear indicators.

				European states to reveal its limitations outside the original 15 (predominantly Western European) cases.	Original policy analysis and coding of limited but clear indicators extrapolated to characterize citizenship regimes.
2009	Marc Morjé Howard	*The Politics of Citizenship in Europe.*	Fifteen EU states.	Measures of *jus soli*, immigrant residency requirements, and dual citizenship allowances.	
2009	Stephen Castles and Mark Miller	*The Age of Migration: International Population Movements in the Modern World.*	Global perspective.	Identifies four prevalent citizenship policy regimes across states: those that integrate members or former members of multi-ethnic empires, those that focus on folk or ethnic dimensions of allegiance such as culture or language,	Qualitative and not clearly specified variable.

(continued)

TABLE 2.1 *(continued)*

Date	Author	Title of study	Countries considered	Aspects of immigration/ integration considered	Method and variables
				those that adopt a republican regime based on allegiance to a constitution or laws, and a multicultural regime which focuses on pluralistic approaches to cultures.	
2010	Sara Wallace Goodman	"Integration Requirements for Integration's Sake? Identifying, Categorising and Comparing Civic Integration Policies."	Fifteen EU states.	Naturalization requirements of country knowledge, language acquisition, and value agreement.	Original policy analysis and coding of limited but clear indicators.
2010	Thomas Janoski	*The Ironies of Citizenship: Naturalization and Integration in Industrialized Countries.*	Eighteen OECD states.	Naturalization Rates.	Standardized calculation and comparison of citizenship policy outcomes.
2011	Keith Banting et al.	"Are Diversity and Solidarity Incompatible?"	Twenty-one OECD states.	Measures the character and strength of multiculturalism policies and across three points in time (1980, 2000, 2010).	Original policy analysis and coding of limited but clear indicators.

Year	Author	Title	Scope	Focus	Sources
2012	Ruud Koopmans et al.	"Citizenship Rights for Immigrants: National Political Processes and Cross-National Convergence in Western Europe, 1980–2008."	Northern and Western Europe (soon non-European settler states).	Nationality acquisition, family reunification, expulsion, anti-discrimination, public-sector employment for non-nationals, political rights for non-nationals, cultural rights in education, cultural and religious rights.	Analysis of policy documents, legal texts, secondary literature, internet websites, and expert information.
2013	Maarten Vink and Rainer Bauböck	"Citizenship Configurations: Analysing the Multiple Purposes of Citizenship Regimes in Europe."	Thirty-six European states.	Creates a citizenship regime typology based on functional components of citizenship laws.	CITLAW database of 2011 citizenship laws, and country-specific expert reports.

Note: We do not include single-country case studies under these typologies. See Freeman (2011) for an overview that includes single-country studies. Nor does the table include encyclopedias of immigration that list a number of countries but do not consider these in a comparative fashion (e.g. Cohen 2010). The focus is on comparative typologies and taxonomies of two countries or more.

of immigrants. Castles and Miller (2009: 44–5) extend this typology of citizenship to four categories: those countries that integrate members or former members of multi-ethnic empires; those that focus on folk or ethnic dimensions of allegiance such as culture or language; those that adopt a republican model based on allegiance to a constitution or laws; and a fourth, multicultural model which focuses on pluralistic approaches to cultures. Others have contested the republican/ethno-national divide either in the modern era, or historically (Wimmer and Glick Schiller 2002; Lucassen 2005; Joppke 2010: 19).

Over the 2000s, researchers developed varied instruments to distinguish between certain types of integration regimes defined by the liberalness or exclusivity of their settlement and citizenship policies. While most of these efforts have entailed analysis of statutes into standardized statistical databases (Koopmans et al. 2005; 2012; Banting and Kymlicka 2006; Bauböck et al. 2006; Migration Policy Group 2006/2011; Howard 2009), Tom Janoski (2010) sets himself apart from these previous efforts by employing Naturalization Rates – an outcome-based indicator – to classify citizenship regimes in eighteen OECD states between 1970 to 2005.

WHAT ARE THE SHORTCOMINGS OF IMMIGRATION REGIME CLASSIFICATIONS?

Despite these contributions, we identify three key shortcomings with existing approaches to classifying immigration regimes that this book addresses. First, existing classifications are limited to OECD states, and especially Western, democratic destinations. Second, existing classifications, in particular those of immigration entry, are weakened by indicators of questionable validity. Third, even those classifications with improved indicators are hindered by approaches that examine admission and integration regimes independently of each other, ignoring a possible immigration–integration policy "nexus." With these shortcomings in mind, we contend that the field of migration politics would benefit from a revised approach to regime classification. We consider each shortcoming in turn.

A Western Democratic Focus

The most glaring shortcoming of contemporary migration policy regime typologies is a general absence of non-OECD countries in the analysis. As is clear from Table 2.1, with only one exception (Segal et al. 2010), only OECD countries – and often, only Western European democracies – are considered in current approaches.[1] This is also true of more recent typologies, which surprisingly, given current trends in global immigration, continue to adopt a Western focus and often follow the early Freeman (1995) model and center their analysis on settler and European states. Indeed, this focus has also led scholars to take for granted the endurance of a settler state model (despite the evidence we present in this book) and instinctively link those former settler states together (despite the divergence we observe between the United States and other former settler states). Therefore, while there have been important single-country and region-specific qualitative contributions to the growing phenomenon of immigration into the Global South[2] (Fong 2006; Baldwin-Edwards 2011; Shah 2011) and some important recent studies that compare democracies and non-democracies globally (Mirilovic 2010; Breunig, Cao, and Luedtke 2012), these systems are not incorporated into the current immigration regime typology literature.

This state of the academic field stands at odds with the reality in which immigration into non-OECD states accounts for around 48 percent of existing global migration stock (Özden et al. 2009: 20).[3] Further, a recent study by the United Nations demonstrates that the fastest rate of growth of international immigration is in the Global South (UN 2013; Abel and Sander 2014).

From Tables 2.2 and 2.3, respectively, we can see that states with the largest stock as a proportion of total populations and the largest absolute stocks are not only Western destination states. Indeed, the Russian Federation, Saudi Arabia, and the United Arab Emirates are among the

---

[1] Dumbravă (2007) considers Eastern European nations in his analysis of citizenship policy and in doing so identifies some of the issues of selection bias in only focusing on Western European nations.

[2] Defined by Solimano (2010: 4) as non-OECD countries. While we realize that the Global South currently features some of the most quickly developing economies, we prefer the "North"/"South" dichotomy as it reflects the conventional division that has defined immigration scholarship until now, rather than purporting as may have historically been the case, a rich North and a more impoverished South.

[3] Although Özden et al. (2009) write that South–South migration is declining as a proportion of total world migration (from 61 percent in 1960 to 48 percent in 2000), they explain that "when the migrant-creating effects of South Asia and the Soviet Union are factored in ... South–South migration remains stable over the period." Yet, their definition of South–South migration does not include intra-Soviet, intra-Russian or intra-Indian sub-continental migration, at the regional level, as distinct from internal migration that is not included in any case.

TABLE 2.2. *Top ten countries, migrants as percentage of total population, 2015*

Rank	Country	Migrants as % of the population
1	United Arab Emirates	88.4
2	Qatar	75.5
3	Kuwait	73.6
4	Bahrain	51.1
5	Singapore	45.4
6	Oman	41.1
7	Jordan	41.0
8	Hong Kong	38.9
9	Lebanon	34.1
10	Saudi Arabia	32.3

Source: UNPD 2015, table 3, countries with population over 1 million.

TABLE 2.3. *Top ten countries, absolute number of migrants, 2015*

Rank	Country	Number of migrants (in thousands)	Migrants as % of the population
1	United States	46,627	14.5
2	Germany	12,006	14.9
3	Russia	11,643	8.1
4	Saudi Arabia	10,186	32.3
5	United Kingdom	8,543	13.2
6	United Arab Emirates	8,095	88.4
7	Canada	7,836	21.8
8	France	7,784	12.1
9	Australia	6,764	28.2
10	Spain	5,853	12.7

Source: UNDP 2015, table 1, countries with population over 1 million.

top five in absolute stock (Table 2.3). When stock is analyzed as a proportion of states' national population (Table 2.2), none of the ten states with the highest proportion are OECD states. The top four are the United Arab Emirates, Qatar, Kuwait, and Bahrain. It is also worth noting that while the United Nations Department of Economic and Social Affairs (DESA) suggests that China has one of the world's smallest migrant populations as a proportion of its populace, China's Bureau of Entry and Exit Administration of the Ministry of Public Security (2011) reports that there are 493,139 foreigners currently resident in the mainland as of

2009 – a number substantial enough to merit the examination of China as a case and significantly greater than many countries currently the focus of immigration research.

As many new immigration-receiving states are non-democratic, observers must recreate frameworks of analysis beyond existing regime typologies that are democratic and state-centric. In many of these states, the social contract between the polity and its constitutive members may be better characterized as an ad hoc economic exchange of required labor for financial compensation. This absence of, or poor adherence to, human rights, complicates analytical frameworks that focus on democracies. Such states may also incentivize or otherwise facilitate alternative forms of human migration – migration to one state in order to reach another (incremental or transit migration), migration with self-imposed temporariness (circular migration), migration with a length of stay subject to government or private sector whims (ad hoc labor migration), and migration of vulnerable people not covered by the Refugee Convention (non-refugee forced migration).

Economic and demographic trends suggest that South–South migration will become more, not less, important over the course of the twenty-first century. As world economic growth shifts toward Brazil, China, India, Russia, the Arab Gulf Region and the African continent, and as countries outside the OECD adopt the same demographic trends of population aging evident within the OECD, we can expect concomitant shifts in migration outcomes. In fact, the United Nations (UN) makes clear that the rate of population aging in key developing nations such as China is greater than that of many developed nations, expediting the need for labor market adaptations (UN 2009: ix). China's working age population will decline by 3.2 percent from 2015 through to 2030 and then 28.5 percent by 2060, requiring mass immigration (or a revolutionary increase in fertility) in order to sustain the labor force (Bruni 2013: 73–4). As such, it is likely that, over the twenty-first century, immigration will become a central mechanism to maintain labor supply in what was once considered the developing world.

Our interest in comparison of demographic migration outcomes across "developed" and "developing" states is not unproblematic. Due to the fact that states – particularly in the Global South – measure the scope and character of their migration profile in different ways, the consideration of migration outcomes across a broad range of countries is methodologically challenging. The incongruence between policy creation and actual policy implementation in non-Western countries, coupled with challenges of data availability, has potentially deterred many scholars from focusing on the developing world (see Global Forum on Migration and Development 2012: 11). These challenges may also explain the documented Western bias in existing analyses and the focus upon laws rather than demographic outcomes in those Western countries. In the final section of this chapter, we outline the approach we adopt to tackle this methodological challenge.

Unclear Indicators

Typologies are only as comprehensive and valid as the indicators of which they are comprised. A central shortcoming of many existing immigration regime typologies is that the policy outcome or output of the immigration regime is not always clearly defined or operationalized. First, particularly within studies of admissions, these typologies often do not clarify their indicators of comparison.[4] It is necessary to disentangle these various features of immigration regimes because otherwise the "building blocks" of a typology are unclear (Collier et al. 2012: 224). Second, existing typologies often do not adequately explain decisions around the aggregation of these variables, at the same time employing single umbrella terms, such as "settler states," "continental European states," or "former emigration states." As Finotelli and Michalowski (2012: 234) note, the consolidation of complex and seemingly divergent policies into broader national models "can impede a nuanced measure of internal differences, rather than helping to empirically compare them" (citing Bader 2007: 875–6). Third, existing typologies generally provide little insight about borderline cases that might be classified in a variety of groupings. This may relate to the discussed tendency to develop country-wide typologies rather than typologies accounting for key dimensions that we unearth in this book.

In the field of citizenship and integration, indicators are significantly clearer. Contemporary scholars have coded extensive policy output data to develop typologies and indices of different national approaches, along with inferential arguments based on these data. Howard (2009) and Goodman (2010) quantify aspects of citizenship and civic integration

---

[4] For example, the seminal article on immigration regimes by Gary Freeman (1995) does not identify whether the variable(s) of interest are the size of immigration intake, the composition of such migration (a migration demographic outcomes variable), the visa categories for immigration (a policy output variable), or the rights accrued following settlement (either a policy or outcomes variable depending upon definition).

policy respectively according to selected policy indicators. The Migration Policy Group (2006/2011) and its collaborators solicit legal experts to code policies related to a range of integration approaches. Banting et al. (2011) code specific policies of immigrant diversity accommodation, which they deem to be reflective (and constitutive) of states' approaches to multiculturalism. Similarly, the International Migration Policy and Law Analysis (IMPALA) Database consortium uses thousands of indicators to code the restrictiveness of national admissions and citizenship laws across nine countries and ten years (Gest et al. 2014; Beine et al. 2015).

Both immigrant admission and settlement regime classifications would benefit from additional indicators based on observable demographic migration outcomes, rather than focusing on policies themselves. There are a number of reasons why, at this stage, concentration on immigration outcomes – as we adopt in this book – may be preferable in the development of immigration taxonomies. First, attempts to synthesize specific policy outputs are currently underway (European Commission 2011; Migration Policy Group 2006/2011; IMPALA 2015; Peters 2017) but at this point, the most comparable cross-national data are on policy outcomes, not policy outputs. While indicators inside these emerging output databases are typically clear, they reproduce a number of the limitations we discuss in this chapter. They tend to be exclusively focused on Western democracies, and a number use expert coders rather than cite actual legal documents, which can lead to decreased reliability (as in Helbling et al. 2017).

Second, outcomes reflect what happens "on the ground" – the reality as experienced by migrants and citizens. While we could otherwise examine the *de jure*, legal policy outputs, these do not always reflect actual de facto circumstances (Money 1999: 22). As a variety of scholars have noted, there exists often within the immigration arena a gap between policy design and the actual outcomes of that policy, which is variously referred to as the "gap" or "implementation hypothesis" (Hollifield 1992: 139; 2000: 143–4; Freeman 1994; Messina 1996). The source of this gap has been attributed to labor market conditions (Hollifield 1992: 139) or interest group lobbyists (Freeman 1995: 885), both of which might drive actual immigration outcomes more than the policy prescriptions of government.

In this way, outcome data may be used to triangulate and confirm observations based solely on policy outputs, or indeed, may even be preferable in offering a more realistic sense of the effects of immigration.[5] Indeed, examining policy outcomes in many cases allows us to avoid validity challenges that emerge over how policy outputs ought to be measured.

The Admissions–Citizenship Policy Nexus

Current typologies tend to examine several admission or naturalization outcomes in isolation. This has led to partial renderings of immigration regimes. Until now, we neither know how different outcomes work with each other, nor what varieties of national immigration regimes exist, once both admission and citizenship are considered in tandem.[6] We argue that social scientists must consciously work to build more comprehensive classifications of migration policy outcomes that allow researchers to consider complementary and contradictory outcomes together.

Chief among these underexplored interactions is the nexus between immigration and citizenship policies. Some may dispute attempts to combine or to consider in tandem measures of immigration selection (e.g. admission criteria, immigration composition, reliance on temporary migration) with measures of settlement (e.g. citizenship, diversity of immigrant populations, and integration policies). Yet, even Hammar (1985: 10), who drew the original delineation between "immigration admission" and "integration" policy also noted that the two work simultaneously in practice.

Taking a cue from this position, it is essential that researchers attempt to incorporate both immigration and settlement-related dimensions into considerations of immigration regimes in order to appraise and acknowledge the extent of what we call an "admissions–citizenship nexus." First, there is reason to believe that the prospects for settlement as well as demographic

---

[5] For example, Howard (2009: 24) uses Naturalization Rates as a "correction" that accounts "for the potential problem of a country appearing to have a very inclusive naturalisation policy, but in reality – whether due to administrative 'discretion' or other barriers or disincentives – being much more restrictive in practice." Koopmans et al. (2005: 38; 2012: 8, note 5) do the same. This demonstrates the reluctance of researchers to take legal outputs, even in Western democracies, at face value.

[6] Such consideration of immigration regime variation based exclusively on one measurement is not substantively different from a consideration of economic policy based exclusively on approaches to trade. Indeed, many capitalist states have protectionist trade policies, but are otherwise quite different in other aspects (such as redistribution, regulation, or fiscal spending). These factors in turn alter the typology of trade regimes (Rodriguez and Rodrik 2000).

outcomes themselves (i.e. prior migratory flows) could constitute a source of pull factors for immigration flows (Thielemann 2006). Second, there may also be a trade-off between the scale of immigration (a measure of immigration control) and the approach toward citizenship and integration, such as the extent of naturalization entitlements (as argued by Ruhs and Martin 2008 and Ruhs 2013). Such a trade-off reflects what several American scholars have referred to as a "grand bargain" (Papademetriou 2002; Cornelius et al. 2004) whereby liberal and restrictive policymakers exchange facilitative naturalization and incorporation regimes for tighter border enforcement. Penninx (2005: 137) adds to this argument in the European Union context, suggesting that "the experience and policies of different countries with integration reflects their experience and policies of immigration" and calls for an examination of this "special relationship."

Third, in terms of practical policies, it is clear that state policymakers do make links between immigration entry and citizenship. Certain types of migrants may be selected because it is anticipated that they will better integrate into the existing polity over the longer term. In fact, this argument is common in the debates over, and preference for, skilled immigrants, who are thought to rely less on public goods than other migrants (Borjas 1999; Hawthorne 2008; Doomernik et al. 2009; Boucher 2016). Likewise, states may turn to more restrictive immigration policy as a response to perceived integration challenges (Alba and Foner 2015: 237). As such, there are strong grounds for the development of typologies that combine the two dimensions of the migratory process. In Chapter 8, we engage in a full analysis of the extent to which such a "nexus" exists between the dimensions we examine: admissions and citizenship.

A GLOBAL APPROACH TO IMMIGRATION REGIMES

At present, we lack a clear typology of immigration regimes and a theory to understand their variation. The existing focus lacks common categories for analysis, clear dimensions for assessment of the various components of each category and often does not consider how, if at all, these dimensions can fit together in a systematic way. Further, existing approaches do not account for migration and settlement into non-democratic and non-Western states and do not attempt to build a common conceptual framework across the different dimensions.

A central agenda of this book is to consider how different variables of immigration regimes interact with each other within as well as across countries. Do states cluster similarly according to different dimensions, allowing us to speak of a single immigration regime typology? Does a different typology arise when expanding or contracting the scope of consideration to the OECD or beyond? What is the relationship between immigrant admission and access to citizenship?

In order to answer these questions, in this book, we develop and focus on a series of dimensions of migration policy outcomes. Some of these are new concepts in understanding immigration demographics while others repurpose established concepts. What constitutes an immigration regime? We identify three primary categories of immigration policy outcomes and seven component measures across these three categories:

(i) Visa Mix
  (1) *Total flows*
  (2) *Work flow (including accompanying family)*
  (3) *Family flow*
  (4) *Humanitarian flow*
  (5) *Free movement flow.*

The first dimension considers the distribution of the annual flow of immigrant admissions through economic, family, humanitarian categories and free movement (which covers free movement through bilateral and supranational arrangements, international agreements and admissions via any small residual visas) as a share of total immigration flows. This distribution varies considerably across states and can be seen as an important indicator of immigration policies. This "Visa Mix," as we call it, has arguably replaced historical ethnicity-based mix as a central issue in immigration selection. The Visa Mix is particularly important when validating claims of a global shift toward more economically selective immigration policies (Shachar 2006; Doomernik et al. 2009). In addition, in some regions, such as across the European Union, or between New Zealand and Australia, free movement may shape the means by which states alter the compositional mix of immigration.[7]

(ii) Temporary Ratio
  (6) Temporary economic migrants as share of total flows.

---

[7] We rely on data from the OECD, the Organization of American States (OAS), the Gulf Labor Markets and Migration (GLMM) dataset, and data we have collected ourselves from national statistics offices to examine this dimension.

The second dimension, the Temporary Ratio, concerns the proportion of immigrants who enter a country with a limited duration of permitted residency as a ratio of total immigration flows. In all immigration regimes, the distinction between temporary and permanent migration is central, but given data restrictions, we only consider this distinction for economic migration. Furthermore, we rely upon the OECD definition of permanent migration rather than only considering those visas that governments define as "permanent," thereby widening the ambit of relevant visas to capture the actual behavior of migrants on the ground.[8]

    (iii)   Naturalization Rate
        (7) Naturalization Rate.

The third dimension considers Naturalization Rates. States with the highest migrant stock as a proportion of their population are conventionally states that offer few paths to permanent residency or inclusion as citizens. For this reason, it is necessary to supplement our consideration of immigrant flows with an analysis of citizenship acquisition. Naturalization Rates are subject to the policies governing citizenship and the hurdles that applicants must overcome, but also the desire of immigrants to pursue their futures in their new community; as such they are a clear policy outcome variable. We measure Naturalization Rates as the percentage of the stock of the foreign-born population that has acquired the citizenship of the given destination country in the reference year – the simplest, most widely available and most conceptually accurate measure of state inclusivity as it pertains to the adoption of nationality. It is worth noting that this rate will include *jus soli* births, as birthright citizenship is a form of naturalization employed in certain states.[9]

Ideally, we would also include irregular immigration in our conceptualization of an immigration regime. Undocumented immigrants enter a state without authorization, overstay the duration of their visas, or violate the terms of their visas. Because it is technically unauthorized, undocumented immigration may be considered to be beyond the scope

---

[8] We draw upon data from the OECD, the Organization of American States, the GLMM dataset, and other national statistics offices from which we have collected information.

[9] Most naturalization data that we include are those collected by the OECD and work by Janoski (2010). However, in considering developing countries and non-democracies, it must be acknowledged that some immigrants never qualify for naturalization or are simply ineligible. Such factors and the idiosyncrasies of regimes must therefore be considered qualitatively alongside available quantitative data.

of a regime's control. However, in reality, many economies depend on de facto tolerance of some level of undocumented migration (Joppke 1998; Massey 2007; Hochschild and Mollenkopf 2009; Trujillo-Pagán 2014). While this level represents a significant proportion of migrant stock and flows in some countries, it is a far smaller proportion in others. In either case, this variation is a key dimension of immigration regime outcomes, but one that is difficult to accurately capture cross-nationally.

In practice, the comparison of undocumented migration across states is problematic for multiple reasons. In countries where undocumented migration is not salient, very little effort is exerted to ensure that estimates are rigorously and regularly calculated. Even in countries like Spain or the United States, where the undocumented migrant population is considerable and which exert substantial effort to quantify the extent of such populations, estimates are disputed and range widely, particularly annual measures. In highly securitized countries like those in the Arabian Gulf region, undocumented immigration is likely to be carefully estimated, but governments are reluctant to release these data out of concern for popular backlash. Concerns about validity and access aside, demographers across countries employ different methods to calculate undocumented migration (for a fuller discussion, see Massey and Capoferro 2004). This makes the standardization of these data – which we are able to achieve in the other, aforementioned dimensions of immigration regimes – impossible for undocumented migration. For these reasons, while we acknowledge the significance of the undocumented in the characterization of immigration regimes and discuss it qualitatively, we choose not to include estimates of undocumented migration in our analysis of immigration regimes.

In Chapter 3, we also introduce two further metrics that gauge the concentration and geographic proximity of immigrants' countries of origin. While this Herfindahl Index and Gravity Measure do not factor into our analysis, they offer a stock-based depiction of the immigrants that different regimes attract – a reflection of how states' historical regulatory practices select people according to their national origins, ethnicity, race, religion, or connection to the country of destination. All stock-based data are collected by the United Nations Population Division. Because stock-based measures and their associated distributions are a reflection of historic trends and policies, we do not analyze them with the annualized flow-based dimensions that we discuss above. Annualized data allow us to freeze state policies and contextual trends at a specific moment in time, permitting a standardized analysis that evaluates the character of different regimes.

Our collection of migration demographic outcomes was a significant undertaking – one that comprises an impediment to broad comparative research prior to this point. In some cases, our data collection involved the aggregation of smaller data sources. In other cases, it relied on the establishment of relationships with independent researchers to gain access to data from particular regions. And in a few further cases, data was accessed as a result of direct correspondence (sometimes in-person) with government officials. In all cases, our data is translated from the original documents and, where possible, standardized to the appropriate institutional methods, such as those employed by the OECD and the United Nations.[10] In all, this work required seven years of data solicitation and collection with the support of many research assistants across five continents. A key contribution of this book is therefore to synthesize available data with original data in order to map the three categories of indicators that we set out above.

CASE SELECTION

Our choice of countries cases in this book is a blend of discretion and convenience. In some countries of immigration, researchers are subject to limitations on access to flow data imposed by governments who either lack the institutional capacity for reliable recordkeeping or perceive a political interest in withholding the results. For this reason, we are necessarily constrained by flow data availability and either depend on direct requests from national statistics agencies or on population research by supranational organizations (which collect stock and flow data from such agencies cross-nationally). Within these constraints of data availability, we then sought to include the most comprehensive array of cases possible to analyze variation in immigration regimes in countries with the most sizable immigration admissions programs.

After extensive examination, we find data are most available in the most prominent migration destinations in any case. Due to the reporting requirements of its bureaucracy, OECD states mostly report complete sets of stock and flow data, with exceptions in countries where immigration has been less significant (e.g. Czechia, Iceland, Poland, Slovakia, Slovenia). Among countries outside the OECD, we made use of data collected by a number of organizations and then solicited data directly

---

[10] It is worth noting that no international institution has standardized methods for the calculation or estimation of undocumented migration across countries.

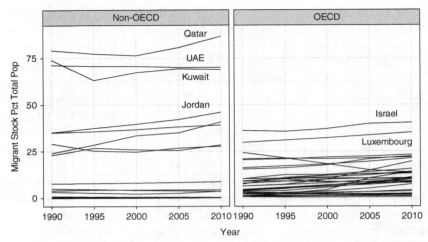

FIGURE 2.1. Total migrant stock over time across the fifty selected non-OECD and OECD countries.
Source: UNPD 2013.

from government agencies. The OECD collects extensive but occasionally patchy immigration data in Russia and Latin America (in the latter case in collaboration with the International Development Bank). The Gulf Labor Markets and Migration (GLMM) group collects noncomprehensive data in the Arab Gulf region. Elsewhere, we were in direct correspondence with national statistics offices in Singapore, Chile, China, South Africa, and a number of Gulf countries to fill in gaps and build a more comprehensive dataset. These data sources and our calculations are outlined in detail in the Methodological Appendix.

Outside the OECD, we selected country cases because they were among the world's most prominent economies and destinations, as evaluated according to two criteria: first, whether a country's migrant stock as a share of total population is comparable to prominent OECD destinations (see Figure 2.1); and second, whether the absolute quantity of migrant stock is comparable to prominent OECD destinations (UNPD 2013). Total migrant stock refers to the United Nations Population Division's mid-year estimate of the number of migrants residing in a country other than the one in which they were born (UNPD 2013). At the most basic level, this total – and its expression as a share of each country's national population – exhibits the role that immigration plays in the composition of a society. Stock excludes people who are of foreign origin but are born inside the given country's borders – the second generation – regardless of their citizenship, which we consider in Chapter 6 in a discussion about Naturalization Rates. Migrant stock also excludes people such as tourists and other short-term visitors for under three months, who are inside the country's borders at the time of measurement but are neither temporary nor permanent residents of the destination country. Because the data are aggregations of admission decisions over time, they tell us nothing about recent policy choices, pull factors, or push factors. Rather, they are a profile of a country's aggregated policy practices over the course of its last few generations of demographic change, as well as the decisions of individual immigrants – a good indicator of the scale of a country's immigration program.

The United Nations Population Division has collected migrant stock measures in a standardized manner for decades (UNPD 2012). While stock data is available for 2015, our measurements reflect results from its 2013 survey, back to 1990, because 2013 is a more accurate reflection of trends in 2011, our principal year of reference. Stock is typically measured as a raw, mid-year count of how many foreign-born people are present within a given state's borders.[11] However, because states are of variable sizes and populations, it is easier to compare states by examining total migrant stock numbers as a share of the given state's total population in the same given year. Yet, this relative calculation may veil the enormous amount of immigrants in large states like Germany, Russia, the United States, and China. For example, China has admitted over 100,000 more foreign-born people than Bahrain, but the island of Bahrain is less than one-tenth of 1 percent of China's size – geographically and demographically. However, this manner of calculating migrant stock as a percentage of the total population more accurately indicates the effect of migration on national population.

Notably, our cases include nine of the top ten countries according to both the absolute and proportionate metrics (see Tables 2.2 and 2.3 earlier in this chapter). We also pursued comparable immigration data from

---

[11] According to the United Nations Population Division, it is important to note that there are differences in data collection practices between countries. Estimates can also be affected by the changing nature of borders, irregular migration and varying degrees of naturalization of the foreign-born (as we discuss in Chapter 6). Stock estimates include migrations across time and therefore capture the cumulative effects over the years. Many developing countries do not allow refugees to become "regular" migrants or naturalize, and therefore the estimates do reflect the stock of refugees over time. Other countries, however, allow refugees to change status, such that the estimates are likely to underestimate the true stock of refugees.

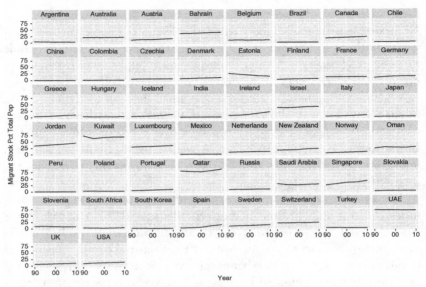

FIGURE 2.2. **Stock as a percentage of total population by country over time.** Total migrant stock over time across the fifty selected countries.
Source: UNPD 2013.

Chinese government sources. While China has among the world's lowest immigration stock as a percentage of its national population, its stock is nonetheless substantial enough to require extensive governance and to merit analysis. South Africa is the only country on the African continent that reports immigration data in a standardized manner and makes it publicly available. It is also the most developed immigration regime on the African continent. Accordingly, it is the only African country included in our dataset. In total, we examine fifteen non-OECD countries, including Argentina, Brazil, Bahrain, China, Colombia, Jordan, Kuwait, Oman, Peru, Qatar, Russia, Saudi Arabia, Singapore, South Africa, and the United Arab Emirates.

Figure 2.2 and Table 2.4 exhibit the case countries' stock numbers as a percentage of their population. Countries with the largest shares are nearly all small countries with strong economies, low outward emigration, and moderate fertility. These include all six Gulf Cooperation Council (GCC) members, Jordan, Switzerland, and the city-states of Luxembourg and Singapore. However, among these, Bahrain, Kuwait, Qatar, and the United Arab Emirates stand apart (see Figure 2.1). They are the only states in the world where the national population is outnumbered – sometimes

TABLE 2.4. Stock as a percentage of total population by country. Total migrant stock over time across the fifty selected countries

Country	1990	1995	2000	2005	2010	Country	1990	1995	2000	2005	2010
Argentina	5.1	4.6	4.2	3.9	3.6	Kuwait	74.0	63.2	67.3	69.2	68.8
Australia	21.0	21.3	21.0	21.3	21.9	Luxembourg	29.8	31.1	32.2	33.7	35.2
Austria	10.3	12.5	12.5	14.0	15.6	Mexico	0.8	0.5	0.5	0.6	0.7
Bahrain	35.1	35.7	36.8	38.2	39.1	Netherlands	8.0	9.0	10.0	10.6	10.5
Belgium	9.0	9.1	8.6	8.5	9.1	New Zealand	15.5	16.1	17.7	20.9	22.4
Brazil	0.5	0.5	0.4	0.4	0.4	Norway	4.6	5.4	6.7	8.0	10.0
Canada	16.2	17.2	18.1	19.5	21.3	Oman	23.0	26.8	26.0	25.5	28.4
Chile	0.8	0.9	1.2	1.4	1.9	Peru	0.3	0.2	0.2	0.1	0.1
China	0.0	0.0	0.0	0.0	0.1	Poland	3.0	2.5	2.1	2.2	2.2
Colombia	0.3	0.3	0.3	0.3	0.2	Portugal	4.4	5.3	6.2	7.2	8.6
Czechia	4.1	4.4	4.4	4.4	4.4	Qatar	79.1	77.2	76.3	80.5	86.5
Denmark	4.6	5.7	7.0	7.8	8.8	Russia	7.8	7.9	8.1	8.4	8.7
Estonia	24.4	21.4	18.2	15.0	13.6	Saudi Arabia	29.2	25.3	24.7	26.8	27.8
Finland	1.3	2.0	2.6	3.3	4.2	Singapore	24.1	28.5	33.6	35.0	40.7
France	10.4	10.5	10.6	10.6	10.7	Slovakia	0.8	2.1	2.2	2.3	2.4
Germany	7.5	11.0	12.2	12.9	13.1	Slovenia	9.2	10.2	8.8	8.4	8.1
Greece	4.1	5.1	6.7	8.8	10.1	South Africa	3.3	2.7	2.3	2.6	3.7
Hungary	3.4	2.8	2.9	3.3	3.7	South Korea	1.3	1.3	1.2	1.2	1.1
Iceland	3.8	4.0	5.7	7.6	11.3	Spain	2.1	2.6	4.4	10.7	14.1
India	0.9	0.7	0.6	0.5	0.4	Sweden	9.1	10.3	11.2	12.3	14.1
Ireland	6.5	7.3	10.1	14.8	19.6	Switzerland	20.5	20.9	21.8	22.3	23.2
Israel	36.2	35.7	37.1	39.8	40.4	Turkey	2.1	2.0	1.9	1.9	1.9
Italy	2.5	3.0	3.7	5.2	7.4	UAE	71.3	70.6	70.6	70.0	70.0
Japan	0.9	1.1	1.3	1.6	1.7	UK	6.5	7.2	8.1	9.7	10.4
Jordan	35.2	37.4	39.7	42.1	45.9	USA	9.1	10.5	12.1	13.0	13.5

Source: UNPD 2013.

37

by a wide margin – by foreign nationals. Elevated shares are also found among settler states like Australia, Israel, New Zealand, and Canada. Smaller shares in Japan and South Korea reflect the restrictive immigration policy regimes of those countries.

Between OECD and non-OECD destinations, we consider a total of fifty immigration countries, although the number differs across the dimensions we examine in the chapters that follow according to data availability. In Chapter 7, we present a classification of immigration regimes by employing a k-means clustering algorithm (Hastie, Tibshirani, and Friedman 2009: 507–11; Grimmer and King 2011; Honaker 2011; Garip 2012). Using this method, we examine relationships between countries sharing similar value combinations across our key indicators. Because the algorithm can only be run with complete datasets, we exclude countries for which we are missing values – even if only one data point is absent. Consequently, this chapter features an analysis of the following thirty countries for which we could access full annualized data: Australia, Austria, Bahrain, Belgium, Brazil, Canada, China, Denmark, Finland, France, Germany, Ireland, Italy, Japan, Kuwait, Mexico, the Netherlands, New Zealand, Norway, Oman, Portugal, Russia, Saudi Arabia, Singapore, South Korea, Spain, Sweden, Switzerland, United Kingdom, and the United States.

The diversity of these cases and their large-scale immigration programs are shaped by demographic trends, geopolitical shifts, and immigration policies over time. In the next chapter, we discuss the history of these trends and policies as they relate to the three dimensions of migration demographic outcomes that concern our analysis.

3

Drivers of Immigration Regimes Over Time

The most striking outcome of immigration over the last one hundred years is the largely continuous scale of movement. While the total stock of migrants has increased six-fold from 36 million in 1910 to 214 million in 2010, if we adjust for demographic growth, people living outside their country of birth have steadily composed between 2 and 3 percent of the world's population (original calculations from UNPD data; also see McKeown 2004: 184). This remarkable constant reflects the stalemate between ever-expanding immigration regulation and ever-evolving means of cheap and rapid transportation coupled with powerful pull factors. However, migrants' destinations have changed dramatically over the same time period. Such shifts in movement are a response to new markets requiring labor, regional conflict, and new relationships of trade and cultural exchange that emerged between different states during different periods. These shifts are also a response to policy changes that have come with significant immigration arrivals and labor shortages.

The earliest systematic attempts to regulate the admission of people to new lands occurred in the late nineteenth century and such policies became commonplace across all developed states over the mid-twentieth century. Since its proliferation, however, immigration policy is thought to be "the crucial element determining immigration patterns" across states (Meyers 2004: 2). This book innovates new concepts in the measurement of the outcomes of such policies. However, these outcomes have been the source of state attention – either explicitly or implicitly – for over a century.

In this chapter, we will begin by reviewing states' early forays into the regulation of migration. The earliest laws focused on controlling the ethnic and racial composition of countries. By the middle of the twentieth century and after a wave of anti-discrimination legislation worldwide, modern immigration policies regulated admission through new strategies that sought to shape the dimensions we consider in this book:

(1) Visa Mix (Chapter 4)
(2) Temporary Ratio (Chapter 5)
(3) Naturalization Rates (Chapter 6)

One by one, this chapter sketches selected historic trends and milestones that exemplify regulation across multiple regions of the world related to each of these outcomes. In the end, we will outline the prominent factors that are thought to explain these dimensions of immigration outcomes across space and time.

EARLY REGULATION OF IMMIGRATION
OUTCOMES

Worlds without Immigration Regulation

For centuries, societies have been subject to consistent and occasionally acute influxes of foreigners due to conflict, trade, inequality, and deprivation; and for much of early human history, migration was not closely regulated. Between 500 BCE and 1400 CE, the expansion and development of the Incan, Macedonian, Roman, Greek, Germanic, and Chinese empires displaced tens of thousands of people due to war, extracted them for slavery, and provided protected paths of free migration along crisscrossing trade routes (Harzig and Hoerder 2009: 20–7). After 1400 CE, the Chinese Empire reached its peak, scattering merchants throughout the Eastern Hemisphere. The discovery of the Americas, the domination of Africa, and the colonization of the Orient each triggered movement from Spain, France, Portugal, Britain, and the Netherlands to exploit new markets and extract resources. Driven by an expanding European population, the flow of free migrants that came to the New World between the years 1760 and 1820 was double the flow that came between 1760 and 1820, but the majority of global migration at the time remained under contract or coercion (Hatton and Williamson 2008: 7). In total, 11.3 million people migrated to the New World between 1580 and 1820, and 8.7 million of them were African slaves. With the decline of the slave trade in the nineteenth century, forty-eight to fifty-two million Chinese and Indian laborers – contracted and indentured – migrated to labor-scarce areas in Burma, Ceylon, British Malaya, Southeast Asia, Manchuria, the Caribbean, the Dutch East Indies, Siam, French Indo-China, South America, the Philippines, and elsewhere (Latham 1986: 11; McKeown 2004: 166). Further colonial migration was subject to imperial facilitation and disease environments (Acemoglu, Johnson, and Robinson 2001).

As states urbanized, migration followed a greater shift from agrarian economics to industrialization, from servitude to free labor. Between 1820 and 1940, migration from Europe to the New World reached fifty-five to sixty million people (King 1993: 20). Another ten to twenty million people moved within the Russo-Siberian region to cities and fertile lands in southern Siberia (Harzig and Hoerder 2009: 38). Within Europe, people emigrated from countries like Ireland and Belgium to more industrialized countries like France and Britain (Hatton and Williamson 2008: 14). And within African colonies, people increasingly moved to larger cities and away from areas of unrest (Mafukidze 2006: 108–13).

For nearly this entire period, state policies and practices facilitating the movement and recruitment of labor were widespread, but restrictive policy remained absent. This was particularly true for settler states, which sought new sources of labor to fuel growing economies and colonize indigenous lands. The United States, by far the largest immigrant recipient of this time, "welcomed newcomers almost unequivocally" (Meyers 2004: 28) from its founding until 1880, constituting what LeMay calls the "Open-Door Era" (1987: 34). Although naturalization policy was restricted in 1795 after an initial period of few requirements, the new law still allowed naturalization for free whites of "good moral character" who fulfilled a number of other requirements including five years of residency (Martin 2011: 75). Canada sought a policy of population expansion and nation-building during the initial decades following its confederation in 1867. Australia and New Zealand likewise sought labor and expansion during their gold rushes and economic success (UNPD 1998: 68). Brazil, Argentina, and Venezuela also actively recruited labor without regulation (Zlotnik 1992: 28–9). At the time, European countries tended to be net-sender states, mitigating the impetus for restriction there (Meyers 2004: 63; Schain 2008: 39).

As these restrictions were absent and as economies expanded during the 1820s and 1850s, the character of migrants evolved and the scale of migration increased. Among those countries viewed as settler states, total migrant stock grew ten-fold in Australia and New Zealand, eleven-fold in Brazil, twenty-one-fold in the United States, and thirty-three-fold in Canada (Hatton and Williamson 2008: 31–2). Migrants were less commonly coerced and indentured, and among the increasing amount of free migrants, people were more likely to be lower skilled laborers and of "dissimilar" ethnocultural origins (Hatton and Williamson 2008: 32). Only with economic recessions towards the end of the nineteenth century did this population growth and diversity finally culminate in the world's first restrictive admission policies.

Prior to the 1880s, the only significant immigration policies gave limited power to executives to expel or exclude certain immigrants. The 1798 Alien and Sedition Acts in the United States gave the president power to deport immigrants deemed to pose a national security threat (Meyers 2004: 28). The Aliens Removal Act of 1848 in Great Britain gave similar power to the Home Secretary (Meyers 2004: 63). Pieces of legislation granting executive power to remove selected immigrants emerged intermittently elsewhere throughout the nineteenth century as well. However, such policies did not amount to either arbitrary – let alone systematic – admission selection.

The landmark legislation widely regarded as the first true piece of immigration restriction policy was the United States' 1882 Chinese Exclusion Act. In the 1840s and 1850s, the United States experienced growing anti-immigration sentiment and political movements directed against the Irish, Germans, Italians, and the Chinese, who were deemed "unassimilable for permanent settlement" (see Hirota 2016). After several decades and with the economy recessing, fierce discrimination and violence against Chinese-American labor migrants mounted (Graham 2004: 30–42; Meyers 2004: 28–30). Amidst calls for federal restrictions and a veto setback in 1879, an Act was passed that suspended all Chinese immigration for ten years – commencing what LeMay (1987: 64) calls the "Door-Ajar Era" of US immigration policy but also a future of increasing racialized regulation around the world. Consistent with the Chinese Exclusion Act, early regulation addressed the distribution of immigrants' national origins before the other flow-based, dimensional outcomes on which this book focuses.

Accounting for the Distribution of Immigrant Origins

The distribution of immigrants' national origins is at least partially an expression of the most basic government attempts at social engineering – the process of population development based in part on how regulatory practices select people according to their nationality, ethnicity, race, religion, or connection to the country of destination. Metrics of resident migrants' number and their origins reveal not only historical bonds of chain migration and demand among immigrants, but also the extent to which governments attempt to discriminate against foreigners from certain parts of the world, no matter what they may be able to contribute to a destination state's society or how desperate their circumstances. In the absence of ethno-national favoritism, these metrics may also reveal an economy's capacity to attract highly skilled labor on a universal – as opposed to local – scale. They reveal the extent to which governments depend on bilateral and supranational agreements that facilitate movement or authorize free movement between certain states. Finally, they also reveal affinities between states as established by previous empires and the legacies of conquest – along with residual linguistic similarities, religious missions, trade links, or senses of obligation. In the way old maps tell the story of a region's history of conquest, the distribution of immigrant origins is a representation of a country's social and political history.

To measure the distribution of immigrants' national origins, we create two different metrics. First, we employ a Herfindahl Index to measure the extent to which destination states attract immigrants from a few specific countries of origin or from many. Second, we employ a Gravity Measure to gauge the extent to which a country's immigrants originate from geographically dispersed or concentrated countries of origin.

Herfindahl Index: A conventional measure of market concentration in economics, a Herfindahl Index is typically calculated by squaring the market share of each company competing in a particular industry and then summing the value outputs (Hirschman 1964). Here, we replace market shares with the percentage of a destination state's total migrant stock from different source countries. Whereas a 100 percent market share would represent a monopoly with a high index score in economics, this would be tantamount to one country being the sole source of a destination state's migrant stock. Czaika and de Haas (2014) previously use a Herfindahl Index but only report regional differences.

Gravity Weighted Diversity Measure: The Gravity Measure[1] accounts for the distance between the given destination country and the countries of origin represented by the total migrant stock. This measures the

[1] The calculation for the Gravity Weighted Diversity Measure is based on the complete 2013 UN stock datasets, broken down into country-specific stock values without imputation. UN estimates are based on official statistics on the foreign-born or the foreign population, classified by sex and age (UN 2013). The statistics utilized to estimate the international

geographic concentration or dispersion of a destination state's migrant stock from original source location. This metric first obtains pairwise distance values by calculating the space between the destination state's capital city and that of the country of origin (e.g. London to Dhaka; Singapore to Kuala Lumpur). The calculation sums each number of immigrants across the different origin countries weighting each by the reciprocal of the distance between the origin/destination squared. An extremely high gravity measure would result if all immigrants to a destination state originated in a contiguous sending state. An extremely low gravity measure would result if all immigrants to a destination state originated in a sending state at the furthest reach of the earth. This measure reveals how geographically local – or proximity weighted – immigration is in our destination cases.

In Figure 3.1, we display Herfindahl Index measures to examine the distributions of destination states' migrant stock across different countries of origin. The calculations reveal a mix of intuitive and unexpected distributions of source countries. Based on our calculations, Figure 3.1 shows that developing destination states with weaker economies and lower GDPs initially attract migrants from very few origins, even if they are not necessarily nearby. States that have developed stronger economies since 1990 such as Czechia, Finland, Ireland, Slovenia, South Africa, and Spain have converged with more traditionally popular destinations. Peru and Brazil are noteworthy exceptions. Both have relatively low stock numbers, but they attract migrants from many origins, near and far. Such exceptions aside, the Herfindahl Index generally separates OECD states from developing states.

The twenty most evenly distributed (least concentrated) stocks are almost exclusively from the world's most established economies. Certainly, these states are not oblivious to issues related to ethnic diversity and intolerance, but it may also be that admissions criteria have been as concerned with skill and fit as origin.

Among these twenty countries, the United States ranks quite low due to its large number of Mexican-born migrants and the predominance of family reunification within its immigration flows. The most evenly

migrant stock were mostly obtained from population censuses, but also population registers and nationally representative surveys (UN 2013). This means that these data typically do not account for the presence of undocumented migrants—a significant factor in some destination states. Distance values were determined from the Geographic Distance Matrix Generator (Ersts 2013), which computes all pairwise distances from a list of geographic coordinates.

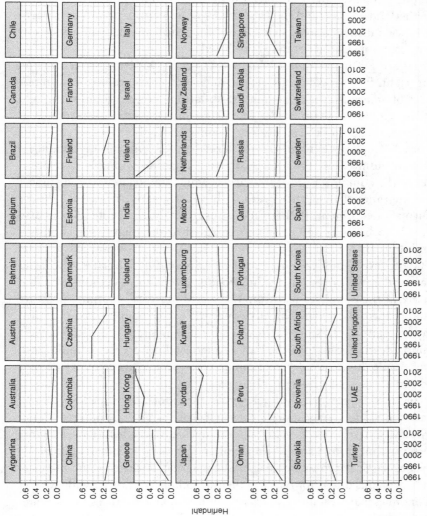

FIGURE 3.1. **Herfindahl Indices by country over time.** Own calculations based on data from UNDP 2013. Higher values represent greater concentrations.

distributed migrant stocks are found in the Nordic states, Canada, and Israel. While Canada and Israel are traditionally viewed as settler states, all three of these countries attract widely in part because they lack affinities to specific territories they once controlled as part of an overseas empire. Still, even those countries with such historic empires (France, the Netherlands, Spain, and the United Kingdom) manage to attract reasonably wide distributions. Their Herfindahl values are likely influenced by how many states their empires produced.

Figure 3.2 lists Gravity Weighted Diversity Measures over time on the right. The calculations reveal unexpected geographic concentration of migrant stock in many destinations conventionally thought to be global in their scope. In particular, European states such as Austria, Belgium, Germany, the Netherlands, Switzerland, and the United Kingdom exhibit greater levels of concentration, revealing a shift in admissions preferences toward regional workers as a product of the common European market, which involves shorter distances for migrants than if they were to have originated from outside the European continent. Perhaps more surprisingly, the United States also proves to be geographically concentrated in the migrants it admits – undoubtedly a product of the immense scale of Mexican, Salvadoran, Cuban, and Dominican migrants that have migrated north in the latter half of the twentieth century. Indeed, our calculations demonstrate that many of the countries featuring the world's largest migrant stocks are among the most geographically concentrated. (Singapore is a noteworthy exception.) Despite far lower absolute migrant stocks, relatively minor destination states in Latin America, Europe, the Middle East, and Asia exhibit broader geographic reach among those migrants they do attract (see also Boeri et al. 2012).

In sum, Figures 3.1 and 3.2 shows that more developed economies have tended to attract more locally but from a range of different countries. Meanwhile, less developed economies have tended to attract more distantly but from a smaller range of countries. A hypothesis influenced by neoclassical economics might suggest that stronger economies are more obvious draws for many of their neighbors over time, while weaker economies have required migrants with stronger motivations to enter (see Massey 1999). The combination of such economic forces and the simple convenience of regional migration to prosperous markets could also drive concentrations of seasonal workers, reunifying families, refugee spillovers, regularized undocumented populations, and people with social affinities, where regional countries share a common language or

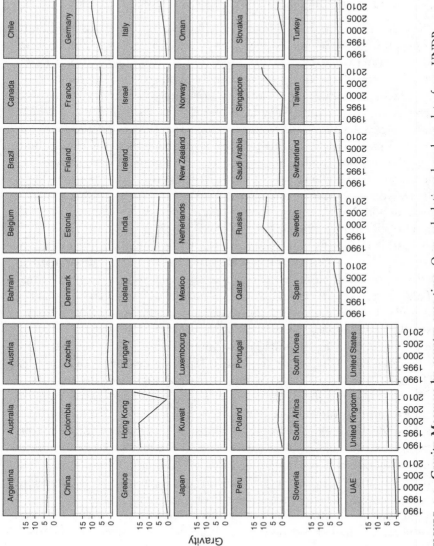

FIGURE 3.2. **Gravity Measures by country over time.** Own calculations based on data from UNDP 2013. Higher values represent greater proximity. Note that Jordan is omitted because its gravity measure is categorically higher than all other states (e.g. 370.18 in 2010).

culture. However, this has not stopped prosperous economies from trying to regulate admission according to immigrants' national origins.

Regulation of Immigrant Origins in Traditional Destinations

The earliest immigration regimes explicitly sought to regulate immigrant origins through race- and ethnicity-based selection policies. The Chinese Exclusion Act in the United States initiated a series of similar policies in other countries receiving large volumes of immigrants near the turn of the twentieth century. The Canadian government attempted to restrict arrivals with its "White Canada" legislation in 1885 and 1910, which first restricted Chinese immigration and later prohibited the entry of immigrants "belonging to any race deemed unsuitable to the climate and requirements of Canada or immigrants of any specified class, occupation, or character" (Hawkins 1991: 16–17; Kelley and Trebilcock 1998: 137–8). David Cook-Martín and David FitzGerald (2014) trace the racist roots of both North American settler states' ethnically selective immigration policies in greater detail.

Australia's first federal immigration law, the Immigration Restriction Act of 1901, established the "White Australia Policy," which used a strict literacy test to effectively prohibit non-Europeans from entering (Lake and Reynolds 2008: 138). In 1904, the original act was slightly liberalized to allow exemptions from the diction test if passports were issued by the Japanese or Indian governments, and in 1905, the diction test was changed to encompass any "prescribed language" rather than a "European language," so that more Japanese migrants could arrive. The same law, however, also banned Asian migrants from bringing their spouses (Lake and Reynolds 2008: 161–2). The White Australia policy endured until its official repeal in 1973.

New Zealand followed a similar whites-only path, restricting Chinese immigrants through head taxes in 1888 and 1896, and establishing a similar diction test in English in 1907 to limit non-whites (Lake and Reynolds 2008: 315). In 1920, New Zealand passed the Immigration Restriction Bill, which required non-British migrants to submit a postal application in advance of arrival and gave the Minister of Customs the authority to single-handedly reject all applicants deemed "unsuitable" (Lake and Reynolds 2008: 315–16).

It was not until 1917 that the United States and others countries acted to slow the growth of migrant admissions in way that did not discriminate against particular nationalities – or at least not quite as openly.

After several attempts, blocks, and vetoes, the United States passed the Immigration Act of 1917, which created categories of "excludable classes" on the basis of criminal history, raised the head tax, imposed a literacy test, and entirely banned immigrants from an "Asiatic-barred zone" (Meyers 2004: 33–4). While the legislation effectively halted most Asian immigration, its non-discriminating principles affected others equally. Indeed, even though head taxes were designed to price out Eastern and Southern Europeans, many Italians, Jews, and Greeks were able to qualify because of improving education and the ethnically unspecific nature of the statute (see Hatton and Williamson 2008: 184).

The United States' 1921 National Quota Act, also known as the Johnson Act, is regarded by many historians to be a definitive turning point in restrictions on migration flows (LeMay 1987: 82; Graham 2004: 46), but it was equally an attempt to manage ethnic composition. The law pegged annual immigrant flows to no more than 3 percent of country-specific nationals living in the United States according to the 1910 Census (Tichenor 2002: 3). By using eleven-year-old numbers, the law particularly favored Northwestern European immigrants and restricted "newer" immigrants deemed inassimilable and burdensome. Migrants from the Western Hemisphere were not subject to the quotas and Northwestern Europeans were fixed to a maximum of 200,000 per year. Southeastern Europeans were limited to 155,000 immigrants per year, and a cap of 1,000 people was placed on newcomers from Asian, African, and Oceanic origins (LeMay 1987: 82; Meyers 2004: 34; Hatton and Williamson 2008: 185). Three years later, the peg was dropped to 2 percent.

By the 1930s, most of the world's primary destination countries were severely curtailing foreigners' entry. The interwar years were characterized by economic instability and xenophobic nationalism (Solimano 2010: 79; Cook-Martín and FitzGerald 2014) that crippled the interdependence and labor-market integration of the previous few decades. Amidst stringently restrictive policies, any international migration tended to be intra-continental and composed almost entirely of refugees between European powers and from Russia following the Bolshevik Revolution (Solimano 2010: 106). According to Hatton and Williamson (2008: 183), this insecurity created by the wars and Great Depression had a much stronger short-term effect on human movement than nascent policy restrictions.

Western European industrial powers emerged from the carnage of World War II in desperate need of foreign labor to bolster depleted workforces (see Castles and Kosack 1973). In their first migration policies as net immigration states, Western European countries regulated admission with explicitly race- or ethnicity-based selection. However, unlike settler states, the industrialized powers regulated admission by forming exclusive bilateral or colony-based agreements with countries featuring more "desirable" populations (see Triadafilopoulos and Schönwälder 2006; Chin 2009). Former colonizer states prioritized immigrants from their colonies. While the British program preferred immigrants primarily from India, Pakistan, Bangladesh, and the West Indies, the Netherlands recruited repatriates from the Antilles, Suriname, and the former Dutch East Indies (Indonesia), and France favored migrants from former North African colonies such as Tunisia, Mali, Senegal, Algeria, Morocco, and Mauritania (Fielding 1993: 51; UNPD 1998: 102; Meyers 2004: 66–7). However, the sudden influx of ex-colony, non-white migrant laborers sparked popular demand for a turn away from former colonies and toward Europe and more temporary residency (Fielding 1993: 45; King 1993: 22–3; Martin 2004: 227).

Countries without former colonial empires instead recruited labor from countries with excess labor supplies, primarily from Southern Europe through bilateral agreements (UNPD 1998: 102). In Germany, temporary agreements stipulated that unskilled workers would register to work and reside in Germany on a temporary, rotating basis and return home at the end of their short contracts. From 1955 to 1973, fourteen million foreign workers arrived in Germany, and about three million returned to their source country (UNPD 2012: 102). Germany – along with other European states – discontinued recruitment programs and agreements and incentivized migrants' return under the pressure of the 1970s oil crisis and recession (Schain 2008: 52). From 1973, the German government closed recruitment offices in Greece, Morocco, Turkey, Spain, and Yugoslavia, and in 1975, encouraged the departure of 655,000 immigrants (King 1993: 31; Martin 2004: 229). Germany also attempted to reduce family reunification by preventing newly arrived spouses from working during their initial years of residence (Martin 2004: 234). Through it all, ethnic Germans from the Soviet Union continued to be welcomed and Germany's immigrant demography was defined by these preferences and the state's inability to implement them (Laurence 2003; 2006).

In one form or another, these origin-conscious policies endured until the 1960s and 1970s when the Civil Rights Era made them unsustainable, but also when imperial centers began to disconnect themselves from their former colonies. In 1965, the Johnson Administration passed amendments to the Nationality and Immigration Act, which eliminated the national origins quota system in the United States, and replaced it with a new selection system, setting an annual ceiling of 170,000 immigrants from the Eastern Hemisphere, with country-specific maximums, and a Western Hemisphere ceiling of 120,000, with further country-specific quotas added in 1976 (Tichenor 2002). In 1962 and again in 1967, Canada enacted a similar shift with its Immigration Regulations, which strove to promote diversity and eliminate ethno-national discrimination. All previous origin-based restrictions were eliminated as Canada moved from a preference for European immigration to a scheme allocating visas to nominated relatives, sponsored dependents, and skilled workers (Hawkins 1988).

Regulation of Immigrant Origins in New Destinations

In the 1980s and early 1990s, Southern European states and East Asian industrial powers like Japan, South Korea, and Taiwan democratized and liberalized their economies. With growing economic prosperity and the collapse of the Soviet Union, Mediterranean states like Spain, Italy, and Greece joined their Northwestern European neighbors and recruited labor extensively from the liberated Eastern Bloc. East Asian economies more conservatively permitted immigrants from territories formerly within the Communist sphere of influence – China, Vietnam, and other parts of Southeast Asia. Singapore did not experience immigration until 1965, Malaysia until the 1970s, Japan until the 1980s, Thailand and South Korea until the 1990s, and Taiwan did not even legalize foreign labor until 1992 (Tsuda and Cornelius 2004: 444; Seol 2005: 87–98).

East Asian destination states have pursued alternative policy regimes that make it more difficult for migrants to reside permanently. Singapore maintains offices in Australia, China, North America, Europe, and India to attract talent, and its government provides clear, easy, and quick employment pass applications, tax incentives, and often a path to naturalization or permanent residence to skilled migrants independent of origins (Fong 2006: 158–9). However, the low-skilled laborers who constructed the city-state's infrastructure are regulated by a system of dependency ceilings and levies imposed on employers to ensure that local workers are not replaced by migrant workers, meaning that such migrants are only present for a short period and may not contribute to the country's migrant stock.² Japan places a high premium on the ethnic and cultural homogeneity of its nation and restricted permanent migration despite a history of severe labor shortages (Tsuda and Cornelius 2004: 449; Seol 2005: 97). Historically, the Japanese government has focused on admitting Nikkeijin or ethnic Japanese expatriates principally from Latin America. Accordingly, while the distribution of immigrant origins in Japan, Singapore, and South Korea is not particularly regionally focused, their immigrants originate from a far more concentrated set of sending states than other comparable economies.

Gulf Arab states have engaged in a determined pursuit to manipulate the distribution of immigrant origins of their massive stocks of migrant workers. During post-colonial prosperity and a period of pan-Arabism, the GCC countries first deliberately recruited migrant workers from the region to create "a single Arab nation in which Arab labor circulates" (Fargues 2011: 276). Initially, Gulf nations recruited Yemenis and Egyptians, but migrant populations included Palestinians after 1948 and Iraqis after the Ba'athist coup in 1968 (Tattolo 2004: 3). By 1970, 85 percent of the 750,000 migrants in the Gulf states had come from other Arab states (Salt 1989: 443). When oil wealth spiked to unprecedented levels and the GCC nations began adopting massive infrastructure projects after 1973, these countries actively preferred and recruited South Asian migrant laborers instead of Arab workers. Compared to fellow Arabs, Asian migrants from Pakistan, India, Bangladesh, Malaysia, and the Philippines were deemed to be a less expensive and more docile workforce with less inclination to settle permanently or demand workers' rights and citizenship (Tattolo 2004: 3; Kapiszewski 2006; Fargues 2011: 278). The turn toward Asian labor was a reflection of government expectations that Asian temporary workers would constitute less of a political or cultural threat to local citizens than other Arabs, and would be less likely to settle permanently (Shah 2006; Hatton and Williamson 2008: 210; Thiollet 2011).

Using migrant contractors, the Gulf states quickly manipulated their labor composition toward Asia and away from Arab origins, while maintaining open doors for highly skilled expatriates from Western Europe and North America. The resulting migration boom increased foreign

² Countries tend to count temporary migrants toward total migrant stock values once they have been resident for over twelve months. However, there is no universal agreement on this measurement. More information can be found at the United Nations Economic Commission for Europe (UNECE 2011).

populations a staggering ten-fold in fifteen years, 4.5 times faster than the growth of their national populations (Fargues 2011: 276–7). By the mid-1990s, the number of South Asian migrants in every GCC country was double the number of Arab migrants and triple that figure by 2010. The average Arab share of the foreign population across the GCC in turn has fallen from 72 percent in 1975 to 32 percent between 2002 and 2004 (Kapiszewski 2006). This politics of immigrant origins thus continues in the Gulf states, but in new ways. In 2013, when Saudi Arabia sought to reduce its migrant stock proportionate to its domestic population, it specifically targeted undocumented migrants from Ethiopia, Somalia, and Yemen for deportation (*The Economist* 2013).

In Israel, the Law of Return has guaranteed admission of Jews to the state of Israel since its independence in 1948 – a unique form of immigrant origin governance that pertains to religion rather than nationality (UNPD 2012: 82). With the collapse of the Soviet Union, 600,000 Jews migrated to Israel between 1989 and 1996. To keep up with demand for low-skilled labor, the government began to recruit temporary laborers too. During the same period from 1990 to 1996, temporary migrant workers to Israel, coming primarily from Romania, the Philippines, and Thailand, increased from 5,000 to 103,000 annually (Zlotnik 1998: 452). Since 2000, immigration to Israel has dropped dramatically. In 2000, over 60,000 new immigrants arrived, the vast majority from the former Soviet Union. However, by 2010, that number had fallen to 16,600, with less than half coming from the former USSR. Israel has also begun to scrutinize its temporary worker programs, tightening restrictions on foreign care workers, reducing its quotas, and piloting a new seasonal worker program in 2010 (OECD 2012).

The turbulent period after the fall of Communism was also characterized by a surge of humanitarian migration that altered the distribution of immigrant origins in many destination states. In light of the population displacement, ethnic conflict and civil wars that erupted with the deterioration of regimes previously propped up by bipolar geopolitics, most applicants came from Latin America, Asia, and Africa. Asylum-friendly countries therefore diversified, despite their reservations. Without strong economies, former Soviet territories like Czechia, Hungary, Poland, Slovakia, and Belarus attracted a number of asylum applicants from the former Yugoslavia and thereafter from Afghanistan, Bolivia, China, Ethiopia, Pakistan, Iran, Somalia, and Vietnam (Okólski 2004: 35–9). Russia also admitted a significant number of displaced people from its former Soviet satellite states. And for much of the late twentieth century,

Nordic countries have been a prominent destination for asylum seekers from the Middle East and Asia (Fielding 1993: 50). The number of asylum applications filed to European countries annually rose from 66,900 in 1983 to 694,000 in 1992 – 70 percent of which came from the developing world, primarily Iran, Turkey, and Sri Lanka (Zlotnik 1998: 442).

Today, origin-conscious immigration programs persist in traditional immigration countries too, albeit less overtly. Following the first oil crisis and economic downturn of the early 1970s, many OECD governments moved to address their established migrant stock through removals and return migration. French legislation, such as the voluntary return program in 1977 and similar legislation in 1980 and 1981, attempted to encourage return migration through payouts and bilateral agreements with sending states (Plewa 2009). In 1983, Germany offered reimbursement of social security contributions and return aid to voluntary return migrants (Schneider and Kreienbrink 2010: 43–4). And as recently as 2009, during the global financial crisis, the Spanish government offered migrants 9,000 euros to return to their homeland; Czechia and Japan provided similar offers to their respective migrants (McCabe et al. 2009). During the same period, Japan offered US$3,000 to workers and US$2,000 to every dependent willing to leave the country. Between 2008 and 2010, the number of Brazilian and Peruvian immigrants in Japan shrank by more than 87,000 combined (Green 2017). Further, between 2005 and 2015, the US government deported more immigrants than it had cumulatively deported in the previous thirty years (Gonzalez-Barrera and Krogstad 2014; Immigration and Customs Enforcement 2015). While these policies did not openly discriminate by country of origin, they were targeted and disproportionately affected North Africans and Turks in the European context and Latin Americans in the North American context (TRAC Immigration 2014). As the regulation of immigration based on national origins has become more subtle, contemporary policies have more overtly focused on controlling the Visa Mix, Temporary Ratio, and Naturalization Rates.

CONTEMPORARY REGULATION OF IMMIGRATION OUTCOMES

The Regulation of Visa Mix

The specification of purposeful visa entry criteria represents the evolution of early, blunter policies that discriminated exclusively according to national origin. "Visa Mix" – the annual distribution of admitted immigrants across visa types – allowed states to select according to familial affinities, labor skills, and on the basis of the need for humanitarian protection. As noted above, the shift coincided with the aftermath of World War II followed by the civil rights movements, when many industrialized powers sought to replenish their depleted labor supply and reunite displaced relatives, but also to transform empires subject to the population movement and conflict associated with decolonization.

Prominent among the earliest Visa Mix-focused legislation was the 1952 McCarran-Walter Act in the United States. It increased visa allocation for relatives of both American citizens and skilled workers, but maintained the stringent national origin quotas established in 1924 and 1927 (LeMay 1987: 104; UNPD 1998: 78; Hatton and Williamson 2008: 229). The Act also established a seven-category preference system, giving admission preference to relatives of US citizens and residents (64 percent); skilled migrants like scientists, professionals, and artists (employment-based categories combined to 30 percent); and refugees, particularly from Communist and Middle Eastern states (6 percent) (UNPD 1998: 79; Meyers 2004: 43; Hatton and Williamson 2008: 229).

Australia followed suit with amendments to its migration legislation that established four categories of immigrant applications: family reunification (at that point the largest), skilled migrants under a points-based system, special eligibility, and humanitarian (UNPD 1998: 70). Canada refined a similar points-based selection system in 1967 to boost employment. The Canadians gave preference to migrants who had pre-arranged employment in Canada, attained higher education and training, spoke proficient English or French, and satisfied other systematic preferences (UNPD 1998: 74; Hatton and Williamson 2008: 231).

After World War II, groups of countries responded with cooperative policies across particular regions. Rather than impose Visa Mix quotas or levels, Nordic states founded the Common Labor Market, which established their citizens' right to free movement without work restrictions and with transferable welfare state benefits, health services, and pensions in 1954 (UNPD 1998: 99; Bartram 2006: 42). As a result, migration flows outside of Soviet-controlled territory were relatively small. In the Eastern Bloc, migration to Western market economies was effectively forbidden, and migration between Soviet-controlled societies was restricted to family reunification. The exceptions were brief influxes to the West that were driven by political events like the 1956 uprising in Hungary, the 1968 Warsaw Pact invasion, and Poland's 1980 liberalization. The Soviet Union permitted thousands of Eastern European Jews to reunify with their families in Israel after the mid-1960s, and admitted about 97,000 African and Middle Eastern labor migrants between 1975 and 1979 (Okólski 2004: 35; Hatton and Williamson 2008: 207, 211). Mix-based policy was slower to develop in Western European states, which were concerned more about recruiting workers and limiting their length of stay.

After the oil shock of 1973, European countries stopped their active recruitment of labor, but post-colonial developments and the deterioration of the Soviet bloc sustained refugee population movements. Indeed, in the 1980s and 1990s, European states accepted increasing numbers of migrants from the Middle East, Asia, and Africa to the point that total incoming migration in Europe exceeded that of the United States since 2005 (Hatton and Williamson 2008: 206–8). With the fall of the Berlin Wall, emigration from Eastern Europe to Western Europe exploded from nearly nonexistent in the 1980s to about 1.2 million per year in the 1990s (Hatton and Williamson 2008: 212). Concurrently, the growth of oil production in Saudi Arabia, the United Arab Emirates, Kuwait, Qatar, and Bahrain spurred Gulf Arab states to increase their migrant stock ten-fold between 1975 and 1991 (Hatton and Williamson 2008), but under a strict regime of temporary labor visas – a further form of regulation.

The Regulation of the Temporary Ratio

Permanent migrant flow is in some ways more easily controlled by states than short-term temporary migration, given the difficulty of removals. Typically, countries have limited the residency of migrant flows in indirect ways with taxes, tests, and bans. After World War II, the world's industrial powers suddenly had pressing labor needs but a persistent unwillingness to alter their ethnocultural composition. Consequently, many states legislated policy that admitted migrants willing to reside only temporarily. The United States acted early to recruit temporary "guest workers" through its 1942 agreement with the West Indies and the 1942 Bracero Agreement with Mexico, which was enacted to ameliorate labor shortages in a manner that would be agreeable to racially-minded southern states that demanded cheap labor unlikely to "threaten" native job-seekers (Meyers 2004: 39; Craig 2014). Switzerland was one of the first countries to enact bilateral labor recruitment agreements after World War II, with a 1948 deal with Italy and other states thereafter (UNPD 1998: 104–5).

However, the largest and most well-known temporary migrant program (*gastarbeiter* or guest worker) was launched by Germany in 1955.

After first arranging an open-door permanent migration policy for ethnic Germans (the bulk of labor until 1961), the government then used inter-governmental agreements with Spain, Turkey, Greece, Portugal, Morocco, Tunisia, and Yugoslavia to recruit temporary workers after 1960 (Fielding 1993: 45–6). The system rested on the principle of rotation. Short-term contracts were negotiated between employers and migrants, and after one-year work and resident permits, foreign workers were expected to return home (Fielding 1993: 45; Martin 2004: 225–7). This system would continue until the first oil strikes took place in the 1970s. In the early 1990s, Germany re-established a more explicitly temporary contract worker program to fill certain seasonal job vacancies. From 1992 to 1999, 2.3 million guest workers were temporarily added to the German workforce via permits of about three months (Kruyt and Niessen 1997: 23; Martin 2004).

The *kafala* system in Gulf Arab states represents an alternate temporary arrangement. Under this approach, the employer-sponsor (known as the *kafeel*) takes full responsibility for the foreign worker, leading to a "structural dependence" in which workers rely upon their employers to live and work in a given Gulf state. Expatriate workers are required to work for the same employer throughout the tenure of their contract; if they choose to break their contract, they typically must pay their own return ticket home (Longva 1999: 22). In 2010, four GCC states (Bahrain, Kuwait, Qatar, and Saudi Arabia) announced that they would abolish the *kafala* system, but there has been little action. These countries believe immigrants' permanent residency will inevitably lead to immigrants' naturalization – a future they are unwilling to accept.

The Regulation of Naturalization Rates

Systematic citizenship laws significantly pre-date systematic admissions policies. Indeed, universal citizenship laws existed in ancient Athens, as discussed in the works of Aristotle (Heater 2004: 21–2). However, with the evolution of human movement's regulation, citizenship became a tool to distinguish entitled members from foreigners. As argued above, temporary migration programs are an implicit way to restrict the acquisition of citizenship, by simply legislating the requirement that migrants return to their origins after a designated period of residence. However, as temporary migration is an evolution of admissions regulation, states developed qualifications for and barriers to naturalization significantly before guest worker programs emerged.

At its most lenient, citizenship was merely a formality in most settler states that sought to occupy land seized from indigenous populations between the sixteenth and nineteenth centuries. Thereafter, each
of the world's settler states considered citizenship to be a territorial or
heritage-based birthright. Many of these policies endure today. Beyond
settler states, the United Kingdom offers a uniquely transparent case
study of how citizenship policies may reflect broader anxieties first about
labor needs and later about diversification and overpopulation. In 1948,
the British Nationality Act decreed that all subjects of Commonwealth
countries were to become British citizens upon stepping ashore in Great
Britain. In 1953, the UK offered Commonwealth laborers work permits
to fill labor shortages (Kruyt and Niessen 1997: 37; Meyers 2004: 67;
Schain 2008: 129). However, legislation in 1964, 1968, and 1971 implemented the racialized system of "partiality," whereby foreigners could
only claim British citizenship if they had a father or grandfather born or
naturalized in the United Kingdom (Fielding 1993: 48; Kruyt and Niessen
1997: 38; Schain 2008: 130–3). In 1981, the British Nationality Act sim-
plified citizenship groups and treated Commonwealth immigrants indis-
criminately from other foreigners (UNPD 1998: 100; Schain, 2008: 138).
This evolution nearly encompasses the spectrum of approaches to citizenship regulation over time – with the exception of the exclusionary
approach adopted in the Gulf states.

With their formally temporary labor admissions programs, Gulf Arab
states are able to almost universally restrict naturalization. The only ave-
nue to citizenship is by executive decree – an edict from the Emir himself
(Baldwin-Edwards 2011). This arbitrary framework is by far the most
restrictive approach to citizenship, particularly among countries with
significant flows of immigrants. The contingency of migrants' presence
in Gulf societies prevents migrants' entitlement to the benefits citizens
derive from local oil rents.

WHAT EXPLAINS REGIME VARIATION?

Given historic trends in policy and immigration outcomes, it is clear that
over the twentieth century, states have exerted increasing effort to control
human movement. However, such attempts vary in their enforcement and
efficacy across space and time. Social scientists have developed several theoretical accounts for what drives this variation, which we consider below.

Before embarking on this sketch of available theories, it is noteworthy
that we treat many of the most prominent possible drivers of migration

demographic outcomes as endogenous to the outcomes themselves; employment rates, economic growth, political stability, and democratic (or autocratic) rule all factor into the migration decisions that produce the outcomes we seek to explain. (For a full discussion of these migration demand determinants, see the Methodological Appendix.) Accordingly, the following review considers factors that are plausibly exogenous to the migration demographic outcomes that we enumerated earlier. We evaluate the extent to which these factors explain our results in Chapter 8.

Colonial Legacies

A number of migration researchers argue that states' colonial histories influence immigration policy outputs and outcomes in a path-dependent fashion. The argument is that ties with former colonies and settler state histories contribute to a greater openness to the presence of foreigners – in light of settler states' desire to occupy indigenous people's land (Freeman 1995; Harper and Constantine 2010), and due to the obligations and industrial links to former colonial empires (Fawcett 1989; Kritz, Lim and Zlotnik 1992; Massey et al. 1998: 40; Cangiano and Strozza 2008: 167–8; Hooghe et al. 2008: 479, citing Portes and Rumbaut 1996: 273). As Massey and his collaborators (1998: 41) argue, "[i]nternational migration is especially likely between past colonial powers and their former colonies, because cultural, linguistic, administrative, investment, transportation, and communication links were established early and were allowed to develop free from outside competition during the colonial era, leading to the formation of specific transnational markets and cultural systems." Correspondingly, a series of quantitative studies covering different states and time periods (Hooghe et al. 2008; Breunig et al. 2012: 851; DeWaard, Kim, and Raymer 2012: 1327; Fitzgerald, Leblang, and Teets 2014) find that colonial histories have a significant positive effect on the size of flows into major destination countries. Randall Hansen (2000: 244) also notes that 1962 marked a turning point in British immigration policy and political elites' attachment to the Commonwealth faded along with public sentiment opposing immigration. As such, this trend may be true of colonizers as well as their requisite colonies.

Colonial legacies have also been shown to affect the composition of migrant stock. For example, the inflow of Antillean and Surinamese immigrants into the Netherlands in the latter half of the twentieth century can be connected to the generous admission and naturalization rules for former colonial subjects in the Dutch Empire (Van Amersfoort and Penninx 1994). In other cases, political and economic turmoil has pushed people to emigrate to the stability of imperial centers, as when immigrants from Angola, Cape Verde, Mozambique, Brazil, and Guinea-Bissau moved to Portugal from the 1980s onwards (Vieira and Trindade 2008: 41). In the British context, the admission of immigrants from the colonies was part of a deliberate strategy to preserve the British Empire and to ward off independence movements, while at the same time British emigration was encouraged to maintain the white quality of British stock (Paul 1995). Inversely, the absence of a powerful colonial history might predict either lower levels of immigration and more targeted recruitment – as in the case of race-conscious Qatar and Bahrain – or more diverse recruitment – as in countries with heterogeneous migrant stock, such as Denmark (Skeldon 2007: 427).

Colonial legacies could also explain the relative openness of a country to naturalization. Janoski's (2010) seminal work on this topic demonstrates that former settler states are the most likely to naturalize immigrants, followed by former colonies and the Nordic countries (the latter being an exception to the path-dependent effects of colonial status, informed by the predominance of social democratic parties). Countries that were neither colonizers nor occupied by a colonial force have the lowest Naturalization Rates. Janoski (2010) argues that colonization requires concessions to the incoming population, suggesting that the length and nature of colonial status may also be important for influencing Naturalization Rates.

Population Aging

Immigration is widely understood to be an antidote to population aging (Alho 2008). However, current research on this subject matter examines immigration as a policy solution for aging, rather than as a causal relationship that may be tested. In particular, Lee and Mason (2011) contend that the admission of temporary immigrants does not specifically counteract structural aging, because migrants also age and temporary visas mandate their ultimate departure when these migrants are no longer of working age or capacity. Irrespective of the demographic reality, governments may defend immigration policies by citing structural aging and as such, we might expect greater immigration in contexts with faster aging rates. Italy, for example, features especially low fertility rates and has already begun to engage in forms of so-called replacement migration

(Billari and Dalla-Zuanna 2011: 114–15). By 2050, over half of the Italian population is predicted to be older than fifty-three (Bermingham 2001: 355–6). Japan has one of the fastest aging populations in the world and is increasingly reliant upon migrant labor to provide workers in the care and health sectors (Green 2017). Other Western nations, such as France, the United Kingdom and the United States, can maintain their current working populations with only marginal increases in immigration (Billari and Dalla-Zuanna 2011: 112). However, East Asian states such as China, Hong Kong, Taiwan, Singapore, Japan, Thailand, and South Korea will all experience around 10 percent population decline during the period between 2010 and 2040. This will leave countries like Japan with over a third of its population over the age of sixty-five by 2050 (Lee and Mason 2011: 198). If immigration mitigates such aging, it is reasonable to expect aging countries to increase the scale of their admissions and, potentially, their focus on economic mix, to address emerging skills gaps.

Natural Resource Wealth

Bearce and Hutnick (2011: 699) argue that resource-rich countries in particular may preference temporary immigration because such migrants place fewer demands upon resource rents than permanent immigrants and citizens. They argue that the economic dependency upon resources in such countries is better viewed not as a "resource curse" but as an "immigration curse" – that the pathologies of resource reliance stem from "labor imports related to resource production." This is especially true in Gulf states since the oil boom of the 1970s, when these countries imported migrant workers to make up for shortfalls in the domestic population (Russell 1989: 27; Chalcraft 2010; Fargues 2011: 275–6). Over time, an increasing reliance on migrant labor and state subsidies has entrenched low citizen employment rates, particularly among women (Kapiszewski 2006). Outside of the Gulf states, but concurrently, Canada (Foster and Taylor 2013; Foster and Barnetson 2015) and Australia (Bahn 2013; Boucher 2016: chapter 7) imported large-scale temporary migrant workers to support natural resource development. As such, we might anticipate that the extent of resource wealth of nations could inform the percentage of labor migration within the Visa Mix and the Temporary Ratio, with a stronger emphasis on temporary economic migration within resource-rich countries, than in other countries.

Economic Freedom

We might expect that countries with liberal economic approaches would also employ liberal approaches to the governance of human movement. Inversely, destinations that are more protectionist economically may extend this protectionism to labor markets and restrict the entry of both low- and high-skilled immigrants. Economic freedom is defined here as "the freedom to benefit from the fruits of one's labor through voluntary exchange while allowing this same right to others" (Ashby 2010: 51). While the scholarship in this area is limited, a number of researchers contend that economic freedom is associated with more lenient immigration programs, when measured in a variety of ways. In an analysis of fifty-eight countries and using bilateral migration stock as the measure of immigration, Ashby (2010) finds that economic freedom, along with relative per capita GDP, are the most significant predictors of migration flows, while Yakovlev and Steinkopf (2014) show that economic freedom is a significant predictor of the inflow of overseas doctors into immigration states, suggesting that improved economic freedom in sending states could reduce brain drain. Other researchers focusing upon internal migration have corroborated these findings (Cebula and Clark 2011; Cebula 2014; Cebula, Foley, and Hall 2015), but also find that economic freedom does not significantly explain international migration to the United States (Watkins and Yandle 2010).

Welfare State Generosity

Contentious public debates often present immigration as a threat to the welfare state (Borjas 2001; Kretsedemas and Aparicio 2004; Banting 2005; Bay and Pedersen 2006; Hinnfors, Spehar, and Bucken-Knapp 2012; Bucken-Knapp et al. 2014). For this reason, the question of whether welfare state design affects immigration policy outcomes is salient not only theoretically, but also practically and politically. The argument frequently presented is that welfare generosity will operate as a magnet for future immigration and therefore raise the overall volume of immigration flows (Brücker et al. 2002: 90; Hanson et al. 2002: 236; Becker 2004; Cigagna and Sulis 2015). It is important to point out that we are primarily referring here to the more fully developed welfare states of advanced industrial democracies, rather than the fledging and hybrid forms of welfare that exist in the developing world (Hort and Kuhnle 2000).

Welfare state generosity is a statistically significant predictor of the size of immigration flows (Boeri et al. 2012: 23; Cigagna and Sulis 2015: 22). Other studies conclude that generous welfare states attract more unskilled immigration to free migration zones such as the European Union, but not to systems with skill-based restrictions (Borjas 1989; Razin and Wahba 2011). This outcome is consistent with the assumption from economic theory that welfare states might exhibit a bias toward low-skilled migration since high-skilled migrants could earn more in countries with lower tax rates that support less generous welfare (Brücker et al. 2002: 68). This finding points to the multidirectional interaction between welfare and immigration policies whereby governments respond to the potential effects of increased immigration upon the welfare state through the introduction of more restrictive immigration selection criteria and less generous welfare policies (Banting 2000; 2005; Bommes 2000; Geddes 2000; Xu 2007).[3]

Political Ideology of the Ruling Government

The scholarship on the relationship between partisanship and immigration policy outcomes is divided. Partisan political position has sometimes been used to explain immigration or settlement policies, particularly across Western Europe (Ireland 2004; Lahav 2004: 133; Zaslove 2004; Givens and Luedtke 2005; Gudbrandsen 2010; Consterdine 2015). And some scholarship identifies the restrictive effects of right-wing governments upon immigration policies (Green-Pedersen and Odmalm 2008; Duncan 2010; Akkerman 2012).

However, this research should not suggest a uni-dimensional political scale with right-wing parties opposed to immigration and left-wing parties supportive of increased flows. As some scholars have argued, the traditional alliance of social democratic parties with unions (and thereby often the protection of domestic worker interests) can complicate the relationship between higher immigration flows and the liberalism of leftist

---

[3] It is important to note that studies on the effects of welfare state design upon immigration outcomes sometimes also control for the varieties of labor market regulation, primarily through a Varieties of Capitalism theoretical model. According to Devitt (2011) for instance, the structure of labor market regulation can in turn inform the skill level and volume of admitted economic migrants. However, the Varieties of Capitalism schema has not been extended to all of the twenty OECD countries that we consider in our final dataset. For this reason, we retained our focus primarily on welfare regime generosity in this book.

ideology (Hinnfors et al. 2012; Berg and Spehar 2013: 156; Bucken-Knapp et al. 2014: 598). Further, others argue that immigration is an area frequently met with bipartisan responses from political parties, in part because conflict over immigration might threaten incumbency (Freeman 1995: 884). Still others suggest that even if rhetorically right-wing governments are more likely to favor immigration restrictions than others, this ideological preference may not impact actual policy outcomes, especially if these parties are positioned within a governing coalition (Akkerman and de Lange 2012). This is an important point because the measure of "policy" in these studies is often the party position on immigration, as reflected in manifesto documents, expert surveys (Van Spanje 2010; Han 2015) or legal documents (Givens and Luedtke 2005) rather than the actual migration demographic outcomes that are the focus of this book.

In contrast, studies that focus upon actual immigration outcomes as opposed to policy provide mixed and questionable results about the role of party position. Toshkov (2014) finds that GDP per capita is a more important predictor of asylum rates than government positions on asylum seekers, while Neumayer (2005) finds that destination unemployment rates explain asylum rates more than government party positions on humanitarian migration. Bolin, Lidén, and Nyhlén (2014) find that the percentage of seats held at the municipal level by the Social Democrats in Sweden has a statistically significant effect upon the acceptance rate of asylum seekers.

Recent work argues that the presence of anti-immigrant parties within the party system can lead to more restrictive immigration policies, even if they do not hold office (Schain 2006; Howard 2010), because their appeal pressures elected parties to pander to these interests (Green-Pedersen and Odmalm 2008; Van Spanje 2010; Fitzgerald et al. 2014; Cetin 2015: 392; Han 2015). In other work, Morales, Pilet, and Ruedin (2015: 1501–2, 1507) find that anti-immigrant mobilization independent from the party system has a greater effect than parties themselves in shaping restrictive immigration policies.

We might anticipate that variation in the party system across the countries analyzed in this book could in part explain immigration regime variation. Yet, none of these explanatory hypotheses have been tested using cross-national, multidimensional immigration data – whether on migration policy outputs or demographic outcomes – because, until now, no such dataset has existed. This book, and its collection of immigration demographic data, presents an opportunity to apply these ideas and better understand what drives the development of immigration regimes – both as they relate to the historically relevant outcomes discussed in the first half of this chapter and to states' current migration profiles. The next three chapters build a conceptual framework for systematically assessing these profiles – one dimension at a time.

4

Visa Mix

A Global Preference for Labor Immigration?

This chapter considers an issue that is central to policymakers, but is often overlooked in immigration research: the "Visa Mix." We define Visa Mix as the relative distribution of immigrants entering a country under designated laws related to labor, family reunification, humanitarian refuge, or free movement. Is there a large-scale inflow of economic migrants? Or do family reunification migrants, entering on the basis of marital status, next-of-kin, or extended familial relationships, predominate? Is the immigration system permissive of humanitarian immigration or free flows across borders, given bilateral or multilateral agreements between sending and receiving states? As a share of total immigration flows, the distribution of visa-holders across these major categories constitute a regime's Visa Mix.[1]

We argue in this chapter that although Visa Mix has not been treated explicitly as a variable of interest in migration studies, it ought to be central to the study of immigration governance for a number of reasons. The composition of immigration visa flows is of key political salience. Debates in both North America and Europe focus on the capacity of governments to transform their immigration programs into more economically oriented intake (Koslowski 2014; Boucher 2016). Public perceptions of greater social welfare costs associated with family unification and, in

---

[1] Given data impediments and reliability concerns, as noted in Chapter 1, we do not consider undocumented or regularizations within the program mix, although in many countries, such migration forms an important part of the overall picture of the Visa Mix (OECD 2012: 39). This is a necessary shortcoming of focusing upon available standardized data exclusively. We do, however, discuss some aspects of undocumented immigration as it relates to Visa Mix qualitatively below.

particular, humanitarian immigration, have fueled a policy preference for economic immigration in many countries. Yet, a central finding of the chapter is that an increasing political focus upon economic migration in democracies has not translated into a greater share of permanent economic visas, but rather a greater share of temporary economic and free movement visas, the latter of which are operating as a de facto form of economic-based entry.

Such free movement immigration is not without controversy, especially in continental Europe where expansion of the European Union has generated debates about appropriate levels of immigration flows from the new accession states, and arguably contributed to the decision of the United Kingdom in 2016 to exit the European Union. This debate carries heightened urgency with the entry of hundreds of thousands of asylum seekers from the Middle East and Africa into the Schengen Zone of borderless travel – a keystone of the common market. Finally, as we demonstrate later in this chapter, the relative percentage of these different categories within immigration flows does appear to affect the gender and ethnic make-up of the immigration body. As such, Visa Mix holds real implications for the maintenance of multicultural and diverse immigration selection programs, a key concern for many democratic governments (Green and Green 2004; Joppke 2005b).

A final salient point of inquiry here is whether the governments of non-democracies, through their capacity both to expel and control family and humanitarian immigration, and effectively limit all non-citizen access to the welfare state, have avoided this challenge, as some commentators have argued (e.g. Breunig et al. 2012). Indeed, we find that most non-democracies in our study enjoy higher rates of economic migration and either low or negligible rates of family, humanitarian, and free movement migration than their Western counterparts.

The first section of this chapter traces several key policy debates over Visa Mix that have emerged over the last thirty years. We then set out our approach to data collection and measurement before finally presenting our major empirical findings regarding Visa Mix across the thirty-three countries for which mix data were available in our reference year of 2011. Further attention is given to the relationships between free movement and economic immigration, and between family reunification and democratic regime status, as well as the question of whether we are in fact witnessing a shift toward economic immigration as posited by some observers. We conclude the chapter by assessing the implications of changes in compositional Visa Mix for the gender and origin diversity of immigration flows. We also present our argument that the main shift in Visa Mix has occurred in the free movement category, along with temporary economic migration visas, a point that we pursue further in Chapter 5.

VISA MIX OVER SPACE AND TIME

When the United States attempted comprehensive immigration policy reform between 2006 and 2018, one of the central issues was the extent to which its large family reunification program would and could be reduced to permit a relative increase in labor immigration. Across Western Europe as well, governments have called for more selective immigration programs with point tests often preferred as a mechanism to select skilled immigrants (OECD 2006). The French government pursued a policy of "immigration choisie" since 2006, where it aimed – ultimately unsuccessfully – to increase economic immigration to over 50 percent by 2012 while stemming family reunification from former colonies (Paul 2013: 131). Meanwhile, Denmark, Germany, Ireland, New Zealand, and the UK have all recently adopted points tests for skilled immigration.

This rhetorical focus of Western governments on economic immigration is in part related to population aging and the perceived role that "pro-active migration policy" can play in ameliorating such demographic trends (OECD 2006: 112). Chaloff and Lemaître (2009: 4) summarize: "Most OECD countries expect growing shortages of highly-skilled labour in the coming decades, and immigration is viewed as one way of addressing these. Most OECD countries have introduced policies aimed at facilitating the recruitment of such workers in recent years and efforts along these lines can be expected to continue." The extent of structural aging in industrial economies is significant. While currently there exists only a scattering of OECD nations where the fifteen to nineteen age bracket is smaller than the sixty to sixty-four bracket, by 2020, "all but Ireland, Mexico and Turkey are projected to experience a decline in the working-age population, based on the current age structure of the population" (Chaloff and Lemaître 2009: 13–14).

In contrast to this political valorization of economic immigration, family immigration has been cast as far less desirable in many Western countries. Trends to reduce or tighten criteria for family reunification are now commonplace across Western Europe (Charsley et al. 2012; Block 2015). As Block and Bonjour (2013: 203) highlight, Austria, Belgium, Denmark, Germany, France, the Netherlands, Sweden, and the UK have all increased requirements for family reunification immigrants; the argument underpinning this shift is that economic immigrants perform better in the labor market than those entering through family visas.

The evidence that changing the compositional mix of an immigration regime also shifts the economic performance of the total immigrant population is contested. For instance, in Australia, where immigration moved from a family to economic focus in 1996, most economists argue that there was an accompanying reduction in the unemployment rate of new immigrants (Richardson 1999; Richardson et al. 2004; Cobb-Clark and Khoo 2006). Similar research supports this view in Canada (Citizenship and Immigration Canada 1994; Green and Green 1995), Western Europe (Zimmermann 2005), and Singapore (Fong 2006: 161). However, other researchers argue that the relative fiscal benefits of focusing upon economic immigration in the Visa Mix are overstated. Economic migrants may face challenges in having overseas qualifications formally recognized. There may be a mismatch between their skills and those required in the labor market. And they may be discriminated against based on their skin color or accent, just like family immigrants. Moreover, without family members to orient them, economic migrants may experience cultural integration challenges both professionally and in other settings that affect salaries (Doomernik et al. 2009: 27; Boeri et al. 2012: 60–1). Over time, family migrants can catch up with economic migrants and make significant financial contributions (Jasso and Rosenzweig 1995; Wanner 2003). Finally, family immigrants may provide significant non-economic, supportive contributions that can liberate other family members to work, such as unpaid care work by female immigrants. This brief summation suggests that the classic demarcation between family and economic-based immigration is more sharply drawn by policymakers than is perhaps reflective of actual economic performance.

The veracity of these arguments aside, there remains a strong political preference for economic immigration in the Visa Mix of many democratic countries. Yet, this preference for high economic immigration flows within democracies may be mitigated by other factors, including court actions that protect family reunification (Guiraudon 1997; Joppke 1998; 1999) or the strength of immigrant lobbies in maintaining existing arrangements (Freeman 1995). As we argue later in this chapter, the proportion of economic immigration can also be limited – or perhaps more accurately, supplanted – by the extent to which free movement is permitted, such as within the European Union.

In autocratic nations, the relationship between policymaker preference and actual immigration outcomes is often more direct than in democracies.

Autocratic nations are more adept at stemming or blocking family reunification than democracies, given that the mechanisms to achieve this outcome often violate migrants' basic political and social rights, such as the
right to family life (Breunig et al. 2012: 829). These regimes are free
of the pressure from independent courts or international human rights
bodies that confer such rights to long-term resident immigrants (see
International Migrants Bill of Rights 2011). When immigration is viewed
exclusively as the provision of human economic capital, as it is in many
autocratic states, family reunification plays a more minor role.

Unsurprisingly then, family immigration is often more strongly restricted
by policy instruments in the Gulf states, China, and Singapore, than in
democracies. For example, Singapore raised marriage duration requirements for spousal sponsorship to discourage certain forms of cross-border
spousal immigration from poorer neighboring countries (Government of
Singapore 2014). In Kuwait, female migrants who bear children may be
jailed or deported following the delivery of the child and forcibly separated
from their infants (Mahdavi 2015: 72–3). Some of these nations have also
faced challenges in altering their Visa Mix to a more economic tilt and, as
noted earlier, even in these nations, we still find traces of family reunification
and humanitarian immigration occurring, albeit at much lower levels than
in democracies. It is important to use standardized measures to compare
these outcomes with Western democracies, which are often treated as polar
opposites to major autocratic immigration regimes and not considered in
comparative perspective.

MEASUREMENT

For the OECD countries analyzed in this chapter, we employ standardized
data on permanent immigration flows, published in the OECD's *International
Migration Outlook* reports since 2006 for the numerator of "Visa Mix." As
Alan Gamlen (2010: 23) notes, this collection "constitutes a kind of industry
standard" that relies upon residence permit data issued from OECD member states (Fron et al. 2008: 2). In contrast to other efforts that standardize immigration flows cross-nationally but do not disaggregate according
to immigration visa status (DeWaard et al. 2012; Abel and Sander 2014),
such a disaggregation exercise was undertaken for the OECD data.[2] Further
details on the OECD's approach is found in the Methodological Appendix.

[2] Although DeWaard and collaborators' (2012) standardization of immigration data for
OECD member states (the Migration Modelling for Statistical Analysis) or MIMOSA
Project can be viewed as more comprehensive and rigorous than the OECD efforts by

Our Visa Mix analysis relies on the categorization of permanent immigration flow data for OECD countries into four major groupings and a similar categorization of temporary data for those countries that only admit temporary work migrants:

(1) Work (including workers' accompanying family)
(2) Family
(3) Humanitarian
(4) Free movement, international agreement, and other.

Work covers all forms of economic visas but also those family migrants who enter with a work-visa holder but are not themselves the agents of migration. It is important to note that these data do not distinguish between skilled and unskilled economic migrants.[3] Family includes any family reunification that follows, but unlike accompanying family, is not tied to the initial economic migration. Rather it constitutes reunification with existing residents or nationals. Humanitarian visas cover those formally recognized as refugees. As asylum seekers may be only included temporarily if their claims are not recognized by the host state, they are only included in the permanent calculation for OECD purposes if they have been granted long-term residency (Fron et al. 2008: 4).

The final category combines free movement, international agreement, and the residual "other" category. Free movement covers those entries "subject to very few restrictions," such as intra-EU migrants (OECD 2006: 117). As the OECD notes, this form of immigration is classified as "free" because "the international treaties concerned have defined new rights of entry for non-citizens, over which signatory countries cannot in principle exercise discretion once they come fully into force" (OECD 2006: 118). As per the Trans-Tasman Travel Arrangement, Australian and New Zealand citizens also enjoy free movement between their countries. "International agreements" refer primarily to bilateral agreements between Latin American countries (OECD/IDB/OAS 2012). In light of the free movement such migrants effectively enjoy, in this book we subsume this particular category within the broader free movement visa category. "Other" covers any residual categories such as ancestry-based visas, retirees, and those entering

---

virtue of its adopted optimization procedure for standardization, these scholars do not disaggregate according to Visa Mix classification or the Temporary Ratio, considered in Chapter 5. As such, we prefer the OECD data.

[3] Comparative cross-national data on skill level is available in stock but not in flow format (Boeri et al. 2012).

via independent means (Fron et al. 2008: 8). Its composition changes from state to state and is also subsumed within free movement. We consider these categories of admission as a percentage of total immigration flows. Further details are provided in the Methodological Annex.

An obvious omission in the OECD data is undocumented immigration. Evidence suggests that undocumented flows play an important role in providing immigrant workers worldwide (e.g. Papadopoulos 2011). Further, if immigrants are entering without documentation, they may provide a disincentive for governments to create legal economic worker channels, as the needs of employers will at least be partially met through clandestine means. As such, the two categories interact in a symbiotic fashion. Although there are no reliable comparative estimates of undocumented flows into our range of selected countries, later in this chapter, we discuss existing qualitative evidence of undocumented stock in key European nations, alongside an analysis of the possible effects of previous amnesties and regularizations upon Visa Mix.

The OECD does not report Visa Mix flow data for all of its member states. For certain countries, data are unavailable or missing in the various years of our analysis.[4] As will become clear in the following section, there are also fewer OECD countries represented in the time series from 2006 through to 2011, than for 2011 alone. Details of data sources for Latin America and South Africa are included in the Methodological Appendix.

For the other non-OECD countries of interest that do not admit immigrants on a permanent basis (primarily autocratic nations), a comparative exercise was complicated by three factors. First, flow data is not always publicly available from governments of these countries. Second, most of these countries do not have any form of recorded permanent immigration entry. Third, most of these countries do not provide information of visa duration, which would allow harmonization of temporary permits according to the discussed methods developed by the OECD. In order to maximize breadth of countries, we include analysis of the Visa Mix of temporary permits for non-OECD countries outside of Latin America (principally the GCC states, China, and Singapore) in this chapter, but present this information in additional tables where it is instructive.[5]

---

[4] For instance, no data are available for the entire time series (2006 through to 2011) for either Turkey or Greece as governments from these countries did not make data publicly available to the OECD (OECD, pers. comm.).

[5] Information on these countries is also provided in the Methodological Appendix. These quantitative data are supplemented and corroborated by secondary data collected via desk analysis, from websites, newspaper articles, and existing secondary analysis.

DESCRIPTIVE RESULTS

How do countries differ in their Visa Mix? Figure 4.1 sets out the major variation in permanent Visa Mix outcomes according to the four major categories for the OECD, Latin America, Russia, and South Africa. It also sets out the Visa Mix for the remaining available countries with exclusively temporary migration for the most recent available year.

Work-Related Admissions

Observing Figures 4.1 and 4.2, it is clear that there is particularly strong representation of work-related migration not only, as predicted, in autocratic states like Qatar, China, and Russia, but also in Mexico. South Korea, a country which is often associated with labor immigration, has comparatively low levels of permanent economic immigration. However, as we will see in Chapter 5's analysis of temporary economic migration, this assessment alters when we also consider temporary labor immigration, as most of the entry on economic grounds into South Korea is on a temporary basis (Seol and Skrentny 2004). Figures 4.1 and 4.2 therefore reflect the relatively low levels of permanent economic immigration to South Korea. It is also likely that the Mexican share of labor migrants is inflated by its underestimation of undocumented humanitarian migrants admitted from South America, the Caribbean, and Africa (Zavis 2016). Many such migrants use Mexico as a country of transit en route to the United States, where they ultimately enter without authorization or claim asylum. And while some could make recognized asylum claims, many are more aptly characterized as non-refugee forced migrants – fleeing conflict, extreme poverty, environmental disasters, and other risks not covered by the Refugee Convention (Human Rights Watch 2016).

Our analysis of the Visa Mix proportions are informed by the inclusion of accompanying family within the work category. Among the OECD countries, work-based immigration is elevated in Australia, Canada, and the United Kingdom by the inclusion of such family members entering on work visas. This reflects a trend in these countries toward skilled immigration, coupled with the maintenance of accompanying family migration rights, especially for nuclear family members. Further, given that policymakers often treat these two categories together for the purposes of calculating economic migration (insofar that accompanying family visa holders are "attached" to a primary economic visa-holder spouse or parent), these two categories can be viewed as representing an

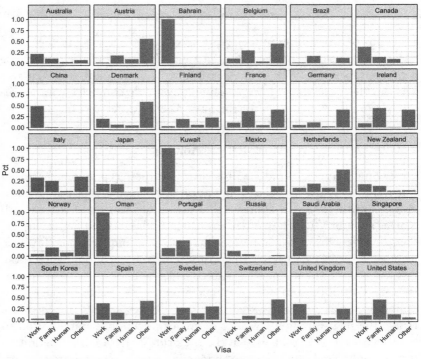

FIGURE 4.1. **Permanent Visa Mix into selected countries, 2011.**
Sources: Statistics South Africa 2012; OECD/IDB/OAS 2012; OECD standard-ized dataset 2013 using 2011 flow data; Bahrain: GLMM 2014a (2011 data). China: Bureau of Entry and Exit Administration of the Ministry of Public Security 2011 (2009 data). Kuwait: GLMM 2013b (2011 data). Oman: GLMM 2014b (2011 data). Saudi Arabia: GLMM 2013a (2010 data). Note that these figures record flow data, as is also the case for the OECD countries.

economic policy focus within those countries (see Kofman and Meetoo 2008; Boucher 2016: chapter 4). As in South Korea, rates of economic temporary immigration are also far higher than those for permanent economic migration in Australia, Canada, South Africa, and the United States (Nakache and Kinoshita 2010; Crush 2011: 11–12; Klotz 2013; Boyd 2014; Boucher 2016: chapter 7). So if we aggregate temporary and permanent entry categories in these countries, the overall economic focus is greater than represented through a focus on permanent Visa Mix alone. As such, an evaluation of the relative shift toward economic migration that has occurred within countries inside the permanent Visa Mix must also be considered alongside our findings in Chapter 5 related to tempo-rary economic migration.

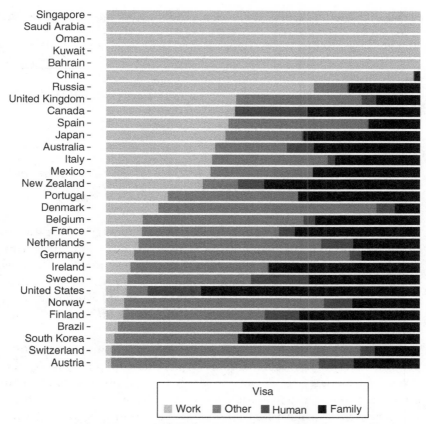

FIGURE 4.2. **Visa Mix into selected countries, 2011.** Visa Mix visualized as a share of all permanent admissions.
Sources: Statistics South Africa 2012; OECD/IDB/OAS 2012; OECD standardized dataset 2013 using 2011 flow data; Bahrain: GLMM 2014a; (2011 data). China: Bureau of Entry and Exit Administration of the Ministry of Public Security 2011 (2009 data). Kuwait: GLMM 2013b (2011 data). Oman: GLMM 2014b (2011 data). Saudi Arabia: GLMM 2013a (2010 data). Note that these figures record flow data, as is also the case for the OECD countries.

Turning to the non-OECD countries, economic visas represent the vast majority of entry into China. Work-related immigration is generally higher in non-OECD states and autocratic nations than in democracies. Bahrain, Kuwait, Oman, and Saudi Arabia all have rates of economic immigration over 79 percent (Figures 4.1 and 4.2). This economic focus across autocratic nations validates observations that leaders in these countries are far less constrained by the norms and rights demands of both immigrants and citizens than in democracies. They are consequently more able to influence immigration outcomes than leaders in democratic

TABLE 4.1. *Accompanying family migration as a percentage of total flows in select GCC states and China, 2006–11*

Country	2011	2010	2009	2008	2007	2006
Bahrain	17	18	18	n/a	n/a	n/a
China	n/a	2	n/a	n/a	n/a	n/a
Kuwait	21	n/a	20	n/a	n/a	n/a
Oman	1	n/a	n/a	n/a	n/a	n/a
Saudi Arabia	n/a	14	n/a	17	18	22

Sources: Bahrain: GLMM 2014a. China: Bureau of Entry and Exit Administration of the Ministry of Public Security 2011. Kuwait: GLMM 2013b. Oman: GLMM 2014b. Saudi Arabia: GLMM 2013a. n/a signifies missing data.

states (Breunig et al. 2012: 827). While these authors focus their analysis on the overall immigrant stock, we can also apply this argument to flow-based Visa Mix. In Chapters 7 and 8, we demonstrate that the type of political regime correlates with variation in Visa Mix distributions, as non-democracies tend to cluster together. To complicate this picture further, we must consider the interaction of economic and accompanying family in available autocratic nations.

As noted earlier, the Work category aggregates both work and accompanying family visas. Table 4.1 above presents collected data on the extent of temporary accompanying family immigration compared with economic temporary immigration across available non-OECD countries. It is important to emphasize that family here is primarily of an accompanying family nature given that independent family reunification is not permitted in these countries in most instances.

These non-OECD countries openly discourage family immigration by imposing very high-income conditions or by assessing fees for accompanying family residency permits (Nagy 2010: 59–60). Further restrictions are placed indirectly upon the reunification of family members with economic immigrants in the Gulf states through requirements that these workers live in employer-controlled housing or in purpose-built work camps that do not accommodate family members (Nagy 2010: 59).

In some instances, residency rights for immigrants and family members are delimited by the occupational classification of the primary worker and his or her related visa conditions. In Bahrain, most economic work permits are in the domestic service and construction sectors, which do not carry accompanying family rights (Nagy 2010: 59). In other Gulf countries, such as Kuwait, some children are allowed to stay with migrant parents but male children over twenty-one are required to leave unless they secure independent employment. Sponsorship rights in Kuwait are also deeply gendered as women in employment are rarely permitted to sponsor their husbands (Shah 2011: 353–4).

Yet, despite Gulf state policies that clearly favor temporary work-related migration and are highly restrictive of family flows, there appears nonetheless to be some quasi-permanent family migration into the region. This includes inflows of settled accompanying family as well as Gulf-born migrant children. Although this group is not reflected in official statistics as reported in Table 4.2, there is strong reason to believe that such family reunification is occurring without official state recognition. Philippe Fargues (2011: 287) provides two means by which this inference can be drawn. First, in several Gulf countries, there are quite high numbers of child non-nationals. Of ten million children under fifteen years of age who presently live in the Gulf, 21 percent are non-nationals. Indeed, in the United Arab Emirates, non-national children represent the majority of children (61 percent). This suggests a tacit tolerance of immigrant children, born either domestically or overseas, even if this is not consistent with government policy or reflected in available immigration statistics.

Similarly, in many Gulf countries, large percentages of the elderly are non-nationals. In fact, in Bahrain, Kuwait, Oman, Saudi Arabia, and the UAE, there are more non-nationals than nationals over sixty-five (Fargues 2011: 288). While it is possible that some non-nationals over sixty-five years old are engaged in paid employment and present on renewed temporary worker permits, it is likely that many are not and that their enduring residency represents a form of de facto permanent family-based migration of elders who were previously migrant workers. Even if we rely exclusively upon existing flow data for the Gulf countries as displayed in Table 4.2, it is clear that not all immigration into the region is work-related. These data suggest that while all the recorded Gulf states have rates of family immigration lower than the democratic nations, they have not restricted family migration entirely. Further, in China, 80,050 persons were recorded as entering on a family basis in 2009, a not insignificant number but clearly dwarfed by the scale of economic flows (Bureau of Entry and Exit Administration of the Ministry of Public Security 2011).

Undocumented Migration

Our understanding of the scope of economic migration within the Visa Mix will necessarily be limited if we do not also consider undocumented migration. As we argue above, irregular forms of economic immigration might act as a partial replacement for formal channels of immigration, creating disincentives for governments to regularize these channels and for employers to sponsor legal migrants. Data restrictions prevent a comprehensive assessment of this issue. However, existing stock data on undocumented migration gives some indication of the scale of undocumented migration within key countries. They thereby stand as a partial corrective of our analysis of flows.

The most frequently cited statistics on undocumented immigration pertain to the United States, with its 11.3 million undocumented migrants, many of whom are employed in low-skilled sectors (Krogstad and Passel 2015). Within the European Union, estimates from the European Database on Irregular Migration reveal that undocumented migrants comprise between 1 percent (Denmark) and 91 percent (Poland) of the foreign immigrant stock of member states (Kovacheva and Vogel 2009; cited in Papadopoulos 2011: 33). Further, as analysts have noted, while legal economic channels provide important gateways for skilled workers, undocumented migration is often the mechanism for the importation of lower skilled workers into the construction and care sectors (Papadopoulos 2011: 34).

Undocumented migration is not limited to immigration states in the Global North. Indeed, Shah (2009: Table 2) estimates that 18 percent of workers in Saudi Arabia, 37 percent in the UAE, and 41 percent in Qatar are undocumented. Martin Baldwin-Edwards (2011: 39–40) explains that the high rates of undocumented migrants within the foreign population in these countries is in part explained by visa trading, whereby employers sell the visa rights of sponsored workers to third parties, leaving the original migrant in an unauthorized posting.

Statistics from recent amnesties also provide additional information on the extent of undocumented flows into receiving states and possible implications of these movements for Visa Mix. For instance, since the 1986 Immigration Reform and Control Act (IRCA) amnesty in the United States, more than 3.7 million unauthorized immigrants have been regularized. Across Western Europe, amnesties have played an important role in immigration policy, especially in Spain, Greece, and Italy, with over five million immigrants regularized across the European Union since 1996 (Baldwin-Edwards 2007; Kerwin, Brick, and Kilberg 2012). The Spain regularization program of 2005 was intended not only to regularize undocumented immigrants and to strengthen immigration enforcement, but also to expand economic immigration channels for previously undocumented workers (Arango and Jachimowicz 2005). As Kate Brick (2011) argues, amnesties may in part act as a substitute for formal humanitarian or low-skilled economic entry programs and, as such, could reduce flows into other parts of the Visa Mix.[6] While it is impossible to know how many of these individuals would have otherwise entered through other immigration channels, it is clear that amnesties can affect the broader composition of Visa Mix. As such, this qualitative material must be considered alongside the quantitative data presented throughout this chapter.

Family Migration

In several countries, family migration is a principal form of entry. It makes up over 40 percent of the Visa Mix in the United States and Ireland and over 20 percent in Belgium, France, Italy, Portugal, and Sweden. While family reunification makes up a large percentage of flows into many countries, it has exceptionally strong representation in the United States. This skewed Visa Mix can be attributed to the elevated flows of extended family members, such as parents, grandparents, brothers, and sisters, and a policy preference for family immigration within permanent immigration (Tichenor 2002).

In contrast, in recent years, many European nations have placed increased restrictions upon family reunification through immigration selection policies (Charsley et al. 2012: 861–2; OECD 2012: 109–10; Wray, Agoston, and Hutton 2014). These policies include those that raise the required age of sponsorship of a family member or spouse, introduce maintenance bonds as a prerequisite to sponsorship of family members, impose integration and naturalization tests upon new immigrants, and curtail welfare provisions to family migrants (Wray et al. 2014). Some of these policies have been introduced under the rubric of the 2003 European Union Family Reunification Directive, which while permitting large interpretative scope by individual member states (Bonjour 2014) has seen a generalized convergence toward more restrictive family reunification policies (Koopmans et al. 2012; Wray et al. 2014).

The natural question to ask is whether such policies have been successful in restricting actual family flows through a reduction in the relative percentage of family visas over time. In Table 4.2, we exclude those states that either prohibit family migration or only admit immigrants on family

---

[6] For an economic defense of this argument, see Karlson and Katz (2010).

TABLE 4.2. *Family migration as a percentage of overall immigration flows into the OECD, Latin America, Russia, and South Africa, 2006–11*

Country	2011	2010	2009	2008	2007	2006
Argentina	n/a	23	25	n/a	n/a	n/a
Australia	10	12	10	10	11	11
Austria	18	18	16	16	18	28
Belgium	29	37	41	24	25	35
Brazil	n/a	16	9	n/a	n/a	n/a
Canada	13	13	15	15	17	18
Denmark	7	11	11	8	13	13
Finland	19	16	15	15	14	14
France	37	39	37	40	41	45
Germany	11	10	9	9	10	11
Ireland	43	32	39	35	34	6
Israel	n/a	n/a	1	10	19	18
Italy	25	24	26	24	15	30
Japan	18	14	14	14	14	14
Mexico	9	10	n/a	n/a	n/a	n/a
Netherlands	18	18	18	18	12	13
New Zealand	13	11	10	10	10	10
Norway	20	17	17	22	21	29
Peru	n/a	26	18	n/a	n/a	n/a
Portugal	36	31	29	33	22	49
Russia	4	11	16	12	13	n/a
South Africa	18	n/a	n/a	n/a	n/a	n/a
South Korea	15	16	15	12	15	15
Spain	16	18	24	19	15	n/a
Sweden	26	31	38	38	34	32
Switzerland	8	10	8	8	8	9
United Kingdom	8	9	10	10	10	10
United States	45	46	47	42	43	46
Median	18					14.5

This table excludes states that do not permit family migration independent of economic flows.

Sources: OECD standardized data, 2006–10; OECD/IDB/OAS (2012); Statistics South Africa (2012). The appearance of n/a signifies missing data. The median is calculated using only countries for which data are available in both 2011 and 2006.

visas if they are accompanying a work-related visa holder. As we explain earlier, such accompanying family counts as economic entry and therefore is not a true form of family migration.

The data show that family immigration has been restricted significantly in certain countries between 2006 through to 2011. In Russia, family immigration dropped from 13 percent in 2007 to 4 percent in 2011. This imbalance appears to be related in large part to high numbers of economic migrants from former Soviet states entering Russia to work, due in large part to the income differential between these countries (Ivanov 2012: 12, 15). In Austria, family immigration decreased from 28 percent in 2006 to 18 percent in 2011, in Italy it fell from 30 percent in 2006 to 25 percent in 2011 and in Portugal it dropped from 49 percent in 2006 to 36 percent in 2011.

There are a variety of ways in which family migration has been curtailed. Some of these reductions can be attributed to policies that seek to limit the right to family unification under international law. These include the imposition of income and assets testing upon migrant sponsors, the raising of age limits for spousal entry, as has been the case in Austria, or even the setting of minimum accommodation standards to reduce the number of people resident in each square-meter of an apartment as introduced in France, Sweden, and Hungary (Salt and Dobson 2013: 15; Wray et al. 2014). Concomitant reductions in the inflow of third country nationals into the United Kingdom (discussed in further detail below) could also inform the extent of subsequent family migration. Collectively these measures could impact the scale of family reunification flows.

The plethora of policies as well as variation across states in their representation of family immigrants in their Visa Mix challenges the idea that such policies are effective to restrict family flows across the board. Indeed, over this same period, family migration has increased in Brazil, Ireland, and New Zealand. When we take the cross-national median for family migration for the available countries for each of the years, we in fact find a very gradual increase in family migration from 14.5 percent in 2006 to 18 percent in 2011. Therefore, while some countries like Russia and Austria have altered their family immigration profile significantly, the overall picture is of recent stability or gradual evolution rather than revolution, with the most significant changes in policy attitudes rather than actual migration demographic outcomes.

A SHIFT TOWARDS ECONOMIC IMMIGRATION?

The interaction between family reunification and economic migration in the Visa Mix can also be analyzed by considering the relative growth in the latter. At the same time that punitive measures have been undertaken against family reunification across some countries, governments have also introduced policy incentives aimed at increasing the proportion of skilled immigrants within their Visa Mix. These policies range from tax credits to opportunities to move from temporary education visas onto permanent visas for the highly skilled (Guellec and Cervantes 2001: 84). Does a purported structural need for skilled immigration and an articulated government preference for economic immigration over family reunification correspond with changes in migration demographic outcomes that in turn prioritize economic migration? An OECD study by Guellec and Cervantes (2001: 74) demonstrates mixed results in this regard. Some countries over the 1990s experienced increases in the proportion of skilled immigration while others saw a relative increase in family immigration. Drawing upon more recent standardized OECD data on allocation of work-based visas, we compare the relative percentage of work-related immigration from 2006 through to 2011.

Table 4.3 demonstrates considerable variation in the relative proportion of permanent work-related immigration, both across countries and time. Work-related immigration in OECD countries includes accompanying family members and ranges from a low of 0 percent of immigration into Sweden in 2006 to 41 percent in Canada in 2010, which is likely a product of the latter's strong focus upon skilled, points-tested migration (Boucher 2016: chapters 4–6). In some countries, such permanent work-related migration has increased over the six-year period. Yet, in other countries including Australia, Finland, Ireland, New Zealand, Norway, and Portugal, there have actually been slight reductions in the relative percentages of permanent economic migration. Over this relatively short five-year period, there is no major shift toward permanent economic migration, and reductions over time in some countries may also be attributable to the global financial crisis that saw reductions in permanent migrant worker programs (Martin 2011). In Australia and New Zealand, these slight reductions in the Visa Mix of permanent economic migration reflect less a shift toward other categories of permanent migrant selection and more the sharp proportionate increase in temporary economic flows over this same period, often through uncapped admissions of temporary workers.

Taking the median of percentages across the countries for each of the five years, we see a change from 8.5 percent of economic migration in 2006 to 9.5 percent of economic migration in 2011. This represents more of an incremental increase over a five-year period across pooled countries than a transformational shift. We therefore observe an interesting, and potentially revealing, policy gap between the intentions of policymakers to strengthen the

TABLE 4.3. *Permanent work-related immigration as a percentage of total flows across time in the OECD, Latin America, Russia, and South Africa, 2006–11*

Country	2011	2010	2009	2008	2007	2006
Australia	22	22	21	21	22	23
Austria	2	2	2	2	2	2
Belgium	10	9	11	12	12	8
Brazil	n/a	1	1	n/a	n/a	n/a
Canada	36	41	36	35	33	36
Denmark	20	22	19	15	20	16
Finland	3	3	4	7	6	4
France	10	11	11	11	8	5
Germany	5	4	3	4	3	3
Ireland	9	5	8	9	8	12
Italy	33	37	32	29	25	20
Japan	18	12	12	13	13	11
Mexico	11	15	n/a	n/a	n/a	n/a
Netherlands	9	9	10	12	8	4
New Zealand	17	20	20	19	19	21
Norway	5	5	5	7	6	6
Peru	n/a	13	12	n/a	n/a	n/a
Portugal	18	23	30	34	18	23
Russia	11	7	3	1	1	n/a
South Africa	8	n/a	n/a	n/a	n/a	n/a
South Korea	3	2	3	2	2	2
Spain	37	29	30	23	23	n/a
Sweden	8	6	3	1	1	0
Switzerland	1	1	1	1	1	1
United Kingdom	35	32	36	25	22	25
United States	9	10	9	10	10	9
Median	**9.5**					**8.5**

Sources: OECD standardized data, 2006–11; OECD/IDB/OAS (2012); Statistics South Africa (2012). n/a signifies missing data. The median is calculated using only countries for which data are available in both 2011 and 2006.

economic component of their immigration intake and actual migration demographic outcomes.

Importantly, this table only considers permanent economic migration as a percentage of total flows. As much of the growth in economic migration has in fact been in temporary admissions, it only represents one side of the picture of economic-based immigration. OECD countries such as Australia, Italy, New Zealand, and South Korea that rely heavily upon temporary labor migration would likely document more significant

TABLE 4.4. *Free movement immigration as a percentage of total flows across the OECD, 2006–11*

Country	2011	2010	2009	2008	2007	2006
Australia	7	5	6	7	6	6
Austria	55	49	50	50	45	26
Belgium	44	35	38	21	23	27
Denmark	51	46	49	58	42	45
Finland	20	18	16	17	16	15
France	31	29	28	28	27	28
Germany	39	24	22	20	18	16
Ireland	39	52	52	55	57	82
Italy	33	30	30	36	48	9
Netherlands	51	48	46	42	23	20
New Zealand	3	3	3	3	3	3
Norway	59	63	57	53	48	40
Portugal	38	32	29	19	48	7
Spain	41	48	43	39	50	n/a
Sweden	29	28	25	28	30	31
Switzerland	44	40	35	47	42	30
United Kingdom	16	14	16	19	21	13
Median	**38.5**					23

Sources: OECD standardized data, 2006–11. The median is calculated using only countries for which data are available in both 2011 and 2006.

increases in economic Visa Mix were temporary migration included in the analysis. This would also be the case if temporary intra-EU workers (seasonal workers and posted and self-employed workers) were included in EU free movement calculations (Barslund and Busse 2014: 119).

Further, within European nations, EU free movement migration is actually operating as a substitute for the importation of permanent economic migrants from third countries. Indeed, if we consider Table 4.4, it is clear that most EU member states have seen a significant increase in free movement immigration as a percentage of their permanent Visa Mix from 2006 through to 2011. Indeed, the median has also almost doubled from 23 percent of the Visa Mix in 2006 to 38.5 percent in 2011, which is the largest increase for any of the mix categories. Flows have elevated (by more than 10 percent) in Austria, Belgium, Germany, Italy, the Netherlands, Norway, Portugal, and Switzerland and to a lesser extent in Denmark, Finland, France, and the United Kingdom. Only Ireland, Spain, and Sweden have seen a decline in the relative percentage of free movement immigration over this period. A central reason for this relates to the high rates of EU immigration over the period. From 2004 through to 2009, Ireland and Sweden, along with the United Kingdom, were two of the only countries to open their labor markets up to free movement immigration from the new member states of Eastern Europe, but other EU-15 countries maintained their restrictions. In 2009, EU-15 countries were required to open their labor markets to the 2004 new member states unless they applied for special permission to continue restrictions until 2011 (which only Germany and Austria did). More broadly, EU enlargement from 2004 through to 2007 has seen a significant increase in free movement immigration across a broader range of member states (OECD 2014a: 23).

These high rates of free movement raise the question of whether there is a trade-off between intra-EU mobility and third country national (TCN) economic migration, especially as at least 50 percent of internal EU migration is believed to be economic in nature (OECD 2014a: 18). One of the key political concerns around free movement of individuals within the European Union is that it has compromised the capacity of some member states to increase the immigration of skilled Third Country Nationals (Boswell 2008; Paul 2013). The OECD (2012: 33) has previously argued that there is a trade-off between free movement and economic migration: In terms of the composition of migration from employment, there seems to be some "trade-off" between labor migration (that is, from outside of free mobility areas) and free movement. Countries, which have large proportions of their migrant intake through free movement, such as Switzerland, Norway and Austria, but also Germany and the Netherlands, tend to have little labor migration. The numbers of Third Country Nationals within the EU dropped from 140,000 in 2000 to around 120,000 in 2008, while the number of EU workers doubled from 2005 through to 2009.

Consistent with a perceived trade-off between these two forms of economic migrants, in some EU member states, EU workers are included in the calculation of the domestic labor force, against which targets for third country economic migration are set (e.g. the United Kingdom, although this will change with the outcome of the Brexit referendum of 2016). As Paul (2013: 130) argues, this so-called Resident Labour Market Test that applies to all but highly skilled workers, "establish[ed] a preference for the widened EU labor pool over a resident minority workforce, frequently from the New Commonwealth." While some scholars have argued that EU harmonization policy, such as the EU Blue Card, could undermine the labor market engagement of existing EU workers (Parkes and Angenendt 2010), in fact large-scale free movement within the EU has not only persisted since the introduction of the Blue Card, it has, in many member states, increased. Indeed, since 2011 when the Blue Card was introduced, permanent economic immigration of TCNs within the EU has continued to fall by 12 percent but internal EU migration has risen by the same amount (OECD 2014a: 18). In Germany, the Resident Labour Market Test applies to all skill classifications, again prioritizing internal EU labor migrants over TCNs (Paul 2013: 133). This privileging of free movement over Third Country Nationals in turn reinforces "origin-based recruitment hierarchies" as most migrants entering from the new EU Accession States are white and Eastern Europeans, whereas the now deprioritized non-EU workers are frequently sourced from former colonies in the Global South (Paul 2013: 136).

Forms of Convergence Across European Immigration States

Part of the policy motivation around the development of the EU Blue Card for Highly Skilled immigrants was to standardize levels of economic immigration across the Union (Carrera et al. 2011; Van Riemsdijk 2011). However, most commentators agree that the EU Blue Card has been largely unsuccessful in this regard, related in part to the broad room for interpretation by member states within the associated EU Directive and its implementation. The EU has also played a limited function in standardizing other forms of labor migration of Third-Country Nationals within the Union, such that large areas of economic immigration remain unharmonized with member states still largely responsible for their own policies. Further, the Lisbon Treaty of 2010 explicitly excluded harmonization of the overall volume of migratory flows, leaving this to individual member states (Cerna 2010; 2013; Carrera et al. 2011: 3, 7; Van Riemsdijk 2011). As Figure 4.1 makes clear, the percentage of economic immigration remains varied across the EU member states, despite the introduction of the Blue Card in 2009. Our analysis reinforces the findings of existing authors that the EU Blue Card has not led to a convergence of Visa Mix across EU member states and that individual domestic factors are the driving force behind policymaking within the EU (Vink 2005).

This pattern of divergence is also reflective of humanitarian immigration within Europe. From Table 4.5, it is clear that humanitarian migration as a share of the Visa Mix ranges within and across the European member states and the OECD more generally. For instance, in 2011, Sweden stands out as the most generous receiver of humanitarian migrants, while

TABLE 4.5. *Humanitarian immigration across the OECD, Russia, and South Africa as a percentage of total flows, 2006–11*

Country	2011	2010	2009	2008	2007	2006
Australia	3	3	3	2	3	4
Austria	9	8	8	9	11	11
Belgium	3	3	3	2	2	3
Canada	8	7	8	8	10	11
Denmark	5	4	3	3	3	4
Finland	5	8	7	5	5	5
France	5	5	5	5	4	3
Germany	2	2	2	7	9	0
Ireland	0	1	1	1	0	1
Italy	2	1	2	2	1	2
Japan	0	0	0	0	0	0
Netherlands	9	9	9	6	8	9
New Zealand	2	2	2	2	2	4
Norway	8	9	12	9	12	10
Portugal	0	0	0	0	0	0
Russia	0	0	0	0	0	n/a
South Africa	5	n/a	n/a	n/a	n/a	n/a
South Korea	0	0	0	0	0	0
Spain	0	0	0	0	0	0
Sweden	14	14	12	13	21	29
Switzerland	3	3	2	3	2	2
United Kingdom	3	1	1	1	2	5
United States	11	9	11	10	8	12
Median	3					4

Source: OECD standardized data, 2006–11; Statistics South Africa (2012). n/a signifies missing data. The median is calculated using only countries for which data is available in both 2011 and 2006.

several countries have such low rates that they round to 0 percent of the Visa Mix (Ireland, Japan, Portugal, Russia, South Korea, and Spain).

At first glance, this variation is puzzling. As Alexander Caviedes (2016) has argued, of all the categories of immigration, humanitarian immigration has been the most subject to supranational governance and, therefore, we might expect the greatest convergence of flows. Yet, variation prevails and this fact demonstrates that attempts at improved burden sharing of asylum flows within the Union, such as the 1999 Amsterdam Treaty, have been largely unsuccessful. This divergence in flows potentially also relates to the wide variation in implementation of EU laws such as the European Council Reception Directive with different approaches to the interpretation of the standards set out in this document as well as differences in recognition rates of asylum seekers (Thielemann, Williams, and Boswell 2010: 138). As such, while common standards have been determined legislatively, the impact of these standards has varied, in part due to discretion exercised at the member state level and the interests of individual member states (Armstrong 2016; Caviedes 2016: 561, 562).

Furthermore, the refugee crisis in the Mediterranean in 2015 and 2016 has exacerbated the challenges of harmonization of asylum flows within Europe. Discrepancies in the financial management of such flows and the challenges of navigating multilevel governance structures provide a partial explanation (Chryssogelos 2015; Caviedes 2016: 561) as do persistent differences in social attitudes toward immigrants (Büchel and Frick 2005: 176).

IMPLICATIONS FOR GENDER AND ETHNICITY

Visa Mix holds implications for the gender and ethnic compositions of immigrant flows and immigrant stock. However, there is no comprehensive global data on immigrant flows disaggregated according to ethnicity and gender. New research maps the ethnic and gender make-up of immigrant stock globally through bilateral data (e.g. Docquier, Lowell, and Marfouk 2009). While several governments publish gender-disaggregated immigration or administrative data of flows, generally they are not available at the visa-specific level and often they do not disaggregate between the first-named primary and second-named accompanying applicants. This is an important distinction because, disproportionately, the second-named applicant is a female spouse, thereby camouflaging the gender dynamics at hand (Boucher 2016: chapter 2). In this final section of the chapter, we rely upon such disaggregated data for the countries in our dataset where it is available.

Gender in the Visa Mix

Female migrant stock reached parity with male migrant stock globally in 2005 (UN 2006). Yet, highly gendered patterns within immigration Visa Mix belie this apparent trend of gender equality in migration demographic outcomes. Immigration scholars have argued for several decades that women are more likely to predominate in family migration flows and men in employment-related migration flows. Several scholars have noted the preponderance of women in family reunion streams (Houstoun, Kramer, and Barrett 1984; Donato and Tyree 1986; Boyd 1994; Boyd and Pikkov 2004). For instance, Monica Boyd (1999: 15) finds that between 1985 and 1994, women outnumbered men seven to one as immigrating spouses to Canada. She highlights how women's familial connections are vital to their immigration success insofar that these women are reliant upon their marital ties in order to gain immigration entry. Conversely, a large scholarship identifies the benefits male applicants derive from skilled-immigration policies. In particular, this scholarship emphasizes how the high levels of human capital, uninterrupted job experience, and expanded training and network opportunities enjoyed by men are also central to skilled immigration selection, thereby preferencing male applicants in the selection process (Dauvergne 2000: 298; Kofman and Raghuram 2006: 295–6; Boucher 2007; 2009; 2016).

As a result of these trends, a United Nations report (1994: 69, as quoted in DeLaet 1999: 4–5) argued that policy decisions over Visa Mix are central to improving gender equity within immigration policy:

Throughout the world, the formulation of migration laws and regulations is influenced by prevailing conceptions of the family and of the roles that different family members ought to play. Women, as spouses or daughters, are traditionally assumed to have primarily non-economic roles under the assumption that their husbands or fathers are responsible for satisfying the family's economic needs. These perceptions are translated into immigration regulations that, in some circumstances, can actually favour female migration by facilitating the admission of dependents. On the other hand, in countries that either restrict or discourage family reunification, or which admit mainly migrant workers, the migration of women will tend to be smaller than that of women.

Such gendered effects are highly visible in the Gulf states, where the Visa Mix is so skewed toward economic visas that it also informs the gender mix of overall migrant populations. For instance, both due to the restrictive family reunification rights conferred on migrants, but also due to the concentration of employment opportunities for immigrants in the construction sector, the majority of migrants in Bahrain are men. In fact, in some Gulf states, such as the United Arab Emirates, male immigration so significantly eclipses female immigration that it skews gender distribution across the entire national population (Baldwin-Edwards 2011: 11). As a result, governments in the region have presented the overrepresentation of male migrants as a security concern that corresponds with increased "robbery, drug traffic, and addiction, prostitution, raping, child abuse" (Fouad 1999: 2, as cited in Lori 2008: 322). That said, the rate of single female labor migration has grown in recent years as the domestic service sector has expanded within Gulf states, suggesting that gender dynamics could rebalance in the future (Nagy 2010: 59).

Donato and her collaborators (2012: 514) show that women's representation in foreign-born stock varies considerably across countries. And indeed, inverse gender trends emerge in countries like the United States, with women overrepresented as immigrants. As Houstoun and her coauthors (1984: 915) document, in the 1970s, adult female migrants to the United States outnumbered adult male migrants by 18 percent. Boyd and Pikkov (2004) find that this overrepresentation can be linked to the preponderance of family visa selection in permanent immigration flows into the United States. This example demonstrates how changes in Visa Mix can hold implications for gender representation within broader migration demographic outcomes.

Origin Diversity in the Visa Mix

Visa Mix also shapes the origin diversity of immigrant flows. Arguably, this issue has received even less scholarly attention than the gender dynamics, perhaps because observers take the non-discriminatory approach of immigration policies since the 1960s at face value (Joppke 2005a). Consequently, the relationship between Visa Mix and origin diversity is typically implicit in public debates over immigration policy, except when concerns are expressed by ethnic communities that changing the Visa Mix might affect them disproportionately. Within the European Union, the preference in some selecting nations (Austria, Germany, and Switzerland) for immigration from new EU accession states can also be viewed as the favoring of "white European" immigration over immigrants from the Global South (Paul 2013: 136–7, citing McDowell 2009). Similarly, as debates over comprehensive immigration reform in the United States highlight, there is a perception among many immigrant communities that reducing opportunities for extended family admission – as supported by the Trump Administration and numerous Republican legislators – would disproportionately impact certain ethnic groups, particularly Latinos and Asians (Rosenblum 2011).

George Borjas (1993) finds that the higher rates of skilled immigrants within the Canadian population were a product not of the policy shift in Canada toward skilled labor since 1967, but rather because the employment-related points system attracted immigrants of different nationalities than those admitted under the United States' family-dominated immigration regime. As Borjas (1993: 40) notes, this argument "has important, if unpalatable, implications for the ongoing debate over the role of skills of visa applicants." The reduction of immigration from Western Europe into the US labor market since 1965, Borjas (1993: chapter 3) argued, contributed to the decline in economic performance of the immigrant population. This would suggest that the family-focused program that has dominated US immigration since the enactment of 1965 immigration legislation has transformed the ethnic mix of US immigration flows. Green and Green (1995: 1029–39) find that the points test for skilled immigration introduced in Canada in 1967 did not have as great an effect upon skill composition as Borjas' work would predict. Rather, origin diversity mix was a large predictor and this was determined by policy factors including the relative role of family reunification policies.

Confirming findings of a relationship between Visa Mix and origin diversity, a study by Hill and Hayes (2011) employs an administrative dataset to measure the possible effects of changes in Visa Mix on the country composition of US immigration flows. In particular, these authors examine the potential impact of the adoption of a points test on the country profile of accepted immigrants into the United States. Their findings are startling, indicating that if Latin American entrants did not have the possibility to enter via family reunification routes, or if these routes are reduced, only 1 percent would pass a points test similar to that considered by Congress as part of proposed comprehensive immigration reforms in 2007 (Hill and Hayes 2011: 15–16). In contrast, 12 percent of immigrants from East Asia, South Asia, and the Pacific, 6 percent from Europe and Central Asia, and 14 percent from Canada would succeed (Hill and Hayes 2011: 16–17). Most recently, a study by economists Tito Boeri and his colleagues (2012: 43) finds that highly skilled migrant stock across the OECD is skewed toward migrants from other OECD nations and the wealthy Gulf states, with migrants from these countries providing 38 percent of highly skilled stock. Migrants from low-income countries were the most underrepresented within highly skilled stock, comprising only 9 percent of that stock, while middle-income countries such as China, India, Mexico, Russia, and countries in Northern Africa provided around 26 percent of highly skilled stock. This analysis suggests that policies that focus on skilled immigration could carry origin diversity effects over the long term. In short, while not conclusive, there is preliminary evidence that changing the Visa Mix can also affect origin diversity, although this important issue deserves far more academic attention in the future.

CONCLUSION

This chapter has taken a first step by defining and analyzing the nature of the permanent Visa Mix. It has also mapped variation in the Visa Mix of immigration regimes across countries, and to the extent possible, time. In contrast to claims of a global shift toward skilled immigration, based on the data analyzed, this chapter identifies enduring variation within states' Visa Mix, from high rates of economic-related migration, to a predominance of family or free movement. With the exception of Sweden, humanitarian admissions remain fairly low despite recent humanitarian crises. Inter-temporal comparison does not reveal significant changes in median family or employment-related immigration over the period from 2006 through 2011, with the single biggest median increases occurring in the free movement space. Based on available data, non-democracies such as China and the Gulf states appear more capable of achieving a work-focused immigration program. However, even in non-democracies, some forms of family reunification occur, especially on an informal basis. As such, this chapter suggests a greater degree of overlap between democracies and non-democracies than researchers might have assumed, even if the channels for entry differ somewhat.

Against claims by Western governments of successful restrictions upon family reunification, we analyzed whether there has been an actual reduction in family immigration outcomes. While some countries, in particular Austria, saw quite significant reductions in the period between 2006 and 2011, generally, the reductions in family reunification were not as great as we might expect given the political opposition to this form of immigration. Overall, there was in fact a slight increase in family reunification within the Visa Mix over this time. Yet, if we consider free movement as a form of economic migration, especially across the European Union, this form of immigration is increasingly prioritized over the immigration of Third Country Nationals, and it is not scrutinized by governments in the same way as family migration.

This chapter has outlined some of the possible consequences of changes in Visa Mix. In particular, we focused on the possible gender and origin diversity implications of changes in visa composition. We explored existing studies on these topics, which suggest that changing compositional mix, especially increasing skilled immigration and free movement at the same time as decreasing family entry, can create clear winners and losers along gender and country of origin lines. This analysis is central to future debates over the diversity of immigration flows and the role of policy in this regard, especially given the rise of free movement across Europe.

These findings notwithstanding, our evaluation of Visa Mix might change were we to include temporary economic flows. As noted earlier, some countries with comparatively low levels of work-related immigration might present differently if their considerable temporary flows were included in the numerator of the Visa Mix. In the next chapter, we address this issue in more depth through our consideration of the Temporary Ratio of economic immigration, which in turn has implications for our presentation of the Market Model in Chapter 7.

5

Temporary Ratio

The Return of the Guest Worker?

In 1986, as the world was turning toward a more liberal model of immigration selection, sociologist Stephen Castles declared the guest worker model of postwar Europe "dead." However, more recently, he argued that temporary labor migration is on the rise again, leading potentially to a new guest worker system in the modern era (Castles 2006). In many countries, temporary labor immigration is the main form of economic immigration. Furthermore, the distinction between entry on a temporary or permanent basis is gaining increasing salience as the latter is associated with fuller legal and de facto rights. As temporary labor immigration is generally tied to a particular employer, temporary migrants' presence is far more contingent, leaving them more vulnerable to abuse, exploitation, or inhumane working conditions than those on permanent visas (Rosewarne 2010: 103–4; Tham and Campbell 2011; Ruhs 2013; Berg 2016).

Some commentators tie the renewed rise of temporary labor migration schemes to global labor market liberalization and the commodification of labor that assists in capital production (e.g. Rosewarne 2010). This process is also the product of sending state policies that promote the export of their citizens in order to stimulate a remittance economy (Rosewarne 2012). Alternately, governments may preference temporary immigration over permanent settlement, as it is seen to reduce the welfare costs to the host society, and extend the period during which states can make determinations about the permanent incorporation of migrants into their polities (Wickramasekara 2013). However, such preferencing by government is not universal and in some countries, including Canada, political controversies over temporary worker programs have undermined confidence in such approaches (i.e. Boucher 2016: chapter 7).

This chapter sketches major trends in the relationship between temporary and permanent labor immigration by accounting for the Temporary Ratio – the share of total immigration flows that is of a temporary economic nature.[1] We focus on the ratio of temporary economic immigration for several reasons: first, as argued in the previous chapter, temporary economic immigration is an area of growing policy concern for governments worldwide. Second, as we outline in further detail below, data on temporary family and asylum flows (to the extent that these are regulated forms of entry) are not available for most countries and, in any case, these types of visas are rare and do not exist in many countries. As such, we cannot conduct an analysis of all forms of temporary and permanent Visa Mix across our country cases. Third, in many of the non-OECD countries considered, temporary economic immigration is the main form of immigration entry and therefore deserving of singular analysis. This interest in temporary economic immigration is not to discount the importance of other forms of temporary immigration. Migration researchers have documented a variety of other forms of temporary migration including that of students (Shu and Hawthorne 1995; Hugo 2006; Hawthorne 2010; McGill 2013) and asylum seekers (Freeman 1994; Bloch 2002; Crock and Ghezelbash 2010). However, as noted, data on these are poor or unsystematic.

In the next section, we consider the interplay of temporary and permanent economic immigration across Western democracies, the Arabian Gulf, and East Asia. This is followed by a discussion of key considerations in measurement. Employing these methods, we then provide a comparative analysis of available data and explore four key issues that emerge: (1) the ambiguity of the temporary–permanent distinction; (2) the relationship between temporary economic immigration and undocumented migration; (3) gender and ethnicity issues that surface within the Temporary Ratio; and (4) the trade-off between rights and numbers in the balance between temporary and permanent economic immigration.

---

[1] To ensure consistency between Chapters 4 and 5, we retain the denominator of total flows, rather than simply economic flows. Some might argue that total economic flow is a better denominator for this chapter given the focus on temporary economic migration. However, we defend this choice on the basis that temporary economic admissions must be contextualized against Visa Mix. Further discussion on the denominator can be found in the Methodological Appendix.

THE TEMPORARY RATIO OVER SPACE AND TIME

In democratic countries, settler states have historically focused on permanent immigration and Western European states on temporary immigration. Koser (2009: 5) links this distinction to the concentration by settler state governments on permanent migration for broader economic growth and welfare provision. In some Western European nations, the focus on labor migration of a short-term rotational nature has a historical legacy in post-war guest worker schemes (Ellermann 2015). Yet, settler states are increasingly adopting new forms of temporary migration schemes as well (Alboim and Cohl 2013; Berg 2016), such that they may no longer be viewed as "settler" states in a traditional sense. Angenendt (2009) argues that industrialized countries are turning toward temporary forms of economic migration as a solution to labor shortages. Temporary economic migration includes forms of circular migration (immigration involving traditionally unregulated cross-border movement such as that of nomads, day laborers, and traders) as well as regulated forms, such as the movement of both high- and low-skilled seasonal workers (Angenendt 2009: 8). Government officials often believe that a key advantage of temporary economic migration is that it reduces the strain on the welfare state because temporary migrants have lower rates of accompanying family immigration (Wickramasekara 2013) and are not eligible to receive most benefits. Accordingly, temporary migration may be seen to avoid some of the political risks that can accompany permanent migration, such as labor market competition or social conflict and accompanying xenophobia. Finally, temporary migration can buy governments time to train domestic labor forces, while, at least theoretically, not introducing permanent immigrant competition on an ongoing basis (Hugo 2009: 39–40).

Debate surrounds whether new regimes of temporary immigration are better in their policy design than the earlier guest worker approaches. Stephen Castles (2006) has suggested that the focus in some countries on highly skilled temporary labor separates these new regimes from the past. However, low-skilled schemes are increasingly being adopted by a variety of governments. Steven Vertovec (2007) argues that despite their benefits, temporary circular immigration regimes raise similar concerns to earlier temporary regimes around the rights and abuse of temporary workers by their employers. As such, forms of worker dependency and exploitative relationships may be inextricable within temporary economic migration, irrespective of regulatory design. Further, in some contexts we see emerging arguments that given the structural dependency of temporary immigrants upon their sponsors, they may in fact garner lower salaries, making them more attractive as prospective employees than domestic workers (Lowell and Avato 2014). In turn, this may contribute to a displacement of the domestic workforce and a rise in unemployment rates over time.

These politicized dimensions of temporary economic immigration have generated increasing electoral traction since the onset of the global financial crisis in 2007 (for debates see Smith 2012). The Migration Advisory Committee (2012) in the United Kingdom recently concluded that non-EU immigration reduced the employment of British workers between 1995 and 2010 (Ruhs and Vargas-Silvia 2015, corroborated by Devlin et al. 2014). While other studies find no effect either way (e.g. Lucchino, Rosazza-Bondibene, and Portes 2012), or even a positive effect of temporary migrant flows on domestic unemployment rates (McLeod and Maré 2013: 5), still others identify a negative impact for those natives with lower levels of education (Dustmann, Fabbri, and Preston 2005; Bond and Gaston 2011). In the next section, we outline some of the key historical cases of temporary labor migration within Western democracies, before turning to developments in the Gulf and Asian regions.

Use of Temporary Labor in Western Democracies

Since the 1940s, the United States has used temporary visas for its unskilled migration program. During World War II, the US government recruited Mexican workers to fill agricultural labor shortages, particularly in California, Arizona, and Texas. Marred with controversies over employers' abuse of workers, the so-called Bracero Program continued until 1964, when its termination foreshadowed the large-scale undocumented migration that has persisted in the United States ever since (Palmunen 2005). Temporary labor migration into the United States has also taken more highly skilled forms. For example, the H-1B visa permits the entry of highly skilled workers and has benefitted the information technology sector (Batalova and Powell 2006; Money and Falstrom 2006), while the H-2A visa has been used extensively in the agricultural sector (Lowell 2011).

Historically, many Western democracies relied upon the large-scale importation of immigrant workers to sustain their economies after World War II, with the 'gastarbeiter' of Germany often identified as the key exemplar (Castles 2006; Chin 2009). Indeed, Germany, Spain, and the

United Kingdom have all utilized temporary labor to fill gaps in lower-skilled sectors such as agriculture, construction, and service (Angenendt 2009: 8). As we note above, Australia and Canada, both of which traditionally eschewed temporary admissions, have also now moved toward large temporary programs that eclipse permanent entry (Berg 2016; Boucher 2016). In Australia, Tham and Campbell (2011: 2) identify it as the greatest shift in the immigration policies of that country over the last decade.

Use of Temporary Labor in Non-Western Countries

Nearly all immigration into the Arabian Gulf is on a temporary basis. For most migrants, their legal status expires at the end of their visa, typically after two years pending renewal (Baldwin-Edwards 2011: 37). The significant scale of temporary immigration into the Gulf region was stimulated by the discovery of oil following World War II and reinforced with the end of Gulf states' protectorate status from the early 1960s onward (Ruhs 2010). Accompanied by rising affluence among the domestic population and an increasing need for foreign labor to support oil production and a growing service sector, these structural factors contributed to large-scale immigration (Fargues 2011: 275). Originally, migrant labor was predominately from other countries within the Arab world (Fargues 2011: 276). However, with time, flows were diversified to the South Asian subcontinent (Gardner 2010: 42; Fargues 2011: 276–7; Shah 2011: 342). Temporary migrant labor was recruited not only in oil-related construction but also in the construction of major cities like Abu Dhabi, Sharjah, and Dubai in the United Arab Emirates (Rhys 2010).

Over this period, states also tightened the rights offered to migrant workers, and the *kafala* system emerged, requiring each foreign worker to have a citizen sponsor (*kafeel*). These rules also severely restricted workers' rights of marriage, family reunification, education for children, and labor conditions (Fargues 2011: 287). In some cases, migrant workers also have their passports confiscated and are housed in remote labor camps (Gardner 2010: 59). There have been reports of physical and sexual abuse of workers on temporary visas (Ali 2010: 95–8; Auwal 2010; Gardner 2010), leading some to argue that the temporary status of workers in this region dictates working conditions as well as mobility rights (Ali 2010: 82–6).

Under the *kafala* system, temporary migration was viewed as a central mechanism to balance competing policy goals of economic growth and ethnic homogeneity (Russell 1989; Shah 2006). In recent years, there have been some attempts to reform the *kafala* system, motivated in part by the global financial crisis and accompanying concerns about the engagement of domestic labor (Ali 2010: 188; Baldwin-Edwards 2011: 48; Shah 2011). Should the reforms extend the length of migrant workers' visas or create new permanent visa classes, this would shift the Temporary Ratio as described in this chapter toward a more permanent focus. However, Human Rights Watch (2014) suggests that many of these reforms are yet to be implemented on the ground.

Asian countries have also experienced the rise of diverse and complex temporary – primarily low-skilled – labor migration programs. Some scholars have argued that given their focus on temporary labor, Singapore, Malaysia, Thailand, Hong Kong, Taiwan, Japan, and South Korea can be grouped together (e.g. Seol 2005: 85). Key attributes of this "Asian guest worker" regime are their reliance on short-term work contracts for migrant workers and restricted civil and political rights including the right to vote, reunify with family, or settle permanently. Yet, for other scholars, this categorization is misleading. Kalicki (2016), for instance, notes that Japan, Taiwan, and South Korea differ in whether they admit low-skilled workers through named visas or informally through other means and also whether these selection criteria policies are explicitly or implicitly ethnicized. Furthermore, the picture is complicated once highly skilled labor immigration is added to the picture. As in many other countries, not only is highly skilled labor preferred in South Korea, but these migrant workers also enjoy access to dual citizenship, which is not otherwise permitted to "guest workers" (Seol 2012).

The division between skilled and unskilled labor structures the rights, privileges, and obligations of temporary workers across Asia. For instance, foreign domestic workers in Hong Kong entering on temporary visas are denied a variety of rights. These migrants are restricted from marrying locals, required to pay a security bond to employers, made to undertake pregnancy tests, and face expulsion if pregnant (Piper and Yamanka 2008: 170). In Singapore, unskilled workers are only granted temporary work permits operative in certain sectors with imposed pay limits (Fong 2006: 158–9). Compared to those entering Singapore on highly skilled visas, workers in middle- and unskilled temporary positions are also conferred shorter stays and limitations on the overall period during which they can be employed (Ministry of Manpower Singapore 2012; see also Fong 2006: 167). Unless they have a monthly salary over S\$4,000, middle-skilled workers are also not entitled to migrate with family members (Singapore Prime Minister's Office 2012), while low-skilled workers are denied this opportunity unconditionally. Middle-skilled workers have some access to both permanent residency and eventually citizenship (Fong 2006: 160).[2] Highly skilled workers have access to indefinite renewal of temporary visas that provide avenues to citizenship as well as family reunification (Yap 1999; Piper 2005).

In Japan, demand for lower-skilled foreign labor led to the admission of immigrants through the so-called trainee program. This program grants trainees similar wages and benefits to native workers, but with fewer rights. The purpose of this program is to meet business demand for low-skilled labor, while at the same time seeking to maintain Japan's cultural and ethnic homogeneity (Seol 2005: 97–9). Still, large numbers of undocumented temporary workers parallel this legal channel (Seol 2005: 99). As permanent residency is available for some high-skill workers but not for unskilled labor migrants (Oishi 2012), the recruitment of low-skilled co-ethnic *Nikkeijin* into Japan provides a de facto form of temporary labor that over time has led to permanent settlement (Goto 2007).

Once predominantly a sending state, South Korea became a country of temporary migration in the early 1990s. There are ongoing concerns about discriminatory practices toward temporary migrants, including underpayment and abuse (Seol 2005: 99). Until recently, there were far more undocumented migrant workers than those on legal visas. Seol (2005: 102) estimates that of the 400,000 foreign workers in South Korea in 2003, 80 percent were unauthorized. However, following the introduction of an Employment Permit System in 2004, undocumented migration has fallen dramatically, with less than 20 percent of foreign low-skilled workers undocumented in 2010 (Tan 2012: 45). Workers can now obtain work permits and change jobs three times in three years, encouraging legal employment (Tan 2012).

In China, permanent residency is very difficult to obtain. According to Xinhua News Agency, China's state-run press agency, by the end of 2011, only 4,752 foreigners were given a Permanent Residence Card – the Chinese equivalent of a Green Card (Lu 2012). However, the eligibility standards for such cards have been liberalized since 2012, when China

---

[2] Note, however, that the process of access to permanent residency for skilled immigrants is not automatic and itself a highly competitive process in Singapore. Every application for permanent residency is evaluated "holistically on a set of criteria which includes factors such as the individual's economic contributions, qualifications, age and family profile to assess applicants' ability to contribute, integrate well into society and commitment to sinking roots" (Singapore Parliament 2011).

introduced regulations stating that holders of this Green Card "shall in principle enjoy the same rights and assume the same obligations as Chinese citizens except for political rights and the specific rights and obligations not eligible according to laws and regulations" (Dongdong, 2012).

Despite official policy preference for temporary immigration, many East Asian countries have also experienced challenges in ensuring immigrants' repatriation to their country of origin. South Korea, for instance, now hosts large numbers of long-term temporary migrants (Seol 2005: 85). This reality suggests a further gap between policies and measured outcome, which directs us to the central issue of definition and measurement of the term "temporary."

MEASUREMENT

The characterization of a visa as either "temporary" or "permanent" is confounded by multiple factors. First, these terms mean different things in different countries. Second, there is reluctance on the part of governments and politicians to acknowledge permanent immigration, leading officials to underplay its presence in official national immigration statistics. In this section of the chapter, we outline our approach to these issues.

As a starting point, we need to define "economic immigration." As we discuss in Chapter 4, permanent economic migration comprises immigration for work purposes and accompanying family members. It excludes admission for the purposes of subsequent family reunification, humanitarian refuge, or free movement, even if some of those immigrants ultimately work or move for the purpose of obtaining a job. Temporary economic immigration is restricted to immigration for the purposes of work. It includes trainees, those entering on working holiday visas,[3] seasonal workers, intra-company transfers, and other forms of temporary workers.

---

[3] For some, the inclusion of working holiday-makers as work-related migrants might be controversial, given that the title of the visa suggests that these migrants are vacationing. However, in many countries, these migrants are also permitted—and do—work for large sections of their visa stay. Further, entry via this category is numerically important, comprising around 20 percent of total temporary entries (OECD 2009: 46). The inclusion of working holiday-makers in the temporary work migration figure elevates the percentage of temporary economic immigration in some countries such as Australia that have high levels of working holiday-makers. That said, the data do not include international students who might also elevate such figures, given their de facto status in some countries as workers (Boucher 2016).

Whereas permanent visas typically allow unrestricted, unconditional opportunities for renewal and in many cases a path to citizenship, "temporary" refers to those visas or permits under which there are conditional opportunities for renewal. The OECD clarifies the distinction:

> By a "permanent" migrant is meant a person who has been granted the right of settlement by the country of destination at the time of entry or who entered the country as a temporary migrant and became a permanent or settled migrant. The definition refers only to legal migration and the statistics for a given year may include persons who actually entered the country in a previous year. The "right of settlement" is generally manifested by the granting of a permit, which, if it is not permanent, is more or less indefinitely renewable, although the renewal may be subject to certain conditions. The right to permanent residence per se may be accorded only after a number of years of residence in the country. A temporary migrant, on the other hand, enters the country with a permit that is either not renewable or only renewable in a limited way. Included in this group are such persons as international students, trainees, posted workers, installers, persons on exchange programmes, working holiday makers, seasonal workers, asylum seekers, etc. (as cited in Fron et al. 2011: 6)

There may be some countries that at first glance do not appear to have any permanent visas. If information regarding permanent status was not available, we asked the relevant domestic agency if they had information about how long on average those with temporary visas remain – in particular, do over two-thirds of these holders stay for over five years? If so, then that category of visa was classified as permanent, as is consistent with the approach undertaken by the OECD (Fron et al. 2011; Kupiszewska and Kupiszewski 2011; Thomas Liebig 2012, OECD Migration Section, pers. comm.).

Because some categories of long-term temporary immigration will accordingly be reclassified as permanent immigration, this method can lead to different calculations of temporary immigration flows than is sometimes presented by national governments themselves. However, this reclassification more accurately represents the reality of the experience of temporary immigrants on the ground. In particular, a temporary migrant worker may not be "temporary" in terms of their actual length of residence or in their intention to remain for a temporary period of time (Tham, Campbell, and Boese 2016). As such, the classification developed by the OECD and adopted here is based on behavioral outcomes rather than legal outputs (OECD 2014a: 150–1). Further, once an immigrant changes status, from temporary to permanent, they are also classified as "permanent" for the purposes of the OECD statistics (Fron et al. 2011; Kupiszewska and Kupiszewski 2011).[4]

---

[4] We extend these measurement standards to other countries. Since 2011, the OECD also collects data for Russia, which are included in this chapter. All Latin American data except

In many countries, temporary figures underrepresent the extent of unauthorized temporary economic immigration, including visa over-stayers formerly on temporary visas. In some countries, this is a significant issue. For instance, Martin Baldwin-Edwards (2011: 38) estimates that by the late 1990s, unauthorized workers comprised around 15 percent of the total workforce in the GCC. In the United States, the undocumented population has been estimated at around 11.3 million, which amounts to around 5.1 percent of the US labor force (Krogstad and Passel 2015). In Japan and South Korea, the scale of unauthorized temporary workers remains significant (e.g. Seol 2005). While we provide some secondary qualitative analysis of this phenomenon, we were unable to collect reliable statistics on undocumented populations across countries and therefore cannot present comparable data on this phenomenon.

DESCRIPTIVE RESULTS

Table 5.1 and Figure 5.1 present the cross-national variation in temporary migration as a share of total labor immigration. Notably, in the Gulf states (Bahrain, Kuwait, Oman, and Saudi Arabia) 100 percent of labor immigration is of a temporary nature. In Brazil, the International Development Bank (OECD/IDB/OAS 2012: ix) notes that the high rates of temporary immigration in 2011 may reflect previous high conferrals of permanent residency to irregular migrants in the immediate preceding period. This rendered less demand for permanent places in the 2010 calendar year. As such, our assessment of the Temporary Ratio may

for Mexico were drawn from an OECD-backed report, *International Migration in the Americas* (OECD/IDB/OAS 2012). The Mexican data were drawn from standard OECD reports. For Bahrain, Kuwait, Oman, and Saudi Arabia, we relied on data from the Gulf Labor Markets and Migration group (GLMM). As there were no publicly available data on the percentage of temporary entrants who remain in these countries on a permanent basis, all entries for the GCC states were treated as temporary. Nonetheless, later in the chapter we present some secondary qualitative evidence of long-term settlement of labor immigrants in the GCC region, although this trend is not recognized within the official statistics.

For China, data distinguishing between temporary and permanent immigration are available, but not those that differentiate between different temporary visa categories. Given that the focus is in this chapter is on temporary labor migration only, these aggregated temporary data were excluded from this specific analysis. Nonetheless, it is reasonable to assume that the vast majority of economic immigration into China is of a temporary nature. Aggregated data across visa classes suggest that fewer than only 20 percent of immigrants into China stay for over five years (National Bureau of Statistics of China 2010: tables 2–4).

As the Singaporean government holds flow data tightly, we relied upon a range of flow and converted stock-to-flow data (for this conversion process, see this book's Appendix).

TABLE 5.1. *Temporary Ratio across countries, 2000s*

Country	Temporary economic entrants	Permanent economic entrants	Temporary economic entrants as share of total flows (%)
Argentina	3,646	1	4
Australia	309,249	56,180	58
Austria	11,252	1,016	16
Bahrain	127,506	0	100
Belgium	12,767	8,954	14
Brazil	43,526	658	72
Canada	180,092	64,356	42
Denmark	4,860	6,426	11
Finland	21,000	1,152	51
France	18,599	24,115	8
Germany	213,045	26,065	42
Italy	15,638	104,138	5
Japan	65,145	22,438	52
Kuwait	508,410	0	100
Mexico	38,813	8,699	60
Netherlands	15,689	10,961	13
New Zealand	80,892	10,194	65
Norway	5,017	3,495	8
Oman	399,237	0	100
Peru	2,312	1,236	24
Portugal	3,438	7,276	9
Russia	2,014,000	272,979	83
Saudi Arabia	1,639,591	0	100
Singapore	70,400	528	99
South Africa	20,673	2,376	51
South Korea	142,141	1,448	71
Spain	17,537	135,876	5
Sweden	21,365	4,754	23
Switzerland	92,674	2,319	43
United Kingdom	140,272	114,020	30
United States	460,565	65,268	30

Sources: Statistics South Africa 2012; OECD/IDB/OAS 2012; OECD 2013; GLMM 2013a; 2013b; 2014a; 2014b. For GCC states, temporary economic entrants includes accompanying family.

be partially tied to particularly low permanent intake in the relevant reference year.

Temporary migrants represent more than 70 percent of all migration flows into Brazil, New Zealand, Singapore, and South Korea. As we note in Chapter 4, the comparatively low numbers of permanent economic immigration into South Korea can at least in part be explained by the

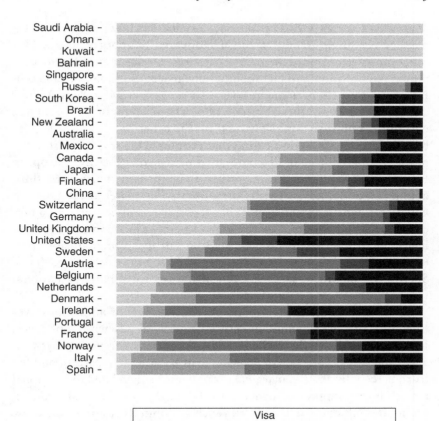

FIGURE 5.1. **Temporary Ratio and Visa Mix, 2011.** This bar graph visualizes Visa Mix in a manner that incorporates Temporary Ratio.
Sources: Statistics South Africa 2012; OECD/IDB/OAS 2012; OECD 2013; GLMM 2013a; 2013b; 2014a; 2014b. For GCC states, temporary economic entrants includes accompanying family.

propensity of labor immigrants to enter via temporary channels (see Figure 5.1). There is another grouping that features over 50 percent of temporary economic migrants and a smaller grouping (France, Denmark, Portugal, Italy, and Spain) that have low numbers of temporary economic immigration as a percentage of total flows (Table 5.1 and Figure 5.1).

A principal observation across this sample of countries is that temporary labor immigration comprises a substantial component of overall migration flows into many of these countries. Drawing upon Figure 5.1, it is important to consider the extent to which the Visa Mix and the Temporary Ratio interact in order to produce these results. For example, compared to other OECD countries, Sweden has low numbers of permanent economic migrants, but a moderate Temporary Ratio. This outcome is determined in part by its low levels of permanent economic immigration and a comparatively generous humanitarian component within its permanent Visa Mix (Swedish Migration Agency 2015), along with the absolute numbers of temporary economic entrants. In Norway and Denmark, on the other hand, we see a quite low Temporary Ratio, indicating that economic labor is being sourced more through internal EU (and in the case of Norway, European Economic Area) immigration rather than through temporary third country national flows. This is corroborated by material presented in Chapter 4, which demonstrates that free movement comprises 59 percent of the Visa Mix in Norway and 51 percent in Denmark. Norway has some of the highest rates of internal European immigration (particularly from Poland) of any country in Europe (Friberg 2012: 316). Such flows might be seen as a substitute for third country national temporary economic migration.

We do not have extensive data on temporary labor admissions over time, and therefore cannot discern long term trends with confidence. Figure 5.2 presents the available data for the 5-year period between 2006 and 2011. The median percentage in 2006 was 36 percent and fell to 30 percent by 2011, a marginal drop that is likely related to the global recession that suppressed demand for labor. Despite the weaker global economy, Gulf and Asian countries such as South Korea and Japan saw relatively consistent trends across time, as did several countries that might typically be associated with high rates of permanent economic immigration – Australia, Canada, New Zealand, and the United States. While some countries such as Italy and Portugal have seen more dramatic fluctuation in their temporary rate, generally the figures are consistent. The OECD (2014: 22) attributes Italy's recent plunge in temporary labor immigration to its slow recovery following the global financial crisis. Italy has also instituted a number of reforms aimed at making it easier to obtain a permanent residence permit, which might encourage permanent economic migration at the expense of temporary migration (OECD 2014: 266). These precarious labor conditions followed a period of consistent economic growth from 1993 to 2006 that encouraged temporary economic immigration. It appears that the adverse economic conditions following the financial crisis made these countries much less attractive as destinations for temporary workers.

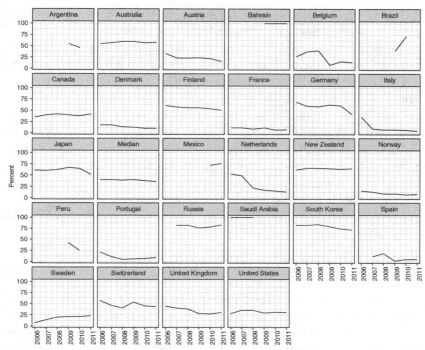

FIGURE 5.2. Temporary Ratio across available countries from 2006 to 2011.
Sources: GLMM 2013a; 2013b; 2014a; 2014b; OECD dataset; OECD/IDB/OAS
2012; Ministry of Manpower Singapore 2015; Singapore Department of Statistics
2007–11; Singapore Prime Minister's Office 2012; n/a denotes missing data.

The relative percentage of temporary labor migration into France
has dropped from 12 percent in 2006 to 8 percent in 2011 (Figure 5.2).
However, this change most likely relates less to cuts to temporary economic migrants that have remained numerically consistent over this
period at around 19,000 per year, and more to increases in the percentage
of permanent economic migrants within the Visa Mix (see Chapter 4).
France has over the last decade moved toward a more selective immigration policy, with a focus within its permanent intake upon skilled economic flows (Chou and Baygert 2007).

In contrast, other countries have seen more stability. Australia has
retained a persistently high Temporary Ratio that has increased from
55 percent in 2006 to 58 percent in 2011. This reflects the uncapped,
"demand"-driven nature of temporary labor flows into Australia and

the strong economic growth during a second mining boom (Boucher 2016: chapter 7). Similarly, the stability of the United States' Temporary Ratio, between 28 and 30 percent, can be linked to the establishment of caps by Congress for many, although not all, temporary labor visas (Freeman and Hill 2006). In Switzerland, it is clear from Figure 5.2 that temporary economic flows have remained fairly high over the full time period. This may relate to extensive entry of temporary visa holders for short-term ambassadorial, consular, and foreign administrative purposes (Fron et al. 2008: 21–2). Indeed, the data reveal high temporary labor immigration across most countries and continuity in these trends across recent years. Nonetheless, when we draw upon secondary qualitative data, it is clear that there is also a great deal of movement between the temporary and permanent categories, particularly in countries that are identified in the tables as having exclusive "temporary" systems.

Ambiguity in the Temporary Ratio

Gulf states are the most immigrant-dominated countries in the world, but the endurance of temporary workers in that region suggests some ambiguity between *de jure* temporary and de facto permanent status (Fargues 2011: 287) – a phenomenon that has been called "permanent impermanence" (Ali 2010: 3).[5] For example, although data on visa stay for temporary residents are limited, we do for instance know that 28.5 percent of immigrants in the United Arab Emirates have been present there for over ten years (Baldwin-Edwards 2011: 32). Baldwin-Edwards suggests on this basis that there is in fact a large minority of effectively "permanent" settlers among the immigrant population in that country. Similarly, Fargues (2011: 280) finds that the number of foreign nationals in Gulf states exceeds number of return migrants, suggesting practically permanent status for large volumes of residents.

Still, there is clearly a qualitative difference between being a long-term temporary immigrant in a Gulf state (even after many renewals of residency) and a permanent resident elsewhere. In the former, an immigrant's presence and renewal is conditional on employer sponsorship, whereas in the latter, a migrant enjoys an independent right to remain,

---

[5] As discussed in the Measurement section above, as we do not have reliable data on the length of stay of temporary visa holders in some countries including those in the Gulf region, we cannot estimate how much of this immigration is actually of a long-term nature that would be classified as "permanent" for the purposes of the OECD methodology. Nor do we have estimates for all GCC countries.

often accompanied with a modicum of other social rights (Goldring and Landolt 2013: 18). This underlies the unstable, contingent nature of long-term temporary immigrants' residency in the Gulf and justifies the enduring characterization of these forms of immigration as of a temporary nature.

The key difference between temporary admissions in autocratic and democratic states appears to be whether opportunities are available to temporary immigrants over time to transition from temporary to permanent visas. Many immigrants eventually wish to undertake just such a conversion. Indeed, the history of guest worker programs in Western Europe demonstrates that today's temporary guest worker is frequently tomorrow's citizen (Joppke 1999). Formalized pathways to adjust from temporary to permanent status are common in states like Australia and Canada where there are established visa categories that facilitate such portability. For instance, the Australian Productivity Commission (2015: 373) estimates that around 72 percent of migrants on Temporary Work (457) visas eventually transition to permanent residency through a variety of permanent skilled visa opportunities. Such pathways to permanency are less common in continental European states where temporary migrants might be tolerated on an ongoing temporary basis as settler state concepts of "permanent residence" are less broadly accepted (IOM 2008: 299). In Japan, which does not offer clear legal pathways for the settlement of people with ethnic Japanese descent, the long-term residency of these individuals is nonetheless well established (Tsuda 1999: 691). The historical record in these countries demonstrates that overtime many have translated guest worker systems into modes of permanent entry, often after legal interventions and advocacy by migrant activists and their representatives (Gurowitz 1999; Joppke 1999).

Temporary Labor Immigration and Undocumented Status

Non-renewal of temporary labor visas generates undocumented workers. While data do not adequately account for the quantity of undocumented workers resulting from visa over-stayers, we can refer to estimates from several key countries to gain insights into the extent of this issue. In the Gulf region, for instance, irregular workers (which include trafficked migrants among the undocumented) are thought to comprise between 10 and 15 percent of the workforce (Khan and Harroff-Tavel 2010: 296). Given *kafala* rules and the low levels of unauthorized entry in Gulf states, it is reasonable to assume that most of the region's undocumented population was once on temporary visas.

Irregular immigration often owes to the inability of temporary visa holders to transition to permanent visas or longer-term temporary status. Such limits lead people to overstay their visa, as was the case historically with the Bracero Program in the United States in the mid-twentieth century (Ruhs 2009). In the Gulf region, Baldwin-Edwards (2011: 39) notes that boys who were once the dependent of an authorized migrant are rendered unauthorized when they reach twenty-one years of age unless they have a sponsor. In Europe, Lenard (2012: 279) argues that the unwillingness of countries to consider legal channels for the permanent conversion of low-skilled temporary labor has encouraged the growth of undocumented immigration across the continent. France and Spain have both struggled with large undocumented populations of former seasonal workers. In recent years, the Spanish government has sought to manage the risk of overstay by primarily granting temporary visas to women with dependent children as they are deemed likely to return (Plewa 2013: 113). Alternately, South Korea has used the liberalization of temporary programs to reduce the size of its undocumented populations, which had grown to over 200,000 by 2007 (Seol 2005: 99–103; Tan 2012: 42).

Implications for Gender and Ethnicity

Existing research suggests that temporary and permanent economic immigration is often stratified not only according to skill, but also gender and origin. The preponderance of unskilled workers on temporary economic visas and of skilled workers on permanent visas is well established in migration research. As Martin Ruhs (2010; 2013) has argued persuasively, countries with fewer social rights for migrants tend to be more willing to admit large numbers of often low-skill temporary workers, while high-skill workers are more likely to enter on a permanent basis with access to a larger array of social benefits. The rationale for this differential treatment, according to Ruhs, is that countries must compete to attract and retain these highly skilled immigrants and must offer greater incentives. Conversely, states may be concerned that low-skilled workers will place a high fiscal burden on welfare systems, and accordingly choose to limit long-term access. Further, states perceive less need to incentivize migration by workers with more easily replaceable skill sets and who are therefore viewed as more disposable.

Complicating the rights versus numbers dynamic further, we argue that temporary unskilled immigrants are more likely to be women and non-white, in democracies and non-democracies. As such, there is a gender and origin diversity dimension to the rights versus numbers trade-off. Women tend to be overrepresented among unskilled temporary visa-holders, particularly domestic worker immigration into the Middle East and Singapore (Rosewarne 2012: 67). There is also a gendered skilled/unskilled demarcation of immigration into developed Western countries. In Canada, women and ethnic minorities are overrepresented in the low-skill Temporary Foreign Worker Program but underrepresented in the more coveted high-skill track of the same program. Only the high-skilled track provides clear portability channels to permanent residency (Boucher 2016: chapter 7).

The gender segregation that operates within the hierarchical sectors of domestic labor markets is exacerbated by the demarcation between temporary and permanent visa status. In particular, migrant women's labor market position can be viewed as a structural effect of temporary labor immigration (Rosewarne 2012: 80). A large part of the gender picture here is the preponderance of female migrant workers in care work that is often classified as "unskilled work" for the purposes of economic visa entry. Outside of Canada, countries generally do not provide permanent opportunities for settlement for care workers (Boucher 2016: chapter 2). This policy question of whether or not to classify care work as "skilled work" (more frequently of a permanent nature) grows in importance as the number of migrant care workers increases globally with structural aging in many Western democracies (Beneria, Deere, and Kabeer 2012: 3).

The Temporary Ratio also divides along country of origin lines. In the Gulf states, highly skilled jobs with more entitlements and greater residency opportunities are often restricted to nationals from high-income Western European countries and former settler states. Correspondingly, migrants from the Global South occupy the lower-skill positions with tighter visa conditions and fewer privileges (Shaham 2008; Baldwin-Edwards 2011). However, this ethnic demarcation between temporary and permanent migrants also plays out in democratic states. For instance, migrants from the Global South are overrepresented in Canada's low-skill Temporary Foreign Worker Program and Seasonal Agricultural Workers Program, both of which limit residency (Sharma 2006).

Employers exercise considerable control over which migrants they select from these programs, meaning that they also possess the capacity to select immigrants on the basis of ethnicity or gender, or those without accompanying family (Hennebry and Prebisch 2012: 25). Workers in the Seasonal Agricultural Workers Program are predominately from Mexico, Jamaica, and Commonwealth Caribbean nations, as these are the countries with which Canada has bilateral contracts (McLaughlin 2010: 82; McLaughlin and Hennebry 2013: 179).

Given the persistent economic inequalities between origin and destination country, immigrants from the Global South may be more likely to remain in these disadvantageous programs (McLaughlin and Hennebry 2013: 182). Critical scholars argue that temporary economic visas reinforce ethnic and class divisions between the Global North and South, amounting to the outsourcing of "dirty work" from the developed regions of the world to developing countries (e.g. Ellerman 2005: 627). Still, this observation is not universally held. While immigrants from European and settler states are overrepresented in the high-skilled Temporary Foreign Worker Program track in Canada, Indian workers are the largest source group in the skilled H-1B track in the United States (predominately on information technology visas) and India is the top country in overall temporary American admissions (Sahoo, Sangha, and Kelly 2010: 301, 303).

CONCLUSION

The data presented in this chapter reveal that temporary economic immigration is in fact the predominant form of economic admission in most immigration regimes – and in some countries, it is the predominant form of all admissions. While the *kafala* systems of the Gulf states have notoriously high rates of temporary labor immigration, this is also true of settler states and many Western European democracies. Even in those countries with lower levels of temporary immigration in our reference year (such as Italy, Spain, and Portugal), there is considerable variation across time. There is also a strong relationship between temporary status and undocumented status. This is the case in autocratic regimes – where we might expect migrants to be more subject to exploitation with impunity – but also in many democracies too. Undocumented labor immigration is an issue in the United States, across Western Europe, and reputedly, increasingly in some former settler states, such as Canada, where the temporary labor population is also growing.

The Temporary Ratio is important not only as a demographic outcome in its own right but also as it informs other indicators considered in this book. Given that permanent status is often the first stepping-stone to naturalization, the extent of permanent immigration holds great influence for citizenship patterns in immigration regimes – the subject of our next chapter.

6

Naturalization

A Final Barrier to Immigration

Access to citizenship represents the acknowledgment of immigrants' full membership after admission. Citizenship renders to immigrants a guarantee of permanent settlement, complete access to constitutionally designated rights, and a stake in the future course of their society through rights of franchise (Vink 2005: 5; Mazzolari 2009: 169; Cort 2012: 510). Conversely, citizenship is also a means of ensuring that certain classes of people are denied such standing. Brubaker (1992: x) viewed citizenship as a "powerful instrument of social closure, shielding prosperous states from the migrant poor" – more a tool for excluding outsiders than granting rights to insiders. Of course, these are two sides of the same coin. And for immigrants, naturalization is a final hurdle to permanent, unconditional immigration.

As the fragile status of foreigners in Gulf states demonstrates, migrants face obstacles long after their initial admission. No matter how long a migrant has been a resident of a given country, only citizenship guarantees unfettered access to a state's territory and protections. Without it, residency is never truly assured, deportation is possible, and readmission is not guaranteed. Thus, citizenship constitutes the final government-imposed barrier that restricts migration and membership. Naturalization Rates measure the frequency with which immigrants may access this membership – a reflection of the ease of accessing membership, but also indirectly, demand for it.

Because immigration selection and naturalization policies are not conventionally thought to align, it is important to include Naturalization Rates in our analysis to render a more complete picture of how states manage immigration. Globalization aside, states have retained their ability to determine membership as a largely sovereign prerogative – independent of the size of immigrant stocks or economic demand. This gives governments a far greater degree of autonomy than they have over admissions outcomes, in light of uncontrollable push and pull factors (Brubaker 1992: 180–1). The most dramatic examples come from Gulf states like Kuwait where migrants make up over 70 percent of the population, yet the Naturalization Rate sits near zero. In contrast, Belgium has a relatively low migrant stock of 10 percent, yet a much higher Naturalization Rate at 2.5 percent. In fact, Janoski (2010: 222) argues that immigration stocks are not positively correlated with Naturalization Rates at all. According to his analysis, countries with the lowest Naturalization Rates often have the highest stocks of immigrants.

Ultimately, immigration selection and naturalization policies work together to determine immigration outcomes. It is therefore important to consider both sets of data to get the most complete picture of barriers to entry and membership. For example, New Zealand featured a fairly liberal naturalization policy between 1977 and 1987. Birthright citizenship was unconditionally universal, the residency requirement was a mere three years, and dual citizenship was permitted. Still, Naturalization Rates during that period remained quite low because restrictive immigration selection policies made it difficult to obtain a New Zealand residency permit, a prerequisite to naturalization (Janoski 2010: 115). Since this time, New Zealand has made permanent residency easier to obtain, and the Naturalization Rate has grown.

As with the two previous chapters, we begin by conceptualizing Naturalization Rates as a dimension of immigration regimes. Next, we explain how we measure Naturalization Rates, accounting for birthright citizenship policies in certain countries, in the context of other methods and approaches. We then present the results of our descriptive analysis of Naturalization Rates cross-nationally over time.

NATURALIZATION RATES OVER SPACE AND TIME

Naturalization dates back at least to ancient Rome, when the Empire bestowed citizenship to integrate (and subjugate) conquered peoples (Janoski 2010: 10). Today, the process has expanded into an institutionalized means to control access to citizenship and its corresponding benefits. However, as Brubaker (1992: 180) highlights, naturalization policy is a uniquely sovereign prerogative and has therefore resisted transnational pressures more effectively than immigration policy. While in many accounts, naturalization is viewed as an essential means of political incorporation for disadvantaged minorities (e.g. Jones-Correa 2005: 75–6), others argue that the process can also work to perpetuate "global racial inequality," depending on the criteria states use to select members (Menzel 2013: 50).

Historically, citizenship has been awarded primarily through place of birth – *jus soli* – and the nationality of one's parents – *jus sanguinis*. Under *jus soli*, all those born in a country (or all those born in a country to citizen or permanent resident parents) are citizens. Under *jus sanguinis*, citizenship is passed from citizen parents to citizen children by inheritance, preventing second-generation immigrants from receiving citizenship as easily as offered by *jus soli*. These two concepts are associated with fundamentally different understandings of national identity, with *jus soli* emphasizing voluntarism and *jus sanguinis* emphasizing ethnicity and heritage (Fahrmeir 2007: 4). Countries that use *jus soli* also often give citizenship via *jus sanguinis* to the children of citizens born abroad.

Jus soli and *jus sanguinis* have been conventionally linked to national ethos or "cultural idioms." Brubaker (1992: 85) notes how France adopted *jus soli* for second- and third-generation immigrants in the late nineteenth century as a response to the anger at the continuing exemption from military service of long-settled foreigners. French openness has also been linked to its early history of democratization, which created a more inclusive view of national identity, and to its early exposure to ethnic diversity through its colonization of territories in Asia, Africa, and the Americas (Howard 2009: 41, 43–6). Britain also has a long history of *jus soli* rooted in the British Empire. The British Nationality Act of 1772 gave citizenship to all born in British dominions, reflecting the reach of the Empire (Janoski 2010: 68). This history of *jus soli* in Britain helped extend the practice to its former colonies in North America (Bloemraad 2006: 20). Today, *jus soli* is most associated with Anglo settler states, although Australia and New Zealand have both modified the practice in recent decades.

The *jus sanguinis* model is often associated with Germany, which adopted the policy in line with its history as a "community of descent" (Brubaker 1992: 115). *Jus sanguinis*, however, is not restricted to Germany; rather it is the predominant logic of naturalization around the world. During the interwar years, *jus soli* countries such as Britain, France, and the United States all emphasized descent over birth as a basis for citizenship (Fahrmeir 2007: 137). Since 1981, the United Kingdom, Australia,

Ireland, and New Zealand have all restricted *jus soli* citizenship to children of a legal resident or citizen (Menzel 2013: 30). *Jus soli* has persisted more vigorously in the settler states of our sample, all of which have some form of *jus soli* and accordingly relatively high Naturalization Rates (Janoski 2010: 93). Although the distinctions have diminished in recent years, *jus soli* and *jus sanguinis* remain key organizing principles of citizenship globally.

However, the emergence of supranational structures has led some to question the value of national citizenship. For example, the 1992 Maastricht Treaty formally created the European Union and conferred many rights on citizens of member states, regardless of where in the Union they resided (Vink 2005: 3). This paved the way for the creation of "postnational membership" (Soysal 1994: 148). However, this has not borne out in practice. Twelve years after the creation of the EU, Vink (2005: 42) noted that it is "still unclear what we should make of the so-called citizenship of the Union." While the Schengen Zone facilitates the free movement of Europeans, states have retained control over their immigration and naturalization policies (Zulean and Roventa 2012: 222). Thus, even one of the most successful supranational organizations of all time has failed to undermine the national roots of citizenship. A concept of dual European and national citizenship was contemplated for the 2004 Rome Treaty, but ultimately removed from the final draft (Vink 2005: 144).

The European Union also exhibits the effect of demand for citizenship on Naturalization Rates. In light of free movement across EU borders, many intra-European immigrants are disinclined to pursue citizenship in their destination state. By virtue of their residency and EU nationality, these immigrants are entitled to admission and already eligible for work and most government-provided services, benefits, and protections. In much of Western Europe, permanent residents might be granted so many rights that immigrants see little reason to naturalize (Bauböck 1992: 102–3). States are increasingly granting welfare and social benefits to permanent residents as well (Ferwerda and Miller 2014). The boundary between residency and citizenship has been further eroded by the granting of some political rights to residents, such as the right of European Union nationals to vote in other EU countries' local and European elections. This extension of rights has gone so far that Tomas Hammar (1990) coined the term "denizenship" to highlight the elevated status permanent residents receive in many countries that makes them closer to, but not full, citizens. Under such circumstances, naturalization offers largely symbolic incentives. This suppresses Naturalization Rates in states that primarily admit other Europeans like Austria, Denmark, and Germany before 2015.

Dual citizenship has also taken on importance in the national context as a barrier to naturalization as laws forbidding dual citizenship, either in origin or destination countries, can dissuade immigrants from naturalizing. Giving up rights in and connections to their home country can discourage immigrants from taking on the nationality of their country of long-term residence. Allowance for dual citizenship can encourage naturalization in receiving countries, increasing the probability of naturalization by 10 percent in one study (Mazzolari 2009: 186). Canada has promoted its policy of permitting dual citizenship as a symbol of the country's multiculturalism (Bloemraad 2006: 276). In contrast, the United States formally requires renunciation of prior citizenship, but has not enforced the policy in practice (Bloemraad 2006: 52). These policies suggest the bureaucratic barriers migrants face to naturalization.

Governments over the last two decades have more actively restricted access to citizenship. Janoski (2010: 37) has classified twelve distinct barriers to naturalization, including the duration of residency requirements and fees.[1] These barriers can have a notable effect on naturalizations. When Germany dropped its residency requirement from fifteen to eight years in 1999, naturalizations temporarily jumped (Schönwälder and Triadafilopoulos 2012: 57). Similarly, when the United States increased the naturalization processing fees it levies on prospective citizens, applications soared immediately prior to the change (Department of Homeland Security 2016). In Japan, naturalization is regarded as arduous, arbitrary, and unfacilitated; while 30,000 permanent resident visas are issued each year, the country processes only 1,000 annual naturalizations (Green 2017).

An especially significant barrier to naturalization in recent years has been the inclusion of language, cultural, and social knowledge on citizenship "tests" administered to prospective citizens. Sara Wallace Goodman collectively refers to these tools as means of "civic integration" (Goodman

---

[1] These include (1) good conduct provisions, (2) provisions concerning immigrants' willingness to integrate, (3) language skills, (4) dual nationality, (5) application complexity, (6) application fees, (7) state discretion in granting citizenship, (8) residency requirements, (9) *jus sanguinis* laws preventing *jus soli* naturalization of children, (10) *jus sanguinis* concerning children of parents born in the country (double *jus soli*), (11) provisions related to women who marry a foreigner, and (12) provisions related to the transfer of citizenship by mothers when married to a foreigner.

2010: 757; Goodman 2012: 659), which – unlike other barriers to citizenship like residency requirements and *jus sanguinis* – restrict who obtains citizenship rather than who is eligible for it. The civic integration model rests on the idea that integration requires in part "individual commitments to characteristics typifying national citizenship, specifically country knowledge, language proficiency and liberal and social values" (Goodman 2010: 754). While the United States has had a civics test since the 1980s, the emergence of these exams in Western Europe marks a novel shift as they emphasize cultural belonging over ancestry as the fundamental basis for citizenship (Goodman 2012: 659). Goodman (2012: 666–74) documents a proliferation of these tests throughout the 2000s with governments increasingly requiring passage of formalized tests on language and integration instead of just evaluating these requirements via interviews.

COMPLICATIONS OF NATURALIZATION RATES

The vagaries and idiosyncrasies of modern governance and immigrant behavior produce a number of complications to the measurement and understanding of Naturalization Rates across countries. Conventionally, Naturalization Rates are thought to offer a measure of "assimilation and adaptation" (Baker 2007: 1) – a reflection of the rationale of naturalization policy. A number of researchers have examined the relationship between state naturalization policy and naturalization outcomes. Reichel (2012: 15) finds a positive correlation between European Naturalization Rates and MIPEX Nationality scores, a measure of the openness of naturalization laws. He argues that policy is a "modest" predictor of Naturalization Rates in general and that it is even better for explaining the naturalization of non-EU citizens. Janoski (2011: 21) goes even further, finding that naturalization laws are the most significant explanation of Naturalization Rates.

In a slightly different vein, other scholars see Naturalization Rates as a reflection of a community's political openness. Koopmans (2004) looks at German Länder (states) and argues that the broad discretion each region has in granting citizenship means that Naturalization Rates will be indicative of their openness to immigrants more generally. This was demonstrated in Hainmueller and Hangartner's (2013) examination of different Swiss cantons, where naturalization decisions vary with applicants' origins and ethnic attributes. Janoski (2010), however, inverts the causation of Naturalization Rates and local politics. While Koopmans views widespread naturalization as a reflection of an open political community, Janoski sees naturalization as a way to increase the political power of immigrants and create more responsive politics. He finds that countries with higher Naturalization Rates, for example, are more conscious of attacks on foreigners and less likely to enact illiberal anti-immigrant naturalization policies due to the stronger political voice of immigrants (Janoski 2010). This argument suggests that Naturalization Rates are more than a mere reflection of naturalization policy but can be the genesis of broader social change. This hypothesis has grown increasingly dubious amidst a rise in populism across Europe and the United States.

Others scholars question the link between naturalization policy and Naturalization Rates. Vink (2011: 11) notes that Naturalization Rates may say something about the general accessibility of citizenship, but they can also be heavily affected by interest in acquiring citizenship. Dronkers and Vink (2012) find that favorable national policies have some effect but that individual factors – like those influencing demand (Howard 2009: 24) – are more important. For example, Diehl and Blohm (2003) highlight how despite few legal benefits to naturalization, Turkish immigrants in Germany who naturalize do so in order to join a per-ceived higher status group. As we underscored earlier in relation to intra-European migrants, demand for naturalization is likely constrained by the ease of repatriation and the portability of benefits in the destination state for permanent residents. Furthermore, administrative arrangements may make naturalization prohibitively time-consuming or expensive.

Technically, Naturalization Rates actually measure the rate at which *foreign citizens* – and not just immigrants – are offered full national membership (Reichel 2012: 22). While this distinction is inconsequen-tial in the United States, Canada, and other countries with liberal *jus soli* practices, Naturalization Rates conventionally measure the rate at which stateless people or foreign citizens – including those born on the territory of a country without citizenship – become citizens. For this rea-son, Brubaker (1992: 81) contends that ascribed citizenship – citizenship acquisitions by virtue of birth (*jus soli*) or descent (*jus sanguinis*) – is far more important than Naturalization Rates, because such policy frame-works fundamentally alter who constitutes a nation. Janoski's (2010) innovative approach to measuring Naturalization Rates, which accounts for *jus soli* citizenship acquisitions, helps solve this problem of compari-son across different naturalization schemes, and increases the utility of Naturalization Rates as a measure of immigrant access to membership.

The complexity of these modifications, however, suggests the further complications involved in measuring Naturalization Rates – a subject we address in the following section.

MEASUREMENT

There are a number of calculations that different scholars call "Naturalization Rates." Consensus only exists on the point that different measures are useful for different research questions. For example, while stock-based rates of naturalized immigrants are most useful for measuring overall incorporation, annual rates better reflect the outcomes of current policies. Individual-level data is necessary to study why people choose to naturalize (Reichel 2012).

The most common measure of Naturalization Rates and the one we use is the annual Naturalization Rate. This is found by dividing the number of naturalizations that occur in a given country in a given year by the population of foreign citizens in that country at the beginning of that year.

Where:

R_Y = Naturalization Rate in year Y
N_Y = Total naturalized aliens in year Y
S_Y = Total migrant stock S calculated in year Y = Total foreign-born individuals who are residents of Country 1 and do not already hold citizenship – not merely the foreign-born population because many foreign-born people have already naturalized, and because some foreign born are *jus sanguinis* citizens born abroad.

$$\text{Naturalization Rate } R_Y = \frac{N_Y}{S_Y} = \frac{\text{Total naturalized aliens in year } Y}{\text{Total migrant stock } S \text{ calculated in year } Y}$$

In light of this measurement's consideration of the total eligible population, this measure of Naturalization Rates is a better reflection of current citizenship policy than those using raw stock numbers alone (Reichel 2012: 3), and is used widely (Clarke, Van Dam, and Gooster 1998; Bloemraad 2006; Howard 2009; Janoski 2010; Reichel 2012).[2]

[2] It is worth noting that for the purposes of measuring Naturalization Rates, foreign stock includes all persons in a country's territory that do not hold that country's citizenship. It does not include dual citizens who also hold their country's citizenship since they have already naturalized or were born into their citizenship by blood or birthright. Likewise, it should not be confused with the immigrant population. Defined broadly, the term "immigrants" includes all that have relocated to a country, including those that have already

This rate represents the most accurate measure of naturalization. Of course, many foreign citizens may be ineligible to naturalize for a variety of reasons (e.g. criminal behavior, debt, language proficiency, etc.), meaning that the denominator over-counts who can naturalize in a given year. However, due to the complicated and varying requirements for naturalization eligibility across countries and the unavailability of more specific cross-national data on such legislative obstacles, we choose to not attempt to adjust our denominator to what statisticians term the "at-risk population" in order to obtain an even more accurate probability.

Looking at the Naturalization Rates of annual flows of immigrant cohorts – which are subject to consistent laws from their date of entry – would be ideal for calculating probabilities, but this is near impossible due to lack of data (Reichel 2011). Jones-Correa (2001) attempts to correct for this in the United States by dividing the number of naturalizations in a given year by the number of immigrants who entered seven years prior. He examines the Naturalization Rates of different immigrant groups within the United States and therefore suggests that seven years is roughly how long it takes to naturalize given America's five-year residency requirement. However, this choice represents an unproven assumption about immigrants' duration of residency and does not apply well to comparative Naturalization Rates for multiple countries. Indeed, such an approach is problematic even within the United States: of the 8.8 million citizenship-eligible US Green Card holders, nearly half have resided in the United States for longer than fourteen years (USCIS 2015). It also allows for Naturalization Rates over 100 percent if immigrants from more or fewer than seven years past choose to naturalize, as Jones-Correa (2001: 1016) finds for Salvadorian immigrants after 1983, which is practically impossible.

ADJUSTMENTS FOR BIRTHRIGHT CITIZENSHIP

As intimated above, calculating comparative Naturalization Rates is also complicated by the difference in what different countries count as "naturalization." A primary discrepancy comes from the enforcement of *jus soli* laws. The Netherlands, for example, allows people born on their territory

naturalized or those who may have possessed citizenship at birth through their parents. Furthermore, "immigrants" also excludes those born in the territory of a country without its citizenship. Even though they are not immigrants, they are still foreigners and thus eligible to naturalize. The foreign stock is therefore the most accurate representation of the population eligible for naturalization.

to opt for citizenship at age eighteen and counts this as naturalization. Of course, if they were born in a country with *jus soli*, these young people would already have citizenship and therefore not be eligible for this relatively easy naturalization procedure. Thus, self-reported naturalization numbers underestimate the openness of countries with *jus soli* since they grant citizenship before people have an opportunity to naturalize. In this section, we consider the magnitude of this underestimation, and justify why we account for it.

Janoski (2010) adjusts for *jus soli* in calculating Naturalization Rates by creating a multiplier that accounts for such birth-based conferrals of citizenship. Doing so requires extensive, patient correspondence with national governments to solicit comparable data, and he undertakes a painstaking series of calculations to produce his adjusted Naturalization Rates. Because data on births to foreign parents is not available for most countries, Janoski (2010: 30) estimates *jus soli* births by multiplying the total birth rate by the foreign population in a given year to estimate how many new citizens are born to foreign parents. Although he acknowledges that this introduces bias due to differences in birth rates across ethnic groups, he argues that it is a fair approximation.

Jus soli laws are not regular across countries. Of the countries in Janoski's study, only the United States and Canada currently grant citizenship to all children born on their territory.[3] In New Zealand, as of January 1, 2006, citizenship is only granted to children born in New Zealand who have at least one parent who is a New Zealand citizen or legal permanent resident.[4] Similarly, the United Kingdom grants citizenship based on birth in the UK to children who have at least one parent who is a British citizen or a "settled" immigrant and to children who lived the first ten years of their life in the UK.[5] Australia has an effectively identical citizenship law.[6][7]

Other countries restrict *jus soli* citizenship based on residency. France offers citizenship to children who have at least one parent who was born in France (commonly called "double *jus soli*") or who meet fairly

---

[3] US Constitution, 14th Amendment, §1; Canadian Citizenship Act, Part I, §1.
[4] New Zealand Citizenship Act 1977 No 61 (as at July 1, 2013), Part 1, §6(1).
[5] British Nationality Act 1981, Part I, §1(1) and (4).
[6] Australian Citizenship Act 2007, §12(1).
[7] For countries that have limits on their application of *jus soli*, Janoski adjusts his birth rate calculation to the relevant population. For the United Kingdom and Australia, for example, Janoski (2010: 30) only applies the full *jus soli* correction to permanent residents and includes a ten-year lag in his calculation for "non-settled" immigrants.

complicated residency requirements depending on their age.[8] Germany
gives citizenship to children who have a parent that has been a German
permanent resident for at least eight years.[9] Belgium grants citizenship to
children who have at least one parent who was born in Belgium (double
jus soli) or were residents for five of the prior ten years and to children
whose parents request it for them before age twelve so long as the parents
lived in Belgium for the prior ten years and the child has lived in Belgium
since birth.[10] In 2004, Ireland restricted its *jus soli* citizenship to children
of permanent residents or persons who lived in Ireland for three of the
prior four years.

While some disagreements exist about the most accurate measures of
Naturalization Rates,[11] it is worth noting that the OECD self-reported
data – which do not account for *jus soli* naturalizations – are only mar-
ginally different from the data produced by Janoski's correspondence-
based approach, which does recognize *jus soli* laws. This gives us
confidence in his estimates that we employ in our dataset. In the far right
column of Table 6.1, using the 2000 to 2005 difference of the OECD
data and Janoski's last published work, we calculate the difference in
the form of a country-specific multiplier that corrects for *jus soli* adjustments. On average, this multiplier has the most impact on Naturalization
Rates in countries with full *jus soli* (although this is largely driven by the
United States), and a very small effect on countries with partial *jus soli*.
We list the average Naturalization Rates during recent five-year intervals
from these countries in Table 6.2. In sum, from this data, we see that
jus soli laws have an appreciable and occasionally significant impact on
Naturalization Rates that might otherwise be underestimated. For this
reason, we account for the marginal increase in Naturalization Rates in

---

[8] Extracts from the French Civil Code, Title 1 bis, of French Nationality, Chapter II,
Section II and Chapter III, Section I. Trans. Georges Rouhette.

[9] "Information in English language – Acquiring German citizenship." *Sachsen.de.*

[10] "Born in Belgium." *Kingdom of Belgium: Foreign Affairs, Foreign Trade and Development
Cooperation.*

[11] These modifications are not universally popular, however. Vink (2011) criticizes Janoski's
adjustments as going beyond Naturalization Rates and therefore measuring more than
just naturalization policy, but concepts of nationality. He also criticizes Janoski for
adjusting for *jus soli* births, but not double *jus soli* since data on non-citizens born in a
country's territory is not readily available. Even though Janoski is unable to capture the
complete magnitude of *jus soli* effects, this generosity is a crucial aspect of citizenship
policy. From 2000 to 2005, Janoski's calculations lead to an average Naturalization Rate
in the United States that is 2.5 times higher than the numbers provided by the OECD.

TABLE 6.1. *Comparison between OECD and Janoski (2010) data,*
with multipliers

Country	Major policy change since Janoski data?	Janoski average Naturalization Rate 2000–5	OECD average Naturalization Rate 2000–5	Janoski-OECD multiplier to account for *jus soli* margins
Full jus soli				
Canada	No	12.3	11.3	1.1
New Zealand	Yes	4.3	–	
United States	No	7.1	2.8	2.5
Partial jus soli				
Australia	No	4.5	3.4	1.3
Belgium	No	5.6	5.2	1.1
United Kingdom	No	5.3	4.7	1.1
France	No	4.9	4.3	1.1
Germany	No	2.6	2.1	1.3
Ireland	Yes	3.1	1.7	1.8
No jus soli				
Austria		4.8	4.8	1.0
Denmark		4.6	5.0	0.9
Finland		4.2	4.3	1.0
Italy		0.7	0.7	0.9
Japan		0.9	0.9	1.0
Netherlands		4.8	5.5	0.9
Norway		4.8	5.0	1.0
Sweden		7.6	7.4	1.0
Switzerland		2.3	2.4	1.0

Sources: Janoski 2010; OECD 2012; OECD 2010 for Ireland; national census data for Australia, Canada, and France (for details, see Appendix). The multiplier is simply the quotient of the Janoski and OECD averages.

jus soli countries and, for countries with *jus soli* laws, replace OECD data with those from Janoski (2016).

DESCRIPTIVE RESULTS

According to these considerations, in Table 6.3, we compiled a dataset for all countries.[12] As demonstrated in Figure 6.1, there was a general

---

[12] Because there is no centralized source for Naturalization Rates, this dataset includes Janoski's data from nine countries featuring some element of jus soli rules, nationality acquisition data from the Organization of American States for four Latin American

TABLE 6.2. *Historical Naturalization Rates for* jus soli *countries*

Country	1970–4	1975–9	1980–4	1985–9	1990–4	1995–9	2000–4	2005–9	2010–12
Australia	5.4	6.9	7.3	8.3	8.6	6.2	4.5	5.3	4.5
Belgium	0.8	0.8	0.8	2.8	2.7	3.4	5.6	3.6	3.2
Canada	10.0	14.7	9.9	8.9	11.3	12.0	12.0	12.5	8.8
France	3.0	2.8	2.8	2.7	2.9	3.5	4.7	4.5	3.7
Germany	0.3	0.3	0.3	0.5	0.5	1.3	1.9	2.0	2.0
Ireland	n/a	n/a	2.3	2.5	1.8	2.1	2.6	2.5	4.1
New Zealand	3.7	6.0	5.6	5.4	4.8	4.2	4.0	4.0	3.2
UK	7.5	5.8	7.3	5.6	3.6	3.5	5.4	4.9	4.5
US	3.6	4.0	3.8	4.0	4.5	9.1	8.5	5.0	4.6

Sources: Janoski (2010: 34) for 1970–99 data; Janoski's (2016) unpublished data for 2000–12. Note: in error, Janoski lists 1995–9 data as "1990–1995".

peak in Naturalization Rates across a number of countries around 2000, and a gradual moderation or decline since then through the most recent measurements in 2014 (also see Figure 7.9 in Chapter 7). Still, different trends emerge within different regions and types of countries. The most pronounced and coherent of these appear among the Gulf states, former settler states, and states with colonial histories – each of which we examine in turn.

Gulf Region

Naturalization in Gulf states is a highly sensitive political issue. Individuals contacted for interviews or data collection in these countries were reluctant to share details, and multiple sources referred to naturalization as a matter of "national security." It is then unsurprising that these states feature among the lowest Naturalization Rates in the world, as displayed in Table 6.3. Citizenship in the Gulf entails access to oil

countries, OECD state-reported data from the remaining twenty-three OECD states, and data collected from national statistics offices for Bahrain, China, Kuwait, Russia, and Singapore. We acquired these latter data either through direct correspondence with officials in these countries or through national reports. Government officials in Oman, Qatar, Saudi Arabia, and the United Arab Emirates declined to report their naturalizations. Ultimately, we estimated rates of zero based on conversations with personnel from national statistics agencies. We are unable to develop reliable estimates about missing values from Argentina, Israel, and South Africa. Even though we collected admissions data from these three destinations, to be consistent throughout the book, we chose not to impute their missing naturalization values.

TABLE 6.3. *Naturalization Rates across fifty countries*

Country	2000	2001	2002	2003	2004	2005	2006	2007	2008	2009	2010	2011	2012	2013	2014
Argentina															
Australia	4.2	4.1	4.9	4.1	4.9	5.0	5.4	6.5	5.7	4.2	5.3	4.4	3.9		
Austria	3.6	4.6	5.1	6.1	5.5	4.5	3.2	1.7	1.2	0.9	0.7	0.7	0.7	0.7	0.7
Bahrain		2.5	2.4	2.1	1.9	1.7	1.5	1.3	1.2	1.1	1.0	1.5			
Belgium	7.2	7.4	5.5	3.9	4.0	3.9	3.4	3.7	3.7	3.1	3.9	2.5	3.2		
Brazil						3.4	3.9	4.2	5.0	5.2	4.9				
Canada	14.7	11.8	10.0	10.9	12.8	12.9	16.3	12.5	11.0	9.7	8.8	10.7	7.0		
Chile										0.2	0.2				
China											0.2	0.0			
Colombia	0.1	0.1	0.1	0.1	0.1	0.1	0.1	0.1	0.1	0.0	0.1				
Czechia	3.6	3.1	2.1	1.5	2.1	1.0	0.8	0.6	0.5	0.4	0.3	0.5		0.6	1.2
Denmark	7.3	4.6	6.5	2.5	5.5	3.8	2.9	1.3	1.9	2.0	0.9	1.1	1.0	0.5	1.2
Estonia		1.5	1.5	1.4	2.4	.2.7	1.9	1.7	0.9	0.7	0.5	0.7	0.6	0.6	0.8
Finland	3.4	3.0	3.1	3.6	6.4	5.2	3.9	4.0	5.0	2.4	2.8	2.7	5.0	4.6	4.0
France	4.9	4.2	4.4	4.8	5.4	5.0	4.7	4.1	4.3	4.2	4.5	3.6	3.0		
Germany	1.2	2.4	2.1	1.9	1.9	2.1	2.3	2.1	1.8	1.8	1.9	2.0	2.0		
Greece								1.9	2.6	2.3	1.1	2.2	2.7	3.8	
Hungary	4.9	7.8	2.7	4.5	4.2	6.9	4.0	5.1	4.6	3.1	3.1	9.8	12.8	6.5	6.2
Iceland					6.6	6.8	6.1	3.5	3.9	3.0	2.1	1.7	2.0	2.8	2.6
India															
Ireland	2.3	3.1	3.1	2.6	2.1	2.4	2.7	2.8	2.4	2.4	2.6	3.9	5.9		
Italy	0.7	0.8	0.7	0.9	1.0	1.2	1.3	1.5	1.6	1.7	1.8	1.4	1.6	2.3	2.6
Japan	1.0	0.9	0.8	1.0	0.9	0.8	0.7	0.7	0.6	0.7	0.6	0.5	0.5	0.4	0.4
Kuwait	0.3	0.2	0.2	0.2	0.3	0.3	0.2	0.1	0.2	0.0	0.0	0.1	0.1	0.4	0.4
Luxembourg	0.4	0.3	0.5	0.5	0.5	0.5	0.6	0.6	0.6	1.9	2.0	1.5	2.0	1.8	2.0

(*continued*)

TABLE 6.3 (continued)

Country	2000	2001	2002	2003	2004	2005	2006	2007	2008	2009	2010	2011	2012	2013	2014
Mexico	7.7										0.8	0.9	1.2	1.2	
Netherlands		7.0	6.6	4.1	3.7	4.1	4.2	4.5	4.1	4.1	3.6	3.8	3.9	3.3	4.0
New Zealand		4.4	3.9	4.0	3.9	4.0	4.4	4.5	3.8	3.1	2.8	3.1	3.7		
Norway	5.3	5.9	4.9	4.0	4.0	5.9	5.4	6.2	3.9	3.8	3.6	4.0	3.0	2.9	3.2
Oman												0.0			
Peru	1.0	1.0	0.9	1.0	1.0	1.1	1.0	0.9	1.1	1.2	1.0				
Poland				3.3				2.8	1.8	4.1	5.9		6.8		
Portugal								1.4	5.1	5.5	4.8	5.2	5.0	5.9	5.3
Qatar	0.4	0.5	0.5	0.4	0.3	0.2	0.9					0.0			
Russia				3.1									19.5	18.9	22.0
Saudi Arabia															
Singapore											0.0	0.0	0.9		
Slovakia				11.8	13.8	6.3	4.4	4.6	1.7	0.5	0.4	0.4	0.4	0.4	0.4
Slovenia											1.8	1.9	0.8	1.4	1.1
South Africa															
South Korea					2.0	3.5	1.6	1.6	1.9	3.0	1.9	1.8	1.3		
Spain	1.5	1.9	2.0	2.0	1.3	1.1	1.5	1.6	1.6	1.4	2.2	2.0	2.0	4.7	1.9
Sweden	8.9	7.6	7.9	7.0	6.1	8.2	10.7	6.8	5.8	5.3	5.4	5.8	7.7	7.5	6.3
Switzerland	2.1	2.0	2.6	2.4	2.4	2.6	3.1	2.9	2.8	2.7	2.3	2.1	1.9	1.9	1.8
Taiwan									6.1						
Turkey										7.8	5.7	5.3			
UAE												0.0			
UK	4.9	4.8	6.0	5.7	5.5	5.9	5.1	4.8	3.6	5.2	4.8	4.2	4.6		
US	12.4	9.4	9.2	5.9	5.7	5.2	4.3	4.2	6.4	4.9	4.3	4.6	4.8		

Sources: OECD/IDB/OAS 2012; OECD 2014; Janoski's (2016) unpublished data; national statistics offices (see Appendix). This table also displays those countries and years for which naturalization data is not available.

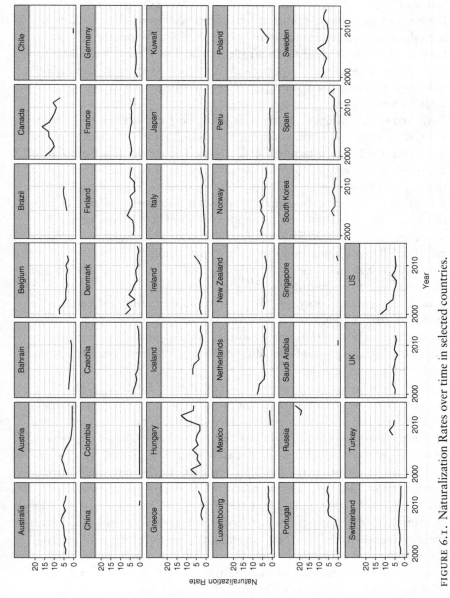

FIGURE 6.1. Naturalization Rates over time in selected countries.

Sources: OECD/IDB/OAS 2012; OECD 2014; Janoski's (2016) unpublished data; national statistics offices (see Appendix).

rent-backed subsidies for housing, education, health care, and employment and is therefore highly coveted, and highly protected. In the city-states of Qatar and Bahrain, and similarly small countries like Kuwait, Oman, and the United Arab Emirates, naturalizations also risk altering the ethnic and tribal composition of the national population. Citizens fear the dilution of their national identity and newcomers' distaste for their dynastic political institutions. With this sensitivity in mind, Gulf governments generally do not publicize naturalizations to citizenries so wary of newcomers.

In 2013, this delicate matter was inflamed by a call to allow some migrants to apply for citizenship in the United Arab Emirates – which, like other Gulf states, requires a declaration from the Emir himself to approve naturalizations. Sultan Sooud al-Qassemi, a member of one of the UAE's ruling families and a prominent Emirati commentator, wrote a *Gulf News* (2013) commentary, suggesting that well-qualified foreign residents should be allowed to apply for citizenship. "Part of the fear of naturalisation is that Emiratis would lose their national identity; we are after all a shrinking minority in our own country," he wrote. Yet an incremental approach, he argued, would not have this effect: "Should the UAE decide to naturalize say 1,000 people a year, on average it would take around 900 years for the naturalised population to outstrip UAE citizens." Citing the success and entrepreneurial contributions of American immigrants, al-Qassemi argued for a more transparent process that rewarded the greatest contributors among long-time residents of the UAE with naturalization.

His call was met with anxiety. Annoyed that the author had "cozied up" to foreigners by writing his thoughts in English, some Emiratis took to social media to condemn the idea (Habboush 2013). While much of the backlash was xenophobic, others were doubtful that expatriates would agree to be ruled by the Emirate's autocratic governing structure and therefore create instability. In a response in the same publication, commentator Jalal bin Thaneya asked, "After being granted citizenship, would political rights be the next step forward?" Businessman Abdulla al-Muhairi told Reuters that naturalized foreigners were unlikely to share Emiratis' belief in the importance of stability above all. "We have no political parties, no political problems," he said. "We have political stability ... How do you guarantee that naturalization will maintain stability?" (Habboush 2013). In many ways, this affair crystallized the difficulty and secrecy surrounding naturalization in the Gulf region.

Kuwait is characterized by similar demographic imbalances as the United Arab Emirates, and similarly constrains naturalization by employing an arbitrary process that ultimately requires the Emir's approval. Uniquely, the Kuwaiti government publicizes data on their annual naturalizations back to the year 2000. In this period, Kuwait has never naturalized more than 4,793 individuals in a year – a 0.3 percent Naturalization Rate. Recent news reports suggest, however, that since 2012, naturalizations may have increased substantially in Kuwait – 110,000 in the five years since 2011 (Izzak 2016). As this is not yet reflected in official statistics, it is not included in our tables above.

Unlike other Gulf states, Saudi Arabia actually employs a points-based system that qualifies migrants to apply for – though not to necessarily be granted – naturalization once they have resided in the country for ten years, hold a bachelor's degree and a master's degree. Qatar has stated an annual cap of fifty naturalizations (Kovessy 2014). Governments have considered liberalizing access to nationality for children with foreign fathers and mothers who are nationals. Saudi Arabia moved to do so in 2013 (*Al-Arabiya* 2013), but consideration of children from mixed marriages is known to be largely ad hoc across the region (e.g. *Khaleej Times* 2012).

The similarly ad hoc nature of naturalization decisions has become especially politicized in Bahrain, where the ruling Al-Khalifa family has balanced demands for consultation and power-sharing from the country's substantial Shia plurality for the past fifteen years. In 2002, the king created a forty-seat parliament that ruled under his supreme authority and loosened restrictions on free speech until 2011, when the king called in Saudi troops to crush the Jasmine Uprising inspired by the Arab Spring. While protesters organized around a broad-based demand for greater democracy, most were from Shia sects. During this period, the government has been accused of using its discretion over naturalization decisions to engineer a Sunni majority in Bahrain (Harrison 2014). This, critics allege, has entailed extending naturalization to a number of expatriates from Sunni countries such as Pakistan, who are expected to defer to the authority of the kingdom's Sunni royal family. Accordingly, a Bahraini parliamentarian estimated that Bahrain approved 60,000 naturalizations between 2001 and 2010 (Baker 2011) – proportionally more than any other Gulf country known during this period. This underpins a logic that naturalization can and often does serve as a political instrument to alter a country's demography.

Former Settler States

Inverse logic underpins the numbers reported by countries traditionally viewed as settler states, which feature the world's highest Naturalization Rates. Countries like Australia, Canada, New Zealand, and the United States historically facilitated citizenship in order to populate vast territories usurped from native populations. The legacy of this leniency endures in Naturalization Rates of 5 percent or higher today. As we describe in detail above, Canada (17.4 percent) and the United States (5.5 percent) naturalize many people born to foreigners by virtue of their full *jus soli* legal regimes, while Australia (5.4 percent) and New Zealand (5.0 percent) have shifted to partial *jus soli* legal regimes since 2006. Consequently, each of their citizen populations have continued to diversify their citizenry, particularly since decolonization and the civil rights era of the mid-twentieth century.

However, as Table 6.3 shows, traditional settler states' elevated Naturalization Rates are now matched by a number of other countries like Brazil, France, and the United Kingdom. Brazil (5.0 percent) is effectively a settler state in terms of its naturalization, where the economy is only more recently developing. However, France (4.8 percent) and the United Kingdom (5.0 percent) have diversified rapidly since decolonization and now recognize the citizenship claims of members of their overseas territories. Whether to compensate for a lingering sense of obligation or to assert ongoing control of post-colonial spaces, naturalization has proven to be an effective means of stabilizing population growth fluctuations by bolstering lagging birth rates in the face of aging. As in settler states like Australia and New Zealand, France and Britain have opted for partial *jus soli* frameworks. And after the fall of various empires, leftist parties and institutions have kept these policies in place, leading to more liberal naturalization outcomes.

Former Colonizers and Non-Colonizers

In his examination of Naturalization Rates in eighteen countries, Janoski (2010) concludes that colonial history is the key determinant of a country's naturalization outcomes. He classifies countries as former colonizers (Austria, France, Netherlands, Spain, United Kingdom), non-colonizers or occupiers (Belgium, Germany, Ireland, Italy, Japan, Switzerland), settler states (Australia, Canada, New Zealand, United States), and perhaps more arbitrarily, the Nordic countries (Denmark, Finland, Norway,

Sweden) as neither colonizers nor occupied nations.[13] His explanation adopts a high degree of path dependency; even though he notes recent shifts in naturalization policy, he argues that outcomes have largely not strayed from a country's category based on its colonial history, or its absence.

This historical approach suggests a reduced role for short-term immigration policy and implementation practices in explaining naturalization outcomes. For example, Irene Bloemraad (2006) examined the divergence in American (4.6 in 2011) and Canadian (10.7 in 2011) Naturalization Rates since the 1970s, despite their similarly liberal naturalization policies. She attributes Canada's rate to the Canadian bureaucracy's normative, extralegal preference for citizenship coupled with public assistance for settlement and integration and an overall policy of multiculturalism. Similarly, Koopmans et al. (2005) acknowledge the effect that informal institutional attitudes can have on outcomes in Germany (2.0 in 2011) and the Netherlands (3.8 in 2011), both of which have arduous citizenship requirements. But while the German naturalization process is drawn out, the Dutch have actively promoted citizenship acquisition. In light of these examples, but also the earlier description of Arab Gulf states' approaches, cultural attitudes are commonly thought to outweigh policies in shaping naturalization outcomes.

IMPLICATIONS FOR GENDER AND ETHNICITY

Because naturalization takes place after admissions decisions by the state, the implications of Naturalization Rates for considerations of gender and ethnicity are of a compound nature. That is, they are typically based on factors beyond the regulation of naturalization alone. Most importantly, trends in the Visa Mix and Temporary Ratio hold transitive effects on the racial, ethnic, origin, and gender composition of those who naturalize. If certain groups are denied admission, or denied access to permanent residence, they will also be restricted from naturalizing.

For those who might be qualified for naturalization, they are now often subject to a range of racialized and gendered barriers that states have developed in order to purportedly ensure citizens are properly integrated into the destination society. Citizenship tests, good conduct provisions, and even public referenda (Hainmueller and Hangartner 2013)

[13] We acknowledge that both Japan and Belgium held overseas territories. For Janoski, these were categorically shorter and less expansive than those held by those states he classifies as former colonizers.

have all been used to screen naturalization applicants, and often lead to ethnicity- or origin-based selection (Janoski 2010). Laws that do not acknowledge dual nationality from certain origins naturally suppress applications from those origins. Further, high citizenship application fees and laws that have economic restrictions and bond guarantees may lead to fewer female applicants. Citizenship tests tend to function as de facto language exams, and many are selectively applied based on origin (see Goodman 2010).

In some cases, ethnicity-based selection is more explicit. Israel restricts admission and naturalization according to religious qualification. Meanwhile, countries like China, Germany, Japan, Korea, and Russia have sought to re-integrate people with ethnic affinities. However, it should be acknowledged that in the European Union, where free movement dominates immigration admissions, immigrants who are non-European are more incentivized to pursue naturalization because they are otherwise denied access to the benefits of European membership. Aside from this countervailing selection effect, naturalization outcomes tend to disproportionately reinforce the dominance of destination states' ethno-religious majorities.

CONCLUSION

In sum, this chapter concludes our separate examination of three principal concepts in the measurement of immigration regimes – Visa Mix (Chapter 4), Temporary Ratio (Chapter 5), and now, Naturalization Rates. While the Naturalization Rate is a conventional metric, it is unconventional to include it as a component of holistic immigration regimes. From this chapter, we see that there is no universally accepted measurement of Naturalization Rates and that this outcome is subject to methodological choices, but also to the policies and institutions of different state contexts. Ultimately, the data and research we present here confirms the broader suggestion of this book, that citizenship represents a final barrier to complete migration imposed by states that are initially reluctant to share the rights, protections, and entitlements of membership. This chapter suggests that there may be further relationships between approaches to immigrant selection and approaches to citizenship acquisition. The next chapter considers these relationships as they are expressed in holistic immigration regimes.

7

The Crossroads Taxonomy of Thirty Immigration Regimes

In the previous chapters, we identified three key dimensions that depict different aspects of a state's immigration regime – the Visa Mix, the Temporary Ratio, and the Naturalization Rate. In this chapter, we exploit the resulting dataset to produce a new taxonomy of immigration regime classification – the first of its kind in multiple ways. As we explained in detail in Chapter 2, earlier attempts at such taxonomies characterize whole national regimes using partial considerations of some aspects without a clear identification of the constituent parts of an immigration regime. Others – very much aware of these limitations – draw conclusions about specific dimensions, such as labor immigration, citizenship, or integration outcomes, but do not contextualize these within a larger understanding or framework of overall immigration regime types. Further, many studies characterize different national policies without regard to how closely these policies are enforced in practice. And even more problematic, nearly all comparative studies choose not to consider emerging regimes of immigration governance in the developing world – where nearly half of the world's migrants now reside.

A key goal of this book has been to address these oversights in the existing field. In this chapter, we synthesize the findings of the three key categories of demographic indicators into a single taxonomy of immigration regimes in thirty of the world's immigration destinations.[1] We begin by setting out the clustering exercise and our methodological choices. The typology we then present demonstrates the convergence of OECD

---

[1] Although across the book we consider fifty countries, given missing data, we only assess thirty countries and twenty OECD countries in the final dataset.

states – particularly Western European states – into an increasingly unified approach to immigration demographics, and their convergence with a set of developing countries that seek even more contingent and concentrated pools of labor. We consider OECD countries in comparison with developing countries and as a grouping in their own right. These results yield an intuitive, demographic data-based taxonomy of immigration regimes that contextualizes traditional destination countries in a more global perspective.

MEASUREMENT

What constitutes an immigration regime? In this book, we developed and focused on seven flow-based component measures of migration policy outcomes, separated into three principal dimensions.

(i) Visa Mix

    Total Flow: Total Migrant Flow: the total number of people who enter a given country in a given year (Chapter 4 and Chapter 5 where this measure is used as a denominator of interest)

    Economic Flow: the total number of people who enter a given country on an economic or labor visa (including accompanying family visas) in a given year, as a share of the total flow (Chapter 4)

    Family Flow: the total number of people who enter a given country on a family reunification visa in a given year, as a share of the total flow (Chapter 4)

    Humanitarian Flow: the total number of people who enter a given country on a humanitarian visa in a given year, as a share of the total flow (Chapter 4)

    Free Movement and Other Flow: the total number of people who enter a given country based on a free movement treaty or other type of visa in a given year, as a share of the total flow (Chapter 4).

The first dimension considers the distribution of economic, family, humanitarian categories, and free movement that combines free movement agreements, international agreements and the residual "other" category. The Visa Mix distribution varies considerably across states and can be seen as an important indicator of immigration policies. This "Visa Mix," as we call it, has replaced historical ethnicity-based mix as a central issue in immigration selection. The Visa Mix is particularly important when validating claims of a global shift toward more economically selective immigration policies

(Shachar 2006; Doomernik et al. 2009). In addition, in some regions, such as the European Union, or between New Zealand and Australia, free movement may limit the capacity for states to radically alter the compositional mix of immigration given that most of the immigration will be "self-selected."[2]

(ii) Temporary Ratio
       Temporary Ratio: the total number of people who enter a given country on a temporary economic visa in a given year as a percentage of total flows (Chapter 5)

The second dimension, the Temporary Ratio, covers the proportion of immigrants who enter a country with a limited duration of permitted residency, compared with those with permanent residency rights. In all immigration regimes, the distinction between temporary and permanent immigration is central, although given data restrictions, we only consider this distinction for labor immigration.[3]

(iii) Naturalization Rate
        Naturalization Rate: the total number of people who become naturalized citizens in a given country in a given year, as a share of the total migrant stock (Chapter 6)

The third dimension considers Naturalization Rates. States with the highest migrant stock as a proportion of their population are conventionally states that offer few paths to permanent residency or inclusion as citizens. For this reason, it is necessary to supplement our consideration of stock with analysis of citizenship acquisition. This indicator considers what percentage of a state's migrants ultimately naturalizes. Naturalization Rates are subject to the policies governing citizenship and the hurdles that applicants must overcome, but also the desire of immigrants to pursue their futures in their new community; as such they are at least in part a clear policy outcome variable. We measure Naturalization Rates as the percentage of the stock of the foreign-born population that has acquired the citizenship of the given destination country in the year of interest – the simplest, most widely available and most conceptually accurate measure of state inclusivity as it pertains to the adoption of nationality. In countries

---

[2] As noted earlier, we relied on data from the OECD, the Organization of American States (OAS), the Gulf Labor Markets and Migration (GLMM) dataset, and data we have collected ourselves from national statistics offices.

[3] We relied on data from the OECD, the Organization of American States, the GLMM dataset, and national statistics offices where we have collected data.

that acknowledge citizenship as a birthright, we include *jus soli* births as a form of naturalization.[4]

Together, these seven outcome categories, across three dimensions, enable an accurate and reasonably comprehensive, annualized characterization of immigration policy outcomes.

K-means Clustering Algorithm

Based on the seven migration demographic outcomes in the thirty selected states, we constructed our taxonomy of immigration regimes using an unsupervised k-means clustering algorithm. K-means clustering algorithms are increasingly used within the social sciences (Hastie et al. 2009: 14.3; Honaker 2011) after growing to prominence in computer science and economics to create taxonomies of people, their behavior, and their choices. We utilize this method to identify states' choices as they relate to the outcomes across our key variables.

Clustering algorithms group a collection of objects into subsets according to a common set of quantitative measurements, such that those within each cluster are more closely related to one another than objects assigned to different clusters (Hastie et al. 2009: 501). Ultimately, this method assigns observations to subsets in such a way that, within each cluster, the average dissimilarity of the observations from the cluster mean is minimized (Hastie et al. 2009: 509).[5] The clustering method attempts to group objects based on the definition of similarity supplied to it, but we do not supervise anything other than the standardization of the variables' respective weights.[6] This way, the data we present determines the nature of the clustering.

A common issue when implementing the k-means algorithm arises from the need to specify the number of clusters that the researcher ultimately adopts. One way to choose the quantity of clusters is to plot the

[4] Our data is based on those collected by the OECD, Janoski (2010), and reports from a number of national statistics offices. In our consideration of developing countries and non-democracies, some immigrants never qualify for naturalization or are simply ineligible. Such factors and the idiosyncrasies of regimes are therefore considered qualitatively alongside available quantitative data.
[5] Using the k-means package in R, we set our initial configuration values to twenty-five and ran 100 iterations to ensure that the algorithm stabilized.
[6] The variables in the analysis have drastically different scales and variation (e.g. GDP per capita versus migrant stock as a share of population). Consequently, to prevent any one variable dominating the k-means analysis, all of the variables are standardized to have a mean zero and unit variance.

within-group sum of squares (the absolute value of the sum or how far each point in a cluster is from each cluster center) against the number of clusters. If there is any discontinuity in the plot – that is, a definitive point where an additional number of clusters stops substantially reducing the sum of squares in each existing cluster – this is used as a guide. However, we did not identify any such point. Consequently, we balance our desire for parsimony with our interest in accounting for nuanced differences across states, in specifying the number of clusters. We opt for seven. In the interest of transparency, we have placed the results for two- through nine-cluster solutions in the Methodological Appendix.[7]

Replication and Expansion

While the methodological nature of clustering algorithms leaves the taxonomy we present open to a degree of subjectivity (in the selection of cluster quantities), clustering solutions are replicable and other scholars can produce alternative taxonomies using the same methods. This versatility and replicability is a virtue because we expect data availability to change over time as countries become better at collecting demographic data and more comfortable with its public release.

With such a template in place, researchers may eventually extend this exercise into the future and back into the past as the required demographic data become available.[8] As such data are more thoroughly and regularly collected across the world, it will be possible to undertake new analyses that account for the transformational changes driven by the 2015 influx of asylum seekers in Europe, the United Kingdom's 2016 vote to depart from the European Union, US President Donald Trump's immigration orders in 2017, and the continual opening of economies in the developing world.

---

[7] We rank-order the demographic outcome data for the purpose of this analysis. Rank-ordering reduces the likelihood that exceptionally high or low values in single dimensions will produce single-country clusters, which are not useful for the purposes of country classification and often exaggerate the true differences between states. From a review of all such outliers, only Canada appears extraordinary enough to merit special attention for the reasons we elaborate later in this chapter.

[8] Notably, we attempted to assemble comparable historical data to perform an analysis of migration policy outcomes over time. However, there was no year or time interval for which comparable data was available for a majority of our selected case countries. Indeed, even a mere eleven years back in time, full data were not even available for all the OECD states we include.

Until that time, we are confident that researchers and public policy-makers may rely on our outcome-based classification of immigration regimes to benchmark immigration policy outcomes, to select cases for analysis and to conceptualize and teach about multidimensional immigration regimes. This will permit the kind of broad comparative research that characterizes studies of labor markets, welfare provisions, health care policy, or carbon emissions and climate change. And researchers may treat this classification system and the data on which it based as a more comprehensive, consolidated baseline point of reference for future analysis.

GLOBAL REGIME TAXONOMY

Based on our assembly of 2011 data and using the k-means clustering algorithm, we generated the following seven-cluster typology:

1 **Neoliberal Regimes**
  Australia
  Canada
  New Zealand
  United Kingdom
2 **Humanitarian Regimes**
  Finland
  Sweden
  United States
3 **Intra-Union Regimes**
  Austria
  Denmark
  Germany
  Netherlands
  Norway
  Switzerland
4 **Extra-Union Regimes**
  Belgium
  France
  Ireland
  Italy
  Portugal
  Spain

5 **Constrained Regimes**
  Brazil
  Japan
  Mexico
  South Korea
6 **Kafala Regimes**
  Bahrain
  Kuwait
  Oman
  Saudi Arabia
7 **Quasi-Kafala Regimes**
  China
  Russia
  Singapore

Each type of regime features unique combinations of the variables across the different annualized dimensions we identify. In order to visualize the results of the algorithm, Figures 7.1 to 7.7 plot the countries of each regime type on overlapping spider graphs to exhibit convergence along these dimensional lines across our seven demographic variables. The results demonstrate a relatively tight overlap between the countries in each cluster.

Type 1: Neoliberal Regimes (Australia, Canada, New Zealand, United Kingdom) are united by high labor-focused selectivity and high Naturalization Rates, which reflect a global free market. Desirable destinations with strong economies and stable societies, these regimes feature relatively high and diverse migrant stock numbers – legacies of their widely acknowledged histories of settling large quantities of people on occupied land (with the exception of the United Kingdom) and more recently, their adherence to non-ethnicized immigration policies. Given their desirability to prospective migrants, neoliberal states have highly discretionary admissions systems that grant large numbers of temporary work visas. Among the permanent visas they distribute, a relatively large share is labor migrants.

This profile exhibits an openness to immigration, and indeed to extending the benefits of citizenship, but only to the extent that doing so advances the competitiveness of the national economy. The diversity and labor-focused admissions of neoliberal regimes is often attributed to points-based methods of selection. A variety of scholars have asserted

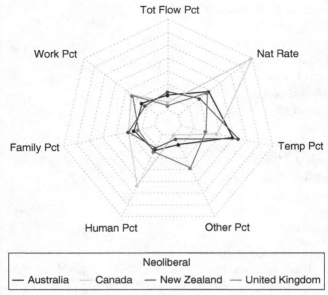

FIGURE 7.1. Neoliberal Regimes spider plot. Ten-point spider plots demonstrate the tight overlap of countries within each of the Global Typology clusters hereafter. The scales on each outward line are standardized across the plots based on the minimum and maximum values observed.

that points-based systems, such as those in Canada and Australia, lead to a diversification of selected immigrants (Hawkins 1988; Joppke 2005b), although increasingly, employer-based modes of selection are preferred (Boucher 2016: chapters 6 and 7). Only Kafala and quasi-Kafala regimes more actively select and exclude immigrants in the interest of maximizing their economic contribution and minimizing the risk of their financial dependence on state resources. The recent focus of Neoliberal Regimes on temporary labor migration creates a migration context adaptive to the short-term needs of employers, but also represents a major departure from their former status as settler states premised on permanent settlement. Writing about Canada, Australia, New Zealand, and the United States, Dauvergne (2016: 118) notes that as the "settler society ethos is stripped away, economics is often left as the only evident explanatory factor remaining."

It is worth acknowledging that Canada appears somewhat of an outlier in this regime grouping. Canada has by far the world's highest Naturalization Rate (Bloemraad 2006), a number that is distinguished even among other former settler states that have historically promoted citizenship acquisition. Different from other Neoliberal Regimes, Canada also features an elevated share of humanitarian migrants. No other regime truly comes close to mimicking Canada's balance – its focus on selecting labor migrants, the compassion it has shown for admitting humanitarian migrants, and its propensity to naturalize large shares of its migrant stock.

The United States is noticeably absent from this regime type, despite its reputation as an original settler state (e.g. Freeman 1995; Dauvergne 2016) coupled with intense capitalism. However, rather than labor, the United States has a permanent migration focus on family admissions and elevated levels of humanitarian admissions, linking it more closely to Nordic countries such as Sweden and Finland. Some analysts expect the United States to adopt labor-favored policies and converge with the Neoliberal Regimes if Washington is ever able to pass the immigration reform bills that have been held up by its polarized Congress (e.g. American Immigration Council 2013b). Although its inclusion at first glance appears counter-intuitive as it was a colonizer rather than a colony, the United Kingdom placement in the Neoliberal Regime cluster relates to its increasing reliance on labor flows and relatively high Naturalization Rates. As the UK moves further away from a reliance on EU-based migration following the Brexit referendum decision, its placement in this grouping will likely extenuate.

Type 2: Humanitarian Regimes (Finland, Sweden, United States) possess the accessibility of Neoliberal Regimes in terms of the proportion of the population comprised of migrants and their rates of naturalization, but are far less focused on labor migration. Indeed, the share of permanent visas distributed to labor migrants is among the lowest among the countries we consider. Rather, Humanitarian Regimes are distinguished by Visa Mixes featuring two of the world's highest shares of humanitarian immigration and three of the world's highest shares of family immigration. In comparison with other members of the European Union, the share of EU migrants in Finland and Sweden is relatively depressed.

In this regard, Humanitarian Regimes appear to be the least overtly economically focused regimes. More than any other regime, they allow admissions as a matter of entitlement – entitlement to family reunification or entitlement based on humanitarian need – while making naturalization about as accessible as Neoliberal Regimes. In the case of Finland and Sweden, such entitlements are supplemented by easy

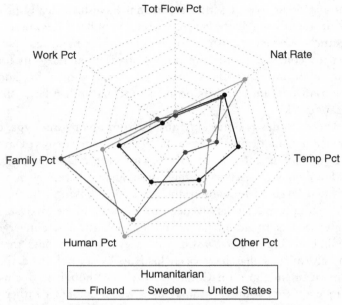

FIGURE 7.2. Humanitarian Regimes spider plot.

access to welfare benefits for immigrants upon their arrival (Barrett and Maître 2011). While variably regarded as generous or naive by their proponents and detractors, they connect with the legacy of earlier settler state governance – although neither Sweden nor Finland were original settler states. However, alternative perspectives on their approach contend that family migrants may yield greater economic productivity and fewer demands on the state than labor migrants because they enter with instantly available networks that swiftly socialize them, connect them with job opportunities, and incorporate them into larger systems of interdependency (American Immigration Council 2013a; OECD 2014b: 2). Alternatively, as noted earlier in this book, economic migrants – particularly those without guaranteed contracts or sponsoring employers – are more likely to arrive without existing support systems and must build such networks on their own.

Type 3: Intra-Union Regimes (Austria, Denmark, Germany, Netherlands, Norway, Switzerland) are immigration systems driven by entitlement to admission, but on the basis of pre-existing membership in supranational unions. All countries in this cluster primarily admit immigrants from other EU member states. (It is worth noting that Norway is not an EU

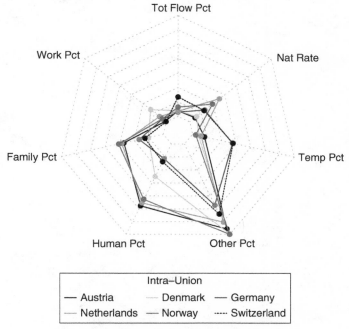

FIGURE 7.3. Intra-Union Regimes spider plot.

member state but is governed by European Economic Area rules.) The predominance of free movement migrants stands in stark contrast to levels of labor visa admissions, suggesting an inverse relationship between the two. Closely managed systems, these countries appear to effectively narrow the market for labor migration to people who are pre-approved for entry.

It is arguable that such an indiscriminate perspective is even more permissive than that of Humanitarian Regimes, which screen applicants for family-based affinities or humanitarian need. The governments of Intra-Union Regimes rather expect European Union migrants to return to their countries of origin if they are unsuccessful in finding work (and many have reduced access to welfare benefits to incentivize this choice). Denmark, for example, replaced unemployment assistance for those who had not resided in the country for seven of the last eight years, with "start assistance," reducing benefits for immigrants and returning Danes (but primarily for immigrants) by 35 to 50 percent (Andersen 2007: 263). Among Intra-Union Regimes, Naturalization Rates are moderate, a

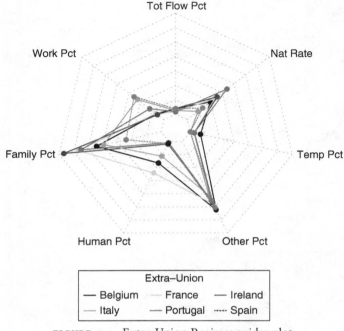

FIGURE 7.4. Extra-Union Regimes spider plot.

product of both selective criteria and the intra-union orientation; many immigrants from EU countries are simply less motivated to naturalize when a new passport changes so little about their lifestyle and privileges (Brochmann 2002: 183).

Type 4: Extra-Union Regimes (Belgium, France, Ireland, Italy, Portugal, Spain) comprise nearly all of Southern and Western Continental Europe – including former imperial centers in Belgium, France, Italy, Portugal, and Spain. Their diverse immigration stock is a residue of colonial histories that led to the incorporation of people from dispersed origins outside of Europe, but possibly also their location mostly on Europe's periphery. They feature moderate levels of immigrant flows proportionate to overall population size – a product of recent economic instability, which both deterred internal European Union immigrants and led many natives to emigrate to Northern European powerhouses in the period immediately after World War II and the recent financial crises (OECD 2014a: 22). Their immigrants' origins are concentrated in countries with colonial affinities, with only a moderate number from the European Union (under

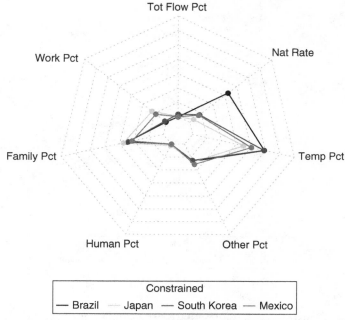

FIGURE 7.5. Constrained Regimes spider plot.

50 percent of permanent flows). By comparison, European Union free movement comprises at least 65 percent of annual flows for Intra-Union Regimes like Austria, Germany, and Switzerland. Extra-Union Regimes make up for this deficiency of EU free movement with some labor, family, and humanitarian immigration flows. They feature among the lowest ratios of temporary migration worldwide (all under 13 percent), and have low or moderate Naturalization Rates (under 4 percent, except in France and Portugal).

Type 5: Constrained Regimes (Brazil, Japan, Mexico, South Korea) are characterized by some of the lowest migrant flows as a share of the country's population among the states we examine. Among the migrants who are admitted by these countries, large proportions are on temporary visas, leaving very small permanent admissions programs. Among permanent migrant flows, there is a moderate percentage of family migrants, some labor migration, and nearly zero humanitarian admissions. Naturalization is nearly non-existent, except in Brazil – which, as a historical settler state, has one of the higher rates in the world.

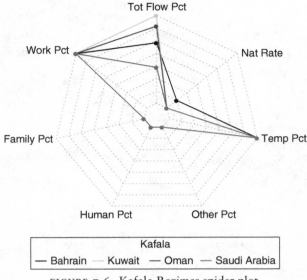

FIGURE 7.6. Kafala Regimes spider plot.

While Constrained Regimes share very similar profiles, these profiles are produced by different sets of constraints. Japan and South Korea have enormous economies and aging populations that stand to benefit greatly from increased immigration flows, but severely restrict admissions to appease xenophobic public attitudes (Sang-Hun 2009; Fackler 2010). Meanwhile, Mexico and Brazil are settler states that date back to the turn of the twentieth century, but feature unstable economies and political circumstances that likely suppress demand to immigrate. Importantly, however, Mexican data do not account for a very high number of undocumented migrants who course through from El Salvador, Guatemala, Honduras, and elsewhere in Latin America. While many seek refuge or opportunity in the United States, others settle in Mexico without authorization (Hamilton and Chinchilla 1991). Depressed flow levels are also to some degree a product of ethnic affinity-based admissions policies in Japan and South Korea (Okólski 2004; Chan et al. 2007; Hatton and Williamson 2008).

Type 6: Kafala Regimes (Bahrain, Kuwait, Oman, Saudi Arabia) represent an extreme among the world's immigration regimes. Their immigration profiles are highly controlled and deliberately transactional. In these states, autocratic governments seek to manage immigration primarily for short-term labor purposes; immigration is a means of maintaining an on-demand, completely contingent labor force. Each country features high

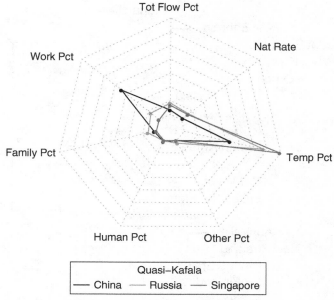

FIGURE 7.7. Quasi-Kafala Regimes spider plot.

concentrations of immigrants from certain origins, a nearly exclusive orientation to labor visas, a nearly exclusive use of temporary visas, and effectively closed citizenship regimes. These outcomes reflect entry policies that treat all foreigners as visitors. Kafala Regimes have prioritized economic gain over adherence to human rights and labor rights (Russell 1989: 32; Baldwin-Edwards 2011: 37).

It is worth noting that Qatar and the United Arab Emirates would almost definitely belong to the same cluster, were they to release annualized flow data. Indeed, more than any other Kafala Regime, Qatar and the United Arab Emirates define this model and rely upon its contingency in light of their enormous migrant stock as a percentage of their overall populations – which both exceed 75 percent, the highest in the world (UNPD 2015). This dependency on large quantities of cheap, foreign labor to fuel their rapid economic development and infrastructure requires a brutal maintenance of the *kafala* system's rules to ensure that government subsidies remain generous and that the naturalized never outnumber native citizens of the same ethno-tribal background.

Type 7: Quasi-Kafala Regimes (China, Russia, Singapore) are similar to Kafala Regimes, but for their far lower population-adjusted flows. In Russia and China, flow levels are only small relative to their large

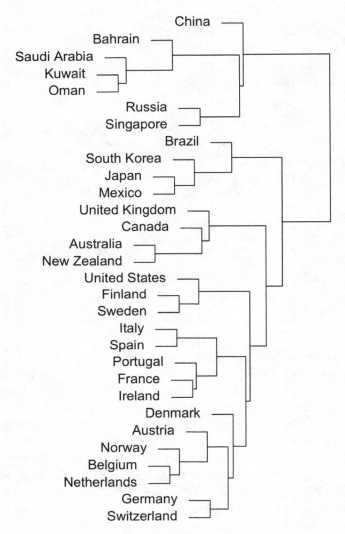

FIGURE 7.8. Global taxonomy dendogram.

populations but large in absolute terms. Reported official statistics also fail to account for sizable quantities of undocumented migrants. Singaporean flows are strictly managed out of concern for overpopulation in the densely settled city-state. These low flow levels aside, Quasi-Kafala Regimes are otherwise similar to their higher flow Kafala Regime counterparts. They feature a high orientation to labor visas, a relatively high reliance upon temporary visas, and effectively closed citizenship regimes. There are of course broader economic and political differences between China and Russia, and the other countries in the Kafala family of regimes. While the others are effectively small city-states with large economies, China and Russia have significant domestic supplies of labor. Whereas China has an interest in suppressing overall population growth, Gulf states have an interest in limiting access to citizenship of non-nationals, but they do not constrain the fertility of their own citizens.

INTERPRETING THE TAXONOMY

The dendogram in Figure 7.8 represents a tree-like, taxonomic visualization of the k-means clustering algorithm's results. It exhibits the arrangement of states' immigration regimes by hierarchical clustering, thereby suggesting the closeness (or separateness) of cluster relationships. In particular, the dendogram exhibits countries' sorting into broader families of regimes that supersede the more nuanced groupings we underscore – akin to taxonomies of biological diversity. Kafala (Bahrain, Kuwait, Oman, and Saudi Arabia) and Quasi-Kafala Regimes (China, Russia, and Singapore) form a greater Kafala family, characterized by their exclusive focus on temporary labor with few outlets to citizenship. Neoliberal (Australia, Canada, New Zealand, and the United Kingdom) and Humanitarian Regimes (Finland, Sweden, and the United States) reflect the legacy and influence of historic settler state models that sustain significant flows under heterogeneous visa types, with high rates of naturalization. Finally, a greater, largely European family emerges from the Intra- (Austria, Denmark, Germany, Netherlands, Norway, and Switzerland) and Extra-Union Regimes (Belgium, France, Ireland, Italy, Portugal, and Spain), which are characterized by free movement at different intensities, limiting the need for permanent labor admissions and reducing demand for citizenship. Through the dendogram, we can also see the way Constrained Regimes (Brazil, Japan, Mexico, and South Korea) affiliate with the stringency of Kafala family.

These families and the more refined regime clusters clarify the way that demographic immigration outcomes reveal the deficiencies of Freeman's historic approach to regime classification. We see that settler states like the United States and Canada diverge within the same branch; that European industrial powers like France, Germany, and the United Kingdom pursue different paths; and the way Freeman's former states of emigration like Italy and Spain are distinct from today's newest destinations, China, Mexico, Saudi Arabia, and South Korea. The near ubiquity of labor-heavy visa mixes and relatively low Naturalization Rates across the other regimes also counter Freeman's teleology toward a settler state model. Indeed, the data suggest the way immigration regimes – particularly those of the newest destinations – perceive immigrants as a means of recruiting increasingly contingent supplies of labor and the creation of a migration market.

OECD REGIME TAXONOMY

The global taxonomy that we set out above is corroborated and informed by our parallel clustering analysis of an OECD-only subset of our selected country cases. This exercise is useful for three reasons. First, doing so allows us to engage with the majority of scholarship on comparative immigration regimes, reviewed in Chapter 2, which focuses exclusively on Western Europe, North America, and Australia. Second, the largest OECD states remain the world's principal concentrated destinations for immigrants. Third, because OECD states are among the most desirable destinations available from the perspective of immigrants, the examination of an OECD-only subset will limit the influence of immigrant demand on flow differences.

Based on our assembly of 2011 data and using the same k-means clustering algorithm, we generated the following five-cluster typology:

1 **Neoliberal Regimes**
  Australia
  Canada
  New Zealand
  United Kingdom
2 **Humanitarian Regimes**
  Finland
  Sweden
  United States

3 **Intra-Union Regimes**
   Austria
   Denmark
   Germany
   Netherlands
   Norway
   Switzerland
4 **Extra-Union Regimes**
   Belgium
   France
   Ireland
   Italy
   Portugal
   Spain
5 **Constrained Regimes**
   Japan
   Mexico
   South Korea

Ultimately, looking only at the OECD states, this analysis identically reproduces the first five groupings observable in the global analysis, reinforcing the earlier results as a durable taxonomy and system of classification. However, in excluding the non-OECD states, this narrower typology does not capture the full diversity of immigration regimes. Indeed, the Kafala and Quasi-Kafala Regimes represent a pioneering – even if ethically questionable – model of governance that may be informing the approaches of less draconian systems in Europe and the former settler states in recent years. Kafala Regimes have heralded and institutionalized the world's increasing emphasis on temporary, labor-focused admissions, with reduced outlets to permanent residency or citizenship, an argument that we pursue in the following section.

THE MARKET MODEL

In his seminal *International Migration Review* article in 1995, Gary Freeman argued that, with the end of the Cold War, the world would observe a general convergence toward expansionary immigration policies, even if countries retained distinctive models. Central to this argument was the idea of a liberal paradox where although the general public might oppose immigration, vested interests in the policy process would successfully push for policy reforms and general immigration openness. These interests would comprise of businesses "that profit from population growth (real estate, construction)" as well as lobbies of ethnic groups that favor increased family migration. The motivation for these groups to advocate for immigration policy over other groups is that such policies "tend to produce concentrated benefits and diffuse costs" for those affected (Freeman 1995: 885).

Similarly, Christian Joppke (2005b) argued that the end of race-based selection in the settler states of Australia, Canada, and the United States heralded a new era of immigration policies with positive contagion elsewhere from the 1960s onwards. Furthermore, he suggested that the principles of public neutrality and equality that underpin modern democracies render overt ethnic selection impossible in contemporary, democratic migration systems (Joppke 2005b: 18–21). He argued that as a nation becomes more diverse as a result of previous immigration flows, the capacity for the state to preclude some from entry would be vitiated by the equality principles that underpin multiculturalism (Joppke 2005b: 21).

For other scholars, the genesis of this "liberal shift" was not lobbying by interest groups at the domestic level, but rather the influence of international human rights norms. Through its diffusion to the nation state level – the argument goes – these norms have "erod[ed] the traditional basis of nation-state membership, namely citizenship" and have forced states to make concessions to immigrants (Jacobson 1996: 9). In particular, the judiciary was seen as playing an important role in securing these rights for migrants at the local level (Jacobson 1996: 2, 10–11). And Yasemin Soysal (1994) argued that international human rights norms have been important for encouraging postnational membership of migrants, although less so at the national level. In particular, she argues that international human rights norms can enable migrants to make claims against the state, which they might not be able to make through domestic politics, creating a form of postnational membership.

When looking at naturalization policies, Howard (2009: 60–1) suggested that the engagement of immigrants, international norms, interest groups, and courts provided latent pressures for liberalization of citizenship policies beyond the sphere of admissions.[9] Joppke (2010: chapter 2)

[9] To be fair, Joppke also argues that public opinion and right-wing parties can be sufficient to block such liberalization (2010: 67), so he does not presuppose the development toward an open liberal model as envisaged by Freeman.

suggested that in the 1980s, there was a liberalization of citizenship laws in Europe as a result of political pressure exercised by immigrants and leftist parties. He acknowledges that, since 2001, there has been a growing restrictiveness of citizenship laws as well as the re-ethnicization of citizenship in some contexts through the retention and reacquisition of citizenship for expatriate communities. Yet despite these trends, he argues that "the restrictive trends occured ... within an overall liberal trend, in some cases even simultaneously liberalizing, framework" (Joppke 2010: 64, 68).

Despite the persuasiveness and moral preference of these arguments, a holistic examination of the data presented in this book suggests a subtle global diffusion of an alternate vision. Instead of a move toward a more liberal, inclusive model, we observe increasingly reduced outlets for permanent residency or citizenship. Indeed, in our analysis, labor-related admissions – whether explicitly through either permanent or more commonly temporary economic labor schemes, or implicitly through free movement agreements – dominate most states' immigration flows. And temporary flows comprise at least 50 percent of all admissions in sixteen of our thirty cases, not only the Kafala and Quasi-Kafala Regimes that feature nearly exclusively temporary flows. Furthermore, Naturalization Rates are quite low worldwide, as shown in Figure 7.9. Outside of the Neoliberal and Humanitarian Regimes, Naturalization Rates are under 4 percent in all of the other countries except Brazil and France. In many of the world's principal destinations, migration is for the purposes of highly contingent, short-term work – a reflection of an increasingly contingent global economy. Contrary to the prediction of Freeman (1995) and others, rather than adopting the key features of settler states (open admissions, multicultural policies, and the long-term settlement of immigrants), states are returning to systems akin to the guest worker approach implemented in Western Europe in the mid-twentieth century – an approach that we refer to as the Market Model.

Our sketch of the Market Model draws from theories of marketization within social and public policy. As a concept, marketization shares many attributes with neoliberalism and is seen by some as an antecedent of neoliberal economic trends, marked by increased market practices and logic in the delivery of services and the use of private actors in providing those facilities (e.g. Anttonen and Meagher 2013: 15; Meagher and Goodwin 2015: 5–6). This process includes broader economic trends such as macroeconomic stabilization, privatization, deregulation, liberalization of foreign trade, and liberalization of international capital flow

– at its core, the idea that the state should disengage from some social and welfare activities (Djelic 2006: 65, 72). It is an ideological position that espouses the belief that markets are of superior efficiency for the allocation of goods and resources.

In the world of migration governance, this Market Model demonstrates states' countervailing acknowledgment of human capital needs and their reluctance to make permanent commitments to newcomers. It reflects new premiums placed on short-term, flexible hiring in an economy of greater expedience and less concern with the rights and stability of people's lives. And it appeals to societies that have experienced nativist and xenophobic backlashes to the way that global migration dilutes demographic homogeneity and diversifies national heritage. In economically unstable times characterized by public concern over various threats to national security, the Market Model permits governments to have it both ways – effectively sanitizing globalization from its purported ills but exploiting the economic benefits of human movement. These points merit an examination of the way the Market Model is expressed in the various dimensions of immigration regimes that we consider in this book.

Visa Mix

The Market Model is discernible in several areas of the Visa Mix. With regard to humanitarian immigration, contingent forms of protection, such as the creation of Temporary Protection Visas, increase the temporality of refugee status (Crock, Saul, and Dastyari 2006: 144; Mansouri, Leach, and Nethery 2009; AHRC 2013). Further, changes in the way that asylum cases are adjudicated, through a method known as "accelerated processing," can reduce adherence to international protection and ultimately may been seen as an effort to minimize the extent of asylum-based claims (Oakley 2007; Kenny and Procter 2014). These procedural changes are linked to the end of the Cold War, which has resulted not only in the decline of ideological justifications for asylum protection but also at the same time, within the proliferation of state creation and civil wars, the rise in and diversification of asylum flows (Hamlin 2012; 2014; Mau et al. 2012: 89).

The EU has seen an increase in internal immigration and a commensurate reduction in that of third country nationals. Dobrowolsky (2007: 640) attributes this change in the Visa Mix to marketization processes insofar as the prioritization of skilled third country national migration meant that unskilled needs could be met through internal migration flows from former Eastern Bloc states, rather than from outside the

European Union. Furthermore, free movement has facilitated high flows of migrant workers accustomed to lower pay and working conditions from recent accession states, contributing to a marketization of the labor market of receiving states (Greer and Doellgast 2013: 9–10). The marketizing effects of free movement therefore lie not only in its focus upon forms of internal migrant labor but also the implications of this labor for the markets of receiving nations.

The focus on economic immigration in the Visa Mix of some countries is a powerful indicator of a Market Model. The non-democratic countries within the Kafala and Quasi-Kafala clusters feature very high rates of economic immigration within their Visa Mix. Nonetheless, some democracies, including the Neoliberal Regimes and Mexico, also have high rates of economic immigration, particularly once accompanying family members are also considered. Nonetheless, other regimes are less marketized than these non-democracies, which supports the argument of some commentators that autocracies possess a competitive advantage in the recruitment of high levels of labor-based immigration (Mirilovic 2010; Breunig et al. 2012).

Temporary Ratio

An essential feature of the Market Model is the rise of temporary immigration as the dominant form of labor immigration across most of the countries considered. The shift toward the temporary importation of labor is in part informed by a desire by governments to enjoy the economic benefits of immigration without open acceptance of the long-term social and demographic transformations that might result. Further, by retaining migrants on a temporary basis, the rhetorical argument follows that those individuals will not be able to make claims on the taxation systems (welfare and health) of host societies. If we review the patterns around the Temporary Ratio considered in Chapter 5, it is clear that temporary economic immigration is now the norm. In many of the destination states considered here, over 50 percent of economic migration is of a temporary nature. In several nations, including most of the Kafala Regimes, 100 percent of economic migration is temporary.

In some respects, the focus upon temporary labor is not new. The guest worker models of the 1960s and 1970s provide a considerable precedent for the current focus upon temporary labor migration that we observe in most of the nations considered. Further, as Catherine Dauvergne (2016: 119) notes, even within the former settler states of Australia,

Canada, and New Zealand (with which she includes the United States), there is a historical legacy of temporary labor migration alongside "'regular' nation-building migration programs." As such, although the "economic focus" within the Neoliberal Regimes is distinctive in recent times, the fulfillment of economic needs has always been foundational for these societies (Dauvergne 2016: 118).

Latin America is often identified as a region with an increasing right to migrate, at least internally, as a result of the Mercosur Agreement. As such, it could be seen to resist the Market Model. However, as Freier and Arcarazo (2015: 44–49) note, several nations within Latin American, including Brazil, Chile, and Ecuador, have not updated their immigration laws in order to match this liberal immigration discourse of permanent residency and free internal movement. Furthermore, Argentina, Uruguay, and Ecuador have retained discriminatory provisions against those who enter illegally or who come from outside Latin America. This sits at odds with a universal right to migrate.

Naturalization Rate

Because naturalization typically culminates a period of residency and qualification for citizenship, there is likely a significant lag between a tightening of admissions regulation and a decline in Naturalization Rates, as the Market Model would suggest. Naturalization Rates are to an extent a product of the type of entry visas distributed by the government, and were a government to significantly reduce the number of permanent visas or temporary visas with outlets to citizenship, the effect of such a change would not be observable for some time.[10] Nevertheless, as we show in Figure 7.9, the overall trend of Naturalization Rates is a subtle downward slope since 2000. Naturalization Rates peaked just after the time that Freeman predicted the expansion of the Liberal Model in the late 1990s, and have generally declined in the world's principal destinations since then.

Despite this statistical trend, Janoski (2010: 261) does not believe that naturalization policies have been tightened as much in the post-September 11

---

[10] It is worth noting that Naturalization Rates are also based on *jus soli* policies that increase access to citizenship, and would therefore be sensitive to the initiation, abolition, expansion, or reduction of such policies. Belgium and Germany limited access to *jus soli* in 2000, and New Zealand did so in 2006.

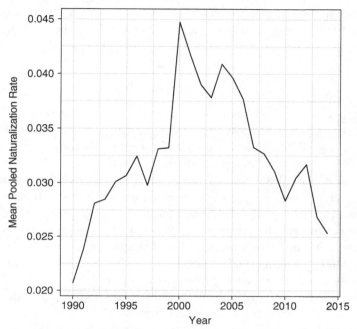

FIGURE 7.9. **Mean Naturalization Rates (1990–2014).** This figure plots the mean Naturalization Rate among countries in the Crossroads database over time, revealing a downward trend since the year 2000. It excludes Russian data, which are not available over the time period.

period. He attributes the subtler marketization we observe to the strong historical factors – colonial legacies in particular – that keep states from reducing the level and conditions of entitlement. However, there is evidence to the contrary. Banting (2014: 82) argues that while some European nations have moved toward a Canadian-style model of multiculturalist citizenship promotion, for others, there has been a number of illiberal shifts through policies such as those which require civic integration courses for naturalization. Works by Sara Wallace Goodman and others have found that the developed states that used to be rather open to naturalization are steadily increasing their demands of immigrants for the sake of assuring their "integration" in advance of naturalization (e.g. Bauböck et al. 2006; Goodman 2010; Janoski 2010). These policies act as deterrents and suppress Naturalization Rates (Van Oers 2013), and often respond precisely to public demands for a market-like transaction whereby immigrants demonstrate their value, contribution, and qualification before being rendered access to membership. The wave of populism and xenophobia since 2016 has only intensified this political trend.

CONCLUSION

Using the concepts, metrics, and data that this book has developed and collected, this chapter presents a taxonomy of immigration regimes derived from standardized, statistical data and informed by substantive knowledge. We create taxonomies of all thirty countries for which we have full data across all dimensions, but also another taxonomy that focuses exclusively on OECD states for comparison. While the methodological nature of clustering algorithms leave this taxonomy open to a degree of subjectivity (in the selection of cluster quantities), this also permits the researcher to balance the calculus of the algorithm (and its inability to consider all factors) with existing knowledge about the countries we study. Reassuringly, clustering solutions are replicable and other scholars will have the ability to produce alternative taxonomies using the same methods. This versatility and replicability is a virtue because we expect data availability to change over time as countries become better at collecting demographic data and more comfortable with its public release.

With such a template in place, researchers may eventually extend this exercise into the future and back into the past as the required demographic data become available. Notably, we attempted to assemble comparable historical data to perform a more comprehensive analysis of migration policy outcomes over time. However, there was no year or time interval for which comparable data was available for a majority of our selected case countries. Indeed, even a mere eleven years back in time, full 2000 data was not even available for all the OECD states we include. As such data is more thoroughly and regularly collected across the world, it will be possible to undertake new analyses that account for transformational changes into the future.

Until that time, we are confident that researchers and public policymakers may rely on temporal analyses from Chapters 4 through 6 and this chapter's outcome-based classification of immigration regimes to benchmark governance, to select cases for analysis, to newly conceptualize and teach about multidimensional immigration regimes. And researchers and policymakers alike may treat this classification system and the data on which it is based as a more comprehensive, consolidated baseline point of reference for their future analysis.

8

What Explains Variation in Immigration Regimes?

Having established the global and OECD immigration regime taxonomies in Chapter 7, we turn to the question: what explains variation in immigration regimes? Indeed, how do the principal explanations for regime differences discussed in Chapter 3 help us to understand why certain countries take similar paths, such that they cluster together in our established taxonomies? Possible explanations include a country's colonial history, demographic aging, economic freedom, and economic dependence on natural resources. To explain the divergence inside of the OECD taxonomy, we also consider the ideological tilt of the executive government over time and the generosity of each country's welfare state. While these variables appear important for some regime clusters in some cases, no universal explanation emerges. Rather, different regime clusters exhibit different relationships. We refer to this as a 'segmented' theory of regime variation.[1]

Our central question here is: What explains the emergence of a Market Model across regime types? Despite enduring differences across the clusters, the data we collect also suggests convergence toward a view of immigration as an economic instrument that serves the national interest, rather than an entitlement of people who are fleeing human rights violations, reunifying with families, or simply migrating out of general desire and interest. On the one hand, many governments have held brutally

---

[1] As a caveat, the reader will recall that the major explanations that could be endogenous to the migration demographic outcomes that we analyzed—largely related to push and pull factors of migration—are not considered here. However, we do account for them separately in the Methodological Appendix.

instrumentalist views about immigrants through time. Even settler states, which admitted migrants for decades with little discretion, did so in order to occupy their frontiers and strengthen their position against indigenous populations and imperial rivals. However, a more overt instrumentalism has emerged that treats immigrants as commodities to recruit, employ, and discard at will. This, we argue, is reflective of a more global marketization and commodification of people across a range of economic sectors, which also allows governments to assuage growing populism, xenophobia, and paranoia about international terrorism.

This chapter proceeds as follows: first, we outline the methods of this explanatory analysis. We then present a series of descriptive statistics related to the variation in regimes and the possible explanatory variables set out in Chapter 3. We contextualize our findings with available qualitative research, and then conclude the chapter by presenting the origins and implications of the Market Model for the dimensions that we consider in this book.

MEASUREMENT

In order to understand the taxonomy developed in Chapter 7, we test the extent to which it is explained by different social, economic, and political factors that have been hypothesized to drive regime variation. We identify and defend the operationalization of each of these variables, first presented in Chapter 3, before presenting bivariate cluster plots that report the relationship between regime clustering and these factors.

Colonial status: In measuring this variable, we drew upon data on colonial status from the Correlates of War Project (2015) that captures colonial status from 1816 through to the present day. We used this dataset to create a scale that differentiates (i) major colonizers, (ii) minor colonizers, (iii) countries that were neither colonizers nor colonized, (iv) short-term colonies, and (v) long-term colonies. Major colonizers are those which occupied median land-masses of over three million square miles (about the size of Australia or Brazil) at the peak of colonization, while minor colonizers occupied less land than three million square miles. Among colonies, we identified the median amount of years (209) that countries were colonized and used that as a point to split the data. Every country that was colonized for more than the median time period was coded as a long-term colony, and less than the median, a short-term colony.

Further details on coding are included in the Appendix. This five-point scale allows for more nuance than existing approaches that only differentiate in a binary fashion between a colonial relationship of seventy-five years or more and nothing (e.g. DeWaard et al. 2012: 1330). Coding colonial status along a scale is also important given evidence that the proximate extent and length of colonial rule matters for immigration and citizenship patterns (Janoski 2010).

Population aging: Demographic aging could affect both the rate and nature of immigration admissions (Alho 2008). In order to analyze this potential relationship, we acquired information on population stock according to the age cohort of people over sixty-five years old from the World Bank (2013a).

Economic freedom: The extent of economic freedom in host societies is a possible factor that could explain variation across immigration regimes. This is because free market approaches to the regulation of trade and commerce also hold implications for the availability and flexibility of labor supplies and human capital. In order to account for this, we take the Overall Freedom Index from Gwartney, Lawson, and Hall's (2015) Economic Freedom Index. This is the most commonly used measure in the scholarship on immigration and economic freedom (e.g. Ashby 2007; 2010). The higher the economic freedom score, the greater the economic freedom. The possible range of values for this Index varies between 3.2 and 8.7.

Natural resource dependency: Reliance upon resource wealth is a possible explanation for migration governance in the Gulf region, as well as in democracies that rely upon migrant labor for mining, construction, and exploration. Where governments use resource rents to subsidize generous citizen entitlements, it is reasonable to expect discretion in who is able to naturalize. Where governments invest resource rents in large infrastructure projects, it is also reasonable to expect greater demand for migrant labor. To calculate economic dependence on natural resources, we rely upon World Bank (2013b) data on total natural resource rents as a percentage of national GDP. Given variation in this figure across time, we took the ten-year average for the period from 2004 through to 2013.

Welfare state generosity: Like natural resources, welfare provision is a scarce government resource that may lead societies to curtail distribution by restricting the number of immigrants that they admit or naturalize. To measure its extent, we took the Combined Generosity Welfare Index from the Comparative Welfare Entitlements Dataset (Scruggs, Jahn, and Kuitto 2014). This variable measures the average generosity across the major possible welfare payments and also considers actual welfare usage data (Scruggs 2014). This variable has been used in a large number of studies on the welfare state (e.g. Bolzendahl 2010; Vis 2010; Rothstein 2011; Easterlin 2013).

Executive partisan position: As noted in Chapter 3, the partisan position of the executive government is thought to inform immigration regimes. In particular, ideologically far-right orientations are often associated with xenophobia. The Comparative Political Data Set (CPDS III) constructs an index from one to five that measures the partisan composition of the governing cabinet (Armingeon et al. 2013: 3) that has been used in a number of studies (e.g. Fisher 2007; Careja and Emmenegger 2009; Nelson and Giger 2011; Falcó-Gimeno and Jurado 2011; Beetsma et al. 2013). Under this approach, one equates to the dominance of a right-wing party and five to the dominance of a left-wing party. In order to capture ideological oscillation over time, we took the average position from 2003 through to 2012 – the decade preceding our observations (nearly all of which are from 2011, the latest of which is from 2013). This also assists in capturing the path-dependent effects of previous governing parties upon present migration outcomes.

In ideal circumstances, the availability of such datasets would permit regression analysis to determine the extent to which they drive the taxonomic variation. However, because countries are our units of analysis, we are ultimately working with thirty observations. This small number of outcomes makes reliable regression results impossible.[2] Instead, we measure bivariate correlations by plotting country-level measures of each explanatory factor and examining the extent to which they vary by cluster.

CORRELATION RESULTS

Colonial Legacies

In Figure 8.1, we plot mean colonial history observations cluster-by-cluster. As a measure of how tightly the country observations cluster, we

---

[2] With so few cases, we experience the convergence of maximum likelihood estimators if we estimate country placement in clusters using a multinomial logit model. And high-standard errors result (and possible omitted variable bias) if we dichotomize taxonomic outcomes and employ a linear probability model (OLS) (Angrist and Pischke 2009; Wooldridge 2013). We address this issue and its limitations further in the Methodological Appendix.

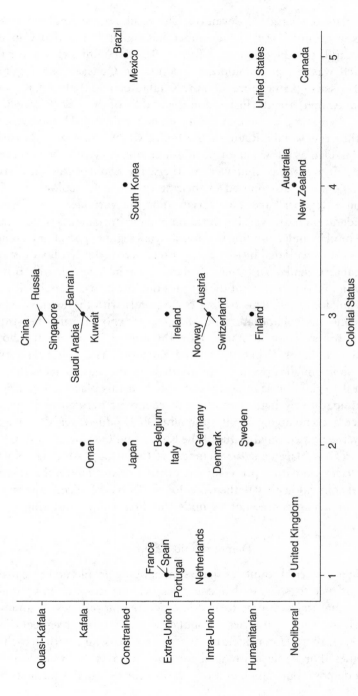

FIGURE 8.1. Colonial legacies and regime clustering results.

also calculate the standard deviation. The results are mixed and reveal several key groups. First, the Neoliberal Regimes (Australia, Canada, New Zealand, and the UK) are all former British colonies except for the UK, which was a major colonizer. Second, the Quasi-Kafala Regimes (China, Russia, and Singapore) and the Kafala Regimes (Bahrain, Kuwait, and Saudi Arabia) are all clustered in the middle of the plot (Figure 8.1), reflecting their status as neither colonizers nor colonies. The sole exception within the Kafala Regimes is Oman, which colonized Zanzibar twice. Classified as either major or minor colonizers (with the exception of Ireland and Norway that were neither), the countries in the Extra-Union Regime are also united in their status as major colonizers. The Intra-Union Regimes have some variation on this variable.

Consideration of the varying duration and territorial mass of colonization is helpful in understanding variation across regime types. For instance, a lengthy British colonial history is consistent across the Neoliberal states of Australia, Canada, and New Zealand. Past inclusion in the British Empire is a unifying feature of these states that are also clustered with the United Kingdom itself. This finding corresponds with the work of Marc Hooghe and his collaborators (2008: 492–3) who identify the strong effects of British colonial status upon the size of immigration inflows in affected countries. While the United Kingdom, as a colonizer rather than a colony, might appear as an anomaly in its placement within the Neoliberal Regimes, it is important to note that this placement is driven by its comparatively high percentage of economic permanent immigration, once accompanying family immigration is added (see Chapter 4). Similarly, the non-colonial status of the Kafala and Quasi-Kafala Regimes explains regime placement for members of that group. Although Kafala Regime states were once protectorates of the British Empire, the absence of official colonial history (either as colonizer or as colonized) appears to matter as much as its presence for understanding regime clustering.

Demographic Aging

While some clustered countries share similar aging profiles, there is insufficient evidence to suggest that countries become more open to immigration or naturalization as their domestic population ages. Examining relationships with countries' population over sixty-five-years old (Figure 8.2), there is considerable variation across and within each of the regimes. For some clusters, there does seem to be a relationship between demographic aging and population clustering. For instance, the

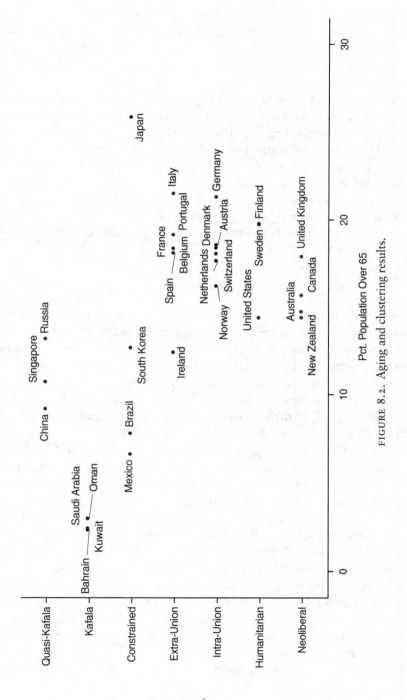

FIGURE 8.2. Aging and clustering results.

Neoliberal Regimes all have similar levels of population aging, ranking them relatively young among the OECD states. This is a product both of higher fertility rates than other OECD countries, and higher relative levels of immigration (see UNPD 2012; SBS 2016). The Kafala Regimes include all Gulf states with young populations, leading to a small relative population under sixty-five but also with high rates of immigration. In contrast, great variation can be found among the Constrained Regimes, with the relatively young population of Mexico coupled with one of the world's fastest aging populations (Japan) that is also increasingly reliant on migrant labor for the provision of care workers (Green 2017). For the remaining regimes, the clustering is spread across the aging spectrum, again suggesting that this variable is not central in understanding the placement of countries within each regime. This indicates that demographic aging is not a key explanation for regime clustering for most of the countries in our dataset.

Economic Freedom

Emerging scholarship argues that openness to the movement of goods and services may be correlated with openness toward the movement of people as well (Ashby 2010; Yakovlev and Steinkopf 2014). It is therefore important to consider whether there is a relationship between the capacity for individuals to benefit from the fruits of their labor and immigration outcomes. If we consider Figure 8.3, countries are varied with regard to their economic freedom scores and regime placement. They range from 6.3 (Brazil) to 8.5 (Singapore). The Neoliberal Regimes all have quite high scores (more economic freedom), while the Constrained Regimes have a mix of lower scores (less economic freedom). Humanitarian, Extra-Union, Intra-Union, and Kafala Regimes are more closely positioned in the middle of the spectrum. The largest variation exists among the Quasi-Kafala Regimes, which include three autocracies (China, Russia, and Singapore) with varying levels of state restrictions over economic freedom. The differences between these countries on economic freedom scores would appear to relate to their differences in political freedom. In particular, Singapore is viewed as having more political pluralism than these other Quasi-Kafala jurisdictions (Roylance 2015). The central argument made by proponents of an economic freedom approach is that greater economic freedom will permit the recruitment of greater numbers of immigrants (Ashby 2010). However, considering the countries with the highest immigrant stock

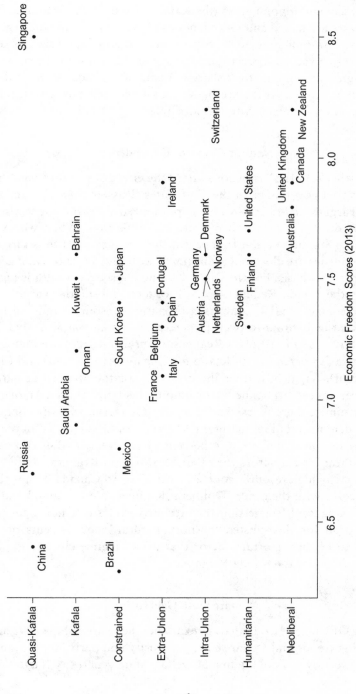

FIGURE 8.3. Economic freedom and regime clustering results.

as a percentage of population (the Kafala Regimes), the economic freedom scores are mixed and indeed, not as high as the Neoliberal Regimes that have lower migrant stock proportionate to population size. As such, while these bivariate correlations do suggest that some of the countries with higher immigrant stock shares (Australia, Canada, New Zealand, and Switzerland) also feature higher economic freedom scores, this is not true of all countries with this attribute.

Natural Resource Dependency

Given other scholars' assertions about the effect of resource wealth on immigration governance in the Gulf states (Russell 1989: 3; Chalcraft 2010; Fargues 2011: 275–6), we hypothesized that this might also be true for other resource-rich migration destinations. When we examine Figure 8.4, however, it is apparent that resource wealth is rare and most countries are clustered accordingly with low levels of GDP generated upon this basis. For the countries where resource wealth is higher, such as the Kafala Regimes, we still observe substantial variation in the percentage of GDP comprised by natural resources ranging from 14 percent in Bahrain to over 40 percent in Oman, Saudi Arabia, and Kuwait. In the Quasi-Kafala Regimes, natural resources are important for Russia (27 percent), but less so for Singapore (0 percent) and China (6 percent). As such, neither the presence nor the absence of natural resources appears to be the factor uniting this latter cluster. Among the other regimes, there is less variation on this factor, as most countries do not demonstrate high natural resource scores. Norway is an outlier. Natural resources make up 16 percent of Norwegian GDP, compared with a mean of 2.4 across the other Extra-Union Regimes. While possessing fairly high resource sources, Australia and Canada do not share these scores with the other Neoliberal Regimes (New Zealand and the United Kingdom), suggesting that resource welfare is not a unifying explanation for this cluster. In short, natural resource rents do not appear to be an important factor that drives regime clustering, other than perhaps for the Kafala Regimes.

Welfare State Generosity

Among OECD states, our analysis examines the relationship between the clustering trends and welfare state generosity and partisan positions of sitting executives. Looking first at welfare state generosity (Figure 8.5),

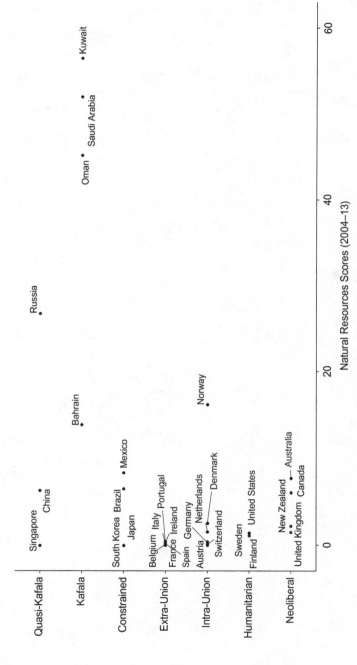

FIGURE 8.4. Natural resources and regime clustering results.

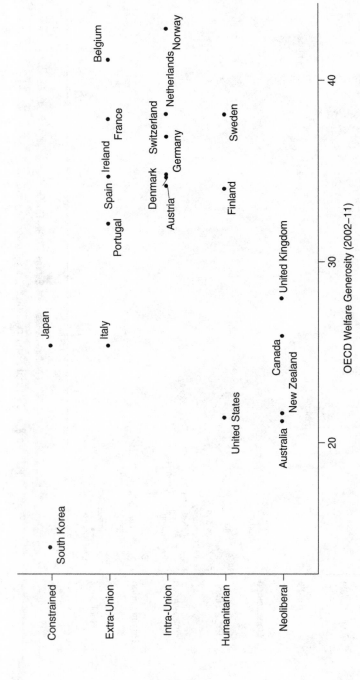

FIGURE 8.5. Welfare state generosity and regime clustering results.

it is clear that the Neoliberal Regimes have fairly similar, low levels of total generosity. This is consistent with common typologies that identify these countries as liberal welfare states (Esping-Andersen 1990). Furthermore, the low level of welfare support from the state for migrants in these countries also interacts with the economic-focus of the immigration programs that aim to bring in self-sufficient, labor-market ready individuals (Boucher 2014; 2016: chapter 4). We might anticipate that countries with greater welfare state largesse would also have more restrictive approaches to naturalization and the inflow of labor immigrants. Welfare state scholars have argued that officials in generous welfare states sometimes manage the magnet effect of generous welfare provision through concomitant immigration and welfare restrictions (Banting 2000; 2005; Bommes 2000; Geddes 2000; Xu 2007). Indeed, in recent times, the Intra-Union Regimes of Denmark, Austria, and Switzerland have introduced welfare restrictions on Syrian asylum seekers. These include the controversial Jewelry Bill in Denmark that allows officials to seize jewelry and other personal items from asylum seekers to cover their immediate maintenance needs (Dearden 2016). Generally, Intra-Union countries report higher welfare generosity scores. Also recall from Chapter 7 that the Extra-Union Regimes have a strong focus on free movement immigration, which might be seen to bring migrants of a largely economic quality who will be less reliant on the welfare states of their host societies.

Welfare state generosity would appear to be important in understanding the Neoliberal Regimes, each of which fall on the less generous end of the spectrum. Similarly, the Intra-Union Regimes feature generosity ratings toward the upper end of the welfare generosity scale. The other clusters demonstrate more variation. For instance, the Extra-Union Regimes include Southern and Northern European nations that feature different welfare models (Esping-Andersen 1990: 26–9). However, for the other regime clusters, no coherent pattern is apparent along the total welfare generosity scores. Among the Humanitarian Regimes, there is large deviation between the frugality of the United States and the social democratic welfare states of Finland and Sweden. Similarly, for the two OECD states that are Constrained Regimes – Japan and South Korea – there is a significant difference. As such, while our OECD taxonomy in some respects mirrors classic welfare state classifications, there is not complete overlap, and the welfare state is a more salient explanation for some regime types than for others. In short, welfare state structure is not a strong predictor of immigration regime type in all instances.

Partisan Political Alignment

A final explanation relates to partisan politics and how this might influence migration outcomes. There is no clear relationship between executive position and regime placement. Even for the Neoliberal Regimes that we might classically associate with more right-leaning governments (Esping-Andersen 1990; Castles and Mitchell 1992: 21), we see variation along the measure of partisan position that we employ, the Schmidt Index (defined below). The Humanitarian Regimes (United States, Finland, and Sweden) group a classically right-dominated party system, with two social democratic nations. For the Extra-Union Regimes, there is variation along the scale. And while the Intra-Union Regimes feature closer clustering towards the right end of the spectrum, there is no overwhelming pattern that emerges.

In considering the partisan position of the governing coalition, we used the Cabinet Composition Schmidt Index, which employs a scale from one through to five, where one indicates hegemony of right-wing parties and five the hegemony of social democratic parties. We took the ten-year average from 2003 through to 2012 for each country to even out any change in governing parties over this time. As is clear from Figure 8.6, the OECD countries presented here demonstrate substantial variation along this index, although the Intra-Union Regimes deviate the least in light of the dominance of center and right-wing parties in Denmark, Switzerland, Austria, and Germany over this period. Interestingly, for the Neoliberal countries that we might historically identify as right-of-center, there is variation across the spectrum, informed in part by the dominance of the right-wing Conservative Party in Canada over much of the period of analysis. While not historically identified as left-leaning nations, Australia, New Zealand, and the UK elected left-wing governments over much of this period as well: the Rudd-Gillard governments in Australia (2007–13), a mixed government and then Helen Clark's Labour in New Zealand (1999–2008) and British Labour in the United Kingdom (1997–2010).

In short, there is no strong correlation between partisanship and regime clustering. In some respects, this is not surprising. While the scholarship suggests that partisanship may influence the rhetoric around government immigration programs, evidence that these discourses in turn shape actual immigration outcomes is more limited. There are two reasons why this might be the case. First, while high-profile dog-whistling by politicians can suggest hardline immigration policies, governments can also be stymied by political factors, implementation gaps, or (in the

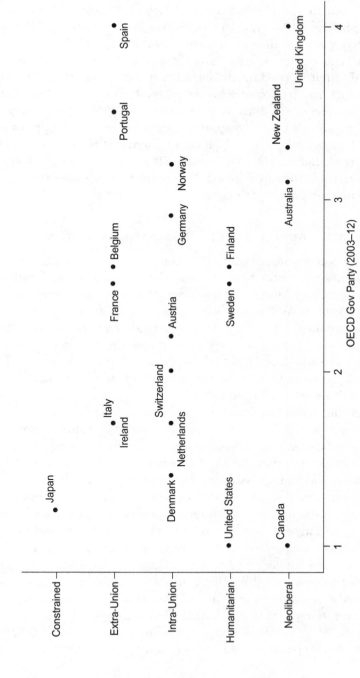

FIGURE 8.6. Executive party position means and regime clustering.

case of EU member states) supranational laws. Immigration scholars have referred to this phenomenon as "control dilemmas" (Guiraudon and Joppke 2001: 12–13, discussed in Wright 2014) whereby governments may publicize their efforts to control immigration in one area, often through border security, in order to distract attention from initiatives that fail to produce the intended outcomes elsewhere. Second, governments may have contradictory perspectives on immigration that result in countervailing outcomes. For instance, right-wing governments can create rhetoric of low immigration to appease xenophobic electorates and at the same time promote high rates of immigration to support business interests. Indeed, the Conservative Howard Coalition in Australia pursued precisely such an approach in its immigration policies from 1996 through to 2007 (Wright 2014).

A SEGMENTED THEORY OF REGIME VARIATION

From this examination of six prominent explanatory hypotheses, it is clear that no single factor drives immigration regimes cross-nationally – a finding consistent with the common rejection of a "grand theory" within migration studies. As Russell King (2012: 31) has argued, instead of a single overarching explanation for understanding migration, we might instead opt for "a range of interlocking theoretical perspectives which, assembled in various combinations, leads us towards a greater level of understanding of the nature and complexity of migration than earlier simplistic theorisations" (King 2012: 31).

A segmented theory of immigration regime development is a more accurate way to understand variation across regime clusters explained by multiple factors. Kafala Regimes are all relatively young, resource-rich, autocratic countries. Regimes that nearly exclusively admit labor migrants on temporary visas, with little to no naturalization, are produced by societies in which membership comes with access to enormous government subsidies fueled by natural resource rents. Accordingly, citizenship is carefully guarded as well. However, the dependence on natural resources also produces a large-scale underemployment among citizens who are unmotivated to work, despite great demand for economic and infrastructural development (Shah, Shah, and Radovanovic 1998; UNDP Kuwait 2011). To accommodate this, Kafala Regimes have the greatest stocks of migrants in the world proportionate to their population. The discretion and aversion to naturalization of Kafala Regimes also appears related to the absence of extended colonial legacies that have, in other countries, imposed a sense of obligation to admitting and naturalizing people from former overseas territories. In contrast, the Kafala Regimes act as free agents, contracting highly contingent labor for short periods from primarily non-Arab populations targeted for their presumed servility and low sense of entitlement among immigrant populations. The Quasi-Kafala Regimes also have authoritarian governments and, like the Kafala Regimes, have made the choice to pursue similar immigration models with low naturalization, high rates of temporary immigration, and an economic focus in the Visa Mix.

Free movement across the European Union constrains the range of immigration policy options that the Intra- and Extra-Union Regime governments can employ. Membership in a free movement agreement typically results in the preference of citizens from other member states in lieu of immigrants from elsewhere in the world. This necessarily shrinks the share of labor and family admissions programs inside of these unions because free movement migrants may be employed to fill most labor gaps and any subsequent family migration is also classified as further free movement. Naturally, this has produced great convergence in the profile of regimes subject to free movement into the Intra- and Extra-Union Regimes. The bifurcation appears at least in part to be a vestige of colonial relationships, which lead countries like Spain, France, and Portugal to exhibit more heterogeneous Visa Mixes and more diverse migrant stock. It may also be a matter of economic freedom and prosperity. Countries like Italy, Portugal, and Spain tend to send free movement migrants, rather than receive them, and subsequently need to recruit externally from their former colonies.[3]

Former settler states inside the Neoliberal Regimes cluster emerge as a byproduct of shared Commonwealth norms that have sharpened their admissions focus over time. Indeed, in many ways, their historic openness and liberalism that once stood in contrast to the relatively draconian Kafala Regimes has inspired immigration regimes that reflect many principal Kafala attributes – a heavy focus on temporary visas and a mix dominated by labor admissions. The primary distinction is the Neoliberal Regimes' highly discretionary approach to labor admissions, focused on the recruitment of high-skilled individuals who are deemed to

---

[3] Outlying European member states like Finland and Sweden made deliberate choices to admit more humanitarian or family migrants, and the United Kingdom has made the deliberate choice to pursue highly selective skilled labor recruitment, much like the former settler states with which it is clustered.

merit naturalization, which is rare in the Kafala Regimes. This neoliberal approach is precisely the kind that United States policymakers have been contemplating for the last two decades, but have been unable to pass as a result of congressional politics. So despite the objectives of the remaining centrists in American government and despite the large quantity of undocumented immigrants, the United States otherwise endures as a relic of its settler state past. The Commonwealth history of all Neoliberal Regimes is unlikely mere coincidence. While policy diffusion is a real phenomenon, particularly among such connected societies, Neoliberal Regimes are also a legacy of the liberalism of the British Empire and its emphasis on power through free trade and wealth.

Finally, the Constrained Regimes have similar demographic immigration outcomes but arrive at that similarity via different paths. In particular, the constrained nature of the Japanese and South Korean regimes is a product of self-imposed restrictions by governments seeking to appease publics that oppose immigration. On the other hand, Mexico and Brazil's constrained outcomes are a product of less demand for entry into their less developed economies, rather than any form of government control.

An Admission–Citizenship Nexus?

By examining demographic outcomes related to both admissions (Visa Mix and Temporary Ratio) and citizenship (Naturalization Rates), we are able to evaluate the relationship between different aspects of the immigration process that are conventionally examined separately (Hammar 1985). Until now, the discrete treatment of immigration and integration policies and outcomes has produced partial renderings of immigration regimes (see critique in Schain 2012). However, as we argue in Chapter 6, naturalization represents a critical factor in state calculations about admission. The prospects for naturalization inform the distribution of visa types, the quotas imposed, and the selection of applicants to fill them. In short, when membership (and all the entitlements that come with it) is likely, states can be expected to select more carefully.

To test this hypothetical relationship, we re-ran the clustering algorithm without accounting for the seventh variable, Naturalization Rates. Doing so allows us to test the extent to which Naturalization Rates distort the results, or rather, the coherence between Naturalization Rates and the admissions-based variables. The more our original clustering results endure, the greater coherence is suggested. Ultimately, this exercise produces precisely the same clustering solution but for one alteration: China shifts to the Neoliberal Regime cluster. This suggests just how close Neoliberal Regimes are to Kafala-like systems, if it were not for their elevated Naturalization Rates. This finding about the coherence between admission and citizenship outcomes allows us to speak of a greater "nexus" between immigration and integration (see Meyers 2004; Freeman 2006: 228), but begs the question of how we can understand the relationships therein? We identify four trends.

First, very high flows place restrictions on access to membership due to the thinner distribution of resources that such high admissions would imply to migrants and citizens across the board. Such an argument is consistent with the finding of Ruhs (2013) that there is a trade-off between high admissions of migrants and the rights conferred upon such individuals, including their rights of membership. Furthermore, and peculiar to the Gulf countries, state reliance on resource rents not only to support public welfare but also to appease citizens means that governments have a stronger incentive to limit immigrants' access to the treasury. The most common way to achieve this is to restrict the number of permanent visas available or to erect barriers to qualification.

Second, high rates of free movement, as seen in the Intra-Union Regimes and to a lesser extent in some Extra-Union Regimes, appear correlated with moderate rates of naturalization. This is because EU citizens enjoy relative parity of access to benefits across the member states (Barrett and Maître 2011) or may not reside in the destination country for a period of time sufficient to warrant naturalization. As such, free movement immigrants may experience less motivation to naturalize.

Third, high humanitarian and family flows correspond with higher Naturalization Rates. Humanitarian and family reunification immigrants have stronger motivations to remain (to evade danger or remain with loved ones) than economic entrants. There are some important exceptions here, such as the Temporary Protected Status provided with great discretion by the United States and Temporary Protection Visas at certain points of time in Australia – both of which ultimately require repatriation by humanitarian migrants once the danger subsides. Short-term family visas such as the Canadian Super Visa for aged parents, offer another counterexample and are becoming increasingly popular with governments precisely due to the reduced state burdens that they represent. However, as noted in Chapter 4, family and humanitarian visas are generally provided on a permanent basis, and countries that emphasize these in their Visa Mix like the United States, Sweden, and France have correspondingly elevated Naturalization Rates.

Fourth, the combination of high economic migration (both temporary and permanent) and high naturalization occurs in those countries where there is also a strong focus on skilled immigration. This is because, in these contexts, immigration selection policies act as a method to rigorously pre-select those immigrants for both entry and membership. In the Neoliberal Regimes, where this pattern is most common, we observe a shift toward temporary economic admission that restricts access to naturalization over the longer term (Boucher 2016; Dauvergne 2016). As such, so long as their temporary migration programs are sustained, the high Naturalization Rates in the Neoliberal Regimes may see reductions in future years.

EXPLAINING THE MARKET MODEL

As we near the conclusion of this book, we identify an emerging logic to the way states build immigration regimes – balancing economic needs, humanitarian obligation, and perceived public aversion. In Chapter 7, this unifying logic is consolidated in what we call the "Market Model" that manages immigrants as consumable human resources. This model emphasizes temporary labor with limited access to permanent residence and citizenship – rendering increasing flexibility to governments and employers, and increasing instability for immigrants and their families. It also reduces naturalization and, where possible, focuses on economic migration either through skilled policies, or more commonly, through free movement agreements. The breadth of this observation makes it difficult to subject to systematic testing. Furthermore, as this book demonstrates, the historical quantitative data that would help trace the emergence of the Market Model is lacking. However, existing research provides a qualitative means of understanding the evolution of the Market Model and the way it relates to today's global environment. Indeed, its emergence is situated in three related contexts.

First, the Market Model may be understood as simply bringing immigrant labor markets into line with other economic sectors, which have been steadily liberalized over the last several decades. A greater shift from Keynesian state regulation to market-regulated sectors is the hallmark of neoliberalism's steady proliferation around the globe (Palley 2004: 20). So that which has been experienced in the worlds of international trade, supply chain management, currency, wage protection, labor standards, and outsourcing can now be seen in the regulation of immigration. Much like companies and consumers, governments want to have more comprehensive discretion on whom they recruit and how long they are contracted. This represents the sharper edge of globalization that initially produced the Liberal Model observed in the immediate aftermath of the Cold War.

Second, and quite ironically, the Market Model helps assuage voting publics that are increasingly wary of globalization's effect on their own economic status. Indeed, the same market pressures that likely contributed to the Market Model in immigration regulation have also made natives' lives more precarious (Gest 2016; Gest and Gray 2016). Governments have found that deepening the instability and contingency of immigrants' residence has (rather artificially) made voting publics feel a greater sense of stability in their own lives. Indeed, tightening immigration admissions and making it more conditional has been a favorite instrument of governments seeking to stave off challenges by populist parties and candidates calling for border closings and protectionism. With such alternating drops in status between working-class natives and their immigrant counterparts, this is a race to the bottom.

Finally, and even more symbolically, the Market Model suggests governments' attempts to exert control over borders in an era defined by paranoia about international terrorism. Since the September 11, 2001 attacks in the United States, there has been heightened awareness of terrorism plotted by followers of radical political movements, particularly those adherent to violent interpretations of Islam (Gest 2010). Such attacks have been rare and many have been perpetrated by native-born citizens, but Muslims' immigrant origins (however far back in time) have propelled an association between immigration and terrorism. Accordingly, governments have justified steps toward the Market Model with frequent references to national security.

More prospectively, the Market Model is likely to have self-reinforcing qualities. As admissions are shifted to temporary visas with no outlet to citizenship, there will be fewer immigrant-origin voters to advocate for immigrant rights and interests such as family reunification, asylum provision, enfranchisement, and migrants' rights more broadly. This will inevitably create a feedback loop into immigrant flows into the future.

IMPLICATIONS OF THE MARKET MODEL

An outstanding question regards the consequences of this new Market Model for the form and composition of immigration regimes globally. Is this new form of migration more stratified? Is it more racialized? It is more gendered? Answering these questions categorically is beyond the remit of this book. However, throughout the preceding chapters, we have sought to demonstrate how gender, race, origin, and class divisions may be a product of some of the migration policies and outcomes that we observe. In this section, we synthesize these arguments.

If we look first at the Visa Mix (Chapter 4), we argued that ethnic divisions have emerged within Visa Mix through the predominance of free movement in continental European countries. Since 2011, permanent economic immigration of third-country nationals within the EU has fallen by 12 percent but internal EU immigration has risen by 12 percent (OECD 2014: 18). The ethnic implications of this shift relate to the source country of third country nationals compared with internal EU flows. Some scholars, such as Adrian Favell (2008: 701), have argued that free movement constitutes "an exploitative dual labour market for Eastern movers working in the West, as well as encouraging a more effective racial or ethnically-based closure to immigrants from South of the Mediterranean and further afield" (see also Paul 2013: 136–7).

Further, we have provided evidence from a range of scholars that a Visa Mix that focuses on economic immigration, particularly skilled immigration, is more likely to preference men (Dauvergne 2000: 298; Kofman and Raghuram 2006: 295–6; Boucher 2007; 2009; 2016). It also contributes to a preference for "masculinized" economic migration over "feminized" family migration (Dobrowolsky 2007: 644). Furthermore, as we argued in Chapter 4, the gendered effects of an economic-focused Visa Mix are most apparent in the Gulf states where they affect the overall gender composition of migrant flows and stocks. Both due to the restrictive family reunification rights conferred on migrants, but also due to the concentration of employment opportunities for immigrants in the construction sector, the majority of migrants in Bahrain are men (Baldwin-Edwards 2011: 11).

With regard to the Temporary Ratio (Chapter 5), it is also clear that the increasing emphasis by governments upon temporary immigration selection carries implications for the gender and ethnicity of selected immigrants. The rights versus numbers trade-off that Martin Ruhs (2010; 2013) identifies implicates temporary immigration insofar that unskilled workers are more likely to be brought in on low-skilled temporary visas with diminished rights. Complicating this picture further, in both democracies and non-democracies, these workers are more likely to be women and ethnic minorities than within highly skilled and permanent economic visa streams (Boucher 2016: chapter 7). As such, there is a gender and ethnic dimension to the rights versus numbers trade-off. Women generally are overrepresented in unskilled temporary flows, particularly domestic worker immigration into the Middle East and Singapore (Rosewarne 2012: 67). This preponderance of women and racial minorities in low-skilled, temporary positions relates to the occupational segregation of the global labor market in more exploitative service sector jobs such as care work (Boucher 2016: chapter 7).

These trends in the Visa Mix and Temporary Ratio compound to hold transitive effects on the racial, ethnic, and gender composition of those who naturalize. If certain groups are denied admission, or denied access to permanent residence, they will also be restricted from naturalizing. Among those who might be qualified for naturalization, many OECD states have developed a variety of barriers that are more stringently applied to or disproportionately affect the capacity for ethnic minorities to access citizenship (Goodman 2010; Janoski 2010). Outside the OECD, naturalization is a rare event aside from Brazil and Israel – both of which originated as settler states – and Russia – which has sought to re-integrate ethnic Russians from former Soviet Republics. Similar policies that favor people with ethnic affinities exist in countries like China, Germany, Japan, and Korea. All Gulf states, China, and Singapore restrict naturalization quite severely, regardless of race, ethnicity, or gender. One countervailing trend emerges from the European Union, where free movement dominates immigration admissions. Here, non-Europeans typically are the immigrants who pursue naturalization because they do not otherwise have access to the benefits of European membership.

CONCLUSION

This chapter concludes an extended exercise in the social science of immigration demography and politics. Indeed, this chapter's content – our attempt to explain the emergence of different immigration regimes and their subtle convergence toward a Market Model – is only possible after the conceptual development that we have undertaken earlier throughout this book. In this light, this book offers four contributions:

(1) We construct a new conceptualization of what constitutes an immigration regime and how one might measure its outcomes in a valid and reliable manner across countries and time. As part of this conceptualization, we develop new dimensions and metrics. These dimensions include the various measures of Origin Diversity, Visa Mix, and the Temporary Ratio. We assemble these new concepts

in measurement alongside conventional metrics like total migrant stock and Naturalization Rates to form a multidimensional understanding of an immigration regime. Unlike earlier attempts, this understanding considers metrics related to both admissions and citizenship. While we view undocumented migration as a further, meaningful dimension of immigration regimes, we lament the lack of accurate and standardized data available cross-nationally.

(2) We build a database according to these dimensions and their constitutive metrics. This database unites available data from the OECD with data from independent reports, national statistics agencies, and news reports, which we standardize to OECD measurements. For the first time, this database permits the broad characterization of immigration regimes across space and time, even though we focus our collection on one period of time. It also permits the standardized consideration of immigration regimes – and each dimension of them – in a full range of OECD countries, but also countries outside the OECD and located in the Global South.

(3) Using this first-of-its-kind database, we produce a taxonomy of immigration regimes derived from standardized, statistical data and informed by substantive knowledge of the policy landscape. We create a taxonomy of all thirty countries for which we have full data across all dimensions, but also another taxonomy that focuses exclusively on OECD states for comparison. While the methodological nature of clustering algorithms leave this taxonomy open to a degree of subjectivity (in the selection of cluster quantities), clustering solutions are replicable and other scholars will have the ability to re-run the analysis using alternative assumptions. This versatility and replicability is a virtue because we expect data availability and country coverage to change over time as countries become better at collecting demographic data and more comfortable with its public release.

(4) Finally, we undertake the first – albeit simple – correlational analysis of this new demographic-data-derived taxonomy. Considering a range of six independent variables hypothesized to relate to immigration regimes and governance, we find that different factors likely explain the pursuit of each type of regime. Neoliberal Regimes like Australia, Canada, and New Zealand are likely informed by their colonial histories that produced a legacy of using immigration and easy naturalization to settle land and build an economy. Kafala Regimes like Bahrain, Kuwait, Oman, and Saudi Arabia are likely informed by desire to withhold government subsidies from oil rents

in rapidly growing economies with high fertility rates on typically small territories. Intra-Union Regimes like Austria, Denmark, and Switzerland are informed by the tension between aging societies and generous welfare states. Extra-Union Regimes are informed by the needs of aging societies and unstable economies with relationships to former colonial possessions offering cheap labor supplies.

Ultimately, we hope that this book's examinations and conclusions will reinvigorate old debates in the politics of migration that may now be substantiated by more complete data, and stimulate new debates that are only possible with access to this information. (Please visit crossroads.earth.) For so long, migration research has been limited to studies of specific regions or specific dimensions of governance. For so long, migration researchers have been unable to conduct the kind of broad comparative research that characterizes studies of labor markets, welfare provisions, health care, or climate change. And for so long, researchers have had difficulty accounting for variation in immigration regime outcomes as an explanatory factor in their analyses of other social, economic, and political phenomena. We hope that the contents of this book render greater direction and new opportunities for studying this world of demographic change.

Methodological Appendix

This appendix outlines our data sources, methodological choices, and any assumptions employed this book, including the non-OECD sources of data and our procedures for data collection, interpretation, and analysis.

DISTRIBUTION OF IMMIGRANT ORIGIN

In measuring the distribution of immigrant origin across states, our data are drawn for all countries from the United Nations Population Division (2013) database POP/DB/MIG/Stock/Rev.2013. As Chapter 3 introduces this concept for the first time, a conventional operationalization does not yet exist. We opt for two different approaches:

Herfindahl-Hirschman Index: A conventional measure of market concentration in economics, a Herfindahl Index is typically calculated by squaring the market share of each company competing in a particular industry, and then summing the value outputs (Hirschman 1964). Here, we consider the percentage of destination state's total migrant stock from different source countries. Whereas a Herfindahl Index of one would represent a perfect monopoly, this would be tantamount to one country being the sole source of a destination state's migrant stock. In the formula below, $\tilde{s}_{ij}$ is the share of immigrants from origin j in destination country i as a percentage of total stock of immigrants in country i. Higher values suggest the greater concentration of migrants from a few countries of origin – that the destination state has a less diversified stock of immigrants. (A similar calculation is employed by Czaika and de Haas 2014.)

$$H_i = \sum_j \tilde{S}_{ij}^2$$

Gravity Weighted Diversity Measure: The Gravity Measure attempts to combine the information in gross stocks of immigrant populations with the distance separating the origin–destination pair, in order to account for the geographic concentration or dispersion of a destination state's migrant stock from original source location. This metric first obtains pairwise distance values by calculating the space between the destination and origin states' capital cities (e.g. London to Dhaka; Singapore to Kuala Lumpur). The calculation sums the share of immigrants across the different origin countries weighting each by the reciprocal of the distance between the origin and destination squared. In the formula below, G_i is the gravity measure, d_{ij} is the distance between destination i and origin j, and s_{ij} is the stock of immigrants from country j in country i. For two countries with similar stocks of immigrants but one across a much smaller set of distances then the other, the former will have a higher value – denoting higher concentration. In this way, higher values suggest that "gravity" must have a much greater force in determining the immigration patterns.

$$G_i = \sum_j \frac{1}{d_{ij}^2} s_{ij}$$

The calculations for Gravity Weighted Diversity Measure were based on UN stock data, broken down into country-specific stock values – all for 2013, which requires no imputation. Distance values were determined from the Geographic Distance Matrix Generator (Ersts 2013), which computes all pairwise distances from a list of geographic coordinates. UN estimates themselves are based on official statistics for the foreign-born or the foreign population, classified by sex and age (UNPD 2013). The statistics utilized to estimate the international migrant stock were mostly obtained from population censuses, but also population registers and nationally representative surveys (UNPD 2013). This means that these data typically do not account for the presence of undocumented migrants – a significant factor in some destination states.

VISA MIX AND TEMPORARY RATIO

Chapter 4 (Visa Mix) relied upon the OECD's categorization of flows as either "temporary" or "permanent." In order to standardize data across countries, the OECD relied upon a reclassification process. For the settler states, this division between "temporary" and "permanent" is a fairly simple exercise as these are clearly delineated visa categories. For the continental European states, the concept of permanent immigration is less applicable, given that migrants are generally tolerated on long-term temporary visas rather than first being admitted on a permanent basis as is common in settler states. For this reason, the OECD adopts a bench-marking exercise in determining whether a visa is permanent or not, rather than relying exclusively upon each domestic definition (Fron et al. 2008). According to this approach, when it is not immediately apparent whether entrants on a visa in practice remain permanently or not, the OECD asks whether over two-thirds of entrants on that visa remained after five years. If they did, the visa was categorized as a permanent visa, even if immigration officials labeled it "temporary." This re-categorization is important not only because it standardizes the definition of "temporary" across states but also because it captures those migrants who, while nominally on a temporary visa – potentially for political reasons – are in fact long-term residents.

It is important to note here that while the OECD data represent a gold standard with regards to both Visa Mix and arguably temporary work flows, aggregating these categories together to constitute total flows for the purposes of the denominator for each country is more challenging. The reason for this is that despite best efforts, statisticians may double-count permanent and temporary records because some immigrants will adjust from temporary to permanent visa status (Thomas Liebig 2012, OECD Migration Section, pers. comm.). This renders direct comparison between temporary and permanent categories difficult. Given this marginal inaccuracy, aggregate measures of total flows are not considered as a stand-alone dimension within this book. In Chapter 4, we report Visa Mix for permanent visas where possible and where this is not possible (for the Gulf countries, for Singapore in some instances, and for China, which do not have permanent forms of migration), we report Visa Mix for temporary visas only. For the purposes of comparison only, we combine temporary and permanent flows as our denominator of interest to calculate percentages of Visa Mix and for the Temporary Ratio in Chapter 5. In Chapter 5, the numerator is temporary economic immigration as the OECD does not provide consistent flow data on non-economic forms of temporary immigration.

In this section, we discuss the sources of non-OECD data utilized in the Visa Mix and Temporary Ratio (Chapters 4 and 5).

Bahrain

Generally, data for Bahrain were gained from the Gulf Labour Markets and Migration (GLLM) website. We relied upon the new visa data sourced from

GLMM (2014a), "Bahrain: New Visa Renewals and Terminations," available online at: http://gulfmigration.eu/bahrain-new-visas-renewals-and-terminations-by-type-of-visa-q3-2008-q1-2014 in http://gulfmigration .eu. Originally from Labour Market Regulatory Authority, Manama, Bahrain.

For the Visa Mix (Chapter 4), the categories "Employer," "Investor," and "Temporary Worker" were coded as our category of "work" while the category "dependent" was coded as our category of "accompanying family" and therefore subsumed within "work." For the purposes of Temporary Ratio (Chapter 5), all economic immigration into Bahrain was treated as temporary. We defend this characterization of all immigration into Bahrain as temporary in Chapter 5. As the Bahrain data differentiated between new visas and renewals, we only utilized new visas.

China

For China, we rely upon data from the Bureau of Entry and Exit Administration of the Ministry of Public Security, 2010. These data are only available for the calendar year of 2009 and published in 2010. The Chinese government does not reveal humanitarian data, so refugee admission is not considered.[1] Available data are aggregated into categories that reflect the OECD classifications. "Business and employment" are combined to represent "work," settlement and others to reflect "other." "Family" represents family reunification as with the OECD data. Further, as the flows in some of these categories are so small compared to the other categories and other countries, they are not reflected in Figure 4.1. The category of "international study" is removed from the Chinese data as the OECD data only considers international study for temporary immigration. Although there were considerable levels of entry through the family category in China in 2009 (80,058 persons), the overall scale of total immigration flows (21,924,427) renders the percentage for this category at close to zero. These flow data were preferred over census data as according to an official in the Shanghai Bureau of Statistics, these census data provide an underestimate (see Bureau of Entry and Exit Administration of the Ministry of Public Security 2011).

[1] The CIA World Factbook estimates that 300,697 Vietnamese, and between 30,000 to 50,000 North Korean refugees reside in China (CIA 2010). Ninety-eight percent of China's Vietnamese refugees are ethnically Chinese, and arrived in the aftermath of Vietnam's 1979 invasion of Cambodia. Despite the fact that they have lived in China for over thirty years, these migrants do not have formal citizenship (Jing 2007).

Aside from international study, other forms of immigration of a temporary nature into China were available, but not that differentiated across visa categories. Therefore, these data were excluded from the Temporary Ratio (Chapter 5). Instead, we assume a 100 percent rate of temporary economic immigration into China. This decision is corroborated by available evidence about the scarcity of permanent residency opportunities for migrants in China. Around a quarter of international migrants stay for more than five years (25.4 percent) (National Bureau of Statistics of China 2010). In the rare event that a migrant holds a "D" Visa, applying for a Chinese "Green Card"/"Green Booklet" allows one to attain residency that lasts up to ten years. The D-Visa system was only instituted in 2004, and is highly selective. Further, restrictions on the fulfillment of eligibility criteria prevent the majority of long-term international migrants from seeking permanent residency (Zou 2012). As of 2011, only 4,752 Chinese Green Cards have been awarded to foreigners since the program's creation in 2004 (Zhang 2011; Lu 2012).

Kuwait

Data for Kuwait are drawn from the GLLM website, in particular: Residence permits by type and purposes of permit, 2009–12, sourced from the Ministry of the Interior (GLMM 2013b), available online at: http://gulfmigration.eu/residence-permits-by-type-purpose-of-permit-and-sex-of-holder-2009-2011-2012 in http://gulfmigration.eu. Originally this data was acquired from the Ministry of Interior in Kuwait City, Kuwait.

For Visa Mix (Chapter 4), we took the aggregate of both sexes, from gender disaggregated data, to calculate data across the various categories. The work category was calculated as encompassing the following categories: "temporary permits," "governmental sector permits," "private sector permits," "business," "domestic help," and "dependent permits." The "study" category was omitted as we do not consider student visas in the Visa Mix. Self-residence permits were coded as "other."

For the Temporary Ratio (Chapter 5) we took: "temporary permits," "governmental sector permits," "private sector permits," "business," and "domestic help" as an aggregate for temporary economic. There is no permanent immigration into Kuwait and therefore we coded permanent economic immigration in Chapter 5 as zero. We defend this decision in the chapter.

Latin American States

Visa Mix data for the Latin American states except for Mexico (which is an OECD country) are sourced from a recent data collection exercise by the Organization of American States, the International Development Bank, and the OECD. To provide consistency with the OECD data, any measures of international study or regularization collected for the Latin American states are taken out of the total measures for analysis, as these categories are not comparable across the remaining countries (OECD/IDB/OAS 2012). The report these organizations produce undertakes the same OECD standardization method for countries in that region (OECD/IDB/OAS 2012), which is necessary for Chapters 4 and 5.

In the OECD/IDB/OAS report, regularization was included as a unique category for Brazil. Given its singularity, we therefore collapsed it into the "other" category. No description of the nature of international agreements was provided for Argentina, Colombia, or Peru. As such, the comparability of international agreement data across these states is unclear. However, this is the best available current data for our purposes and we therefore assumed that "international agreement" was a coherent category across these countries and included it under "Other" for the purposes of our coding for Visa Mix. No permanent Visa Mix data was available for Colombia. Supplementing the IDB sources, some additional data for Brazil were gained from the following sources: Refugee data were gained from the National Immigration Council, Ministry of Labor and Employment, available online at: maisemprego.mte.gov.br/portal/pages/trabalhador.xhtml.

Oman

For Oman, data are drawn from the GLLM website; in particular: GLLM (2014b), "Oman: Residence permits by type of permit (employment/family reunion/domestic labour) (2007–2013)," available online at: http://gulfmigration.eu/oman-residence-permits-by-type-of-permit-employment-family-reuniondomestic-labour-2007–2013 in gulfmigration.eu. Originally from Royal Oman Police, Muscat, Oman.

For Visa Mix (Chapter 4), "Employment," "Domestic Servant," and "Business" were categorized as "work," and "family joining" was categorized in the "accompanying family" group and therefore incorporated into the Work category as well. For Temporary Ratio (Chapter 5), the categories "Employment," "Domestic Servant," and "Business" together constitute total "temporary" economic migration. Like Kuwait, there is no permanent immigration into Oman and therefore we coded permanent economic immigration in Chapter 5 as zero. We defend this decision in Chapter 5. It is important to note that some of these data could include visa renewals as the source data for Oman does not distinguish between new issues, renewals, and transfers of sponsorships. However, we could not access data that provided further differentiation between these categories.

Saudi Arabia

Data for Saudi Arabia are drawn from the GLLM website; in particular, "Residency permits issued by purpose of entry (Saudi Arabia 1984–2011)" (2013c) and "Permits issued by type (residence/ work) (Saudi Arabia, 1984–2011)" (2013b), available online at: http://gulfmigration .eu/permits-issued-by-type-residence-work-saudi-arabia-1984–2011 in http://gulfmigration.eu. Originally from the Ministry of Interior, Riyadh, Saudi Arabia.

For Visa Mix (Chapter 4), the work category includes residency permits issued to "workers" and "accompanying persons." For the Temporary Ratio (Chapter 5), the temporary economic category includes "workers." As for the other GCC countries, we defend the decision to code all entry as temporary in Chapter 5.

Singapore

We could not include Singapore in the Visa Mix (Chapter 4) as we did not have access to complete data across the different categories of the immigration mix (e.g. work, family, and humanitarian). For Singapore for Chapter 5, no flow data were available and for this reason we relied upon a range of flow and converted stock to flow data, using the following formula adopted from Roberts and Camarena (2012):

$$\text{Stock} > flow$$

Estimates and methodology:

$$\text{Flow}(t) = \text{Stock}(t) - \text{Stock}(t\text{-}1)$$

In order to make these calculations, for the Temporary Ratio (Chapter 5), temporary stock data were acquired for 2007–12 from the Ministry of

Manpower Singapore (2015), "Foreign workforce numbers," available online at: www.mom.gov.sg/statistics-publications/others/statistics/Pages/ForeignWorkforceNumbers.aspx and converted to flow data. Temporary migration was defined as (Total Temporary Migration) minus the number of foreign workforce, which comprised of a number of economic visas according to permit type, including Employment Pass (EP), S Pass, and Work Permit, as these latter permits were of a longer residency period and were categorized as permanent visas. Permanent economic data for Singapore included both economic immigrants and accompanying family members (spouses, children, and aged parents). For this reason, to calculate the amount of permanent immigration that was of an economic nature only, we used the estimate provided by the Singapore government of forty-eight percent of this total amount: http://population.sg/resources/immigration-framework/.

We did not use data from before 2011 for historical analysis in Chapter 5 as we did not have full data for the denominator (total migration flows) prior to that year. Further, according to Singaporean national experts, data prior to this period are unreliable due to a considerable change in admissions policy in that country between 2006 and 2010 (Nadica Pavlovska, pers. comm.).

South Africa

For South Africa, we relied on published permanent immigration data (Statistics South Africa 2012). These data are presented with the tables on OECD countries below, as they comprise permanent immigration flows, which are analogous to counterparts across the OECD. Flow data were only available in standardizable fashion for 2011 and were drawn from the following document: Statistics South Africa (2012), "Documented immigrants in South Africa." Our decision to focus upon 2012 is consistent with the analysis of Budlender (2013), which makes clear that other immigration data sources and earlier data sources in South Africa are unreliable for a number of reasons, rendering historical analysis impossible. For the reference year 2011 for the South African data, the original South African coding of "Relations" was recoded as Family; "Refugees" as Humanitarian; and "Retired," a category that appears to serve wealthy European and South Korean retirees, as "Other." "Business and Work" were coded together as Work.

DATA SOURCE YEARS

For Chapter 7, our reference year was 2011 for all OECD data (unless missing, in which case the most recent year was used). For all other countries we used 2011 except for Mexico (2010), China (2009), South Africa

(2012), and Singapore (2011–12), as these were the most proximate available years to the reference year. For the stock and origin diversity measures in Chapter 3, we used 2013 data. For Naturalization Rates for all countries, we used 2011 unless otherwise noted. More details are provided below.

NATURALIZATION DATA

As we discuss in Chapter 6, there are a number of calculations that different scholars call "Naturalization Rates." The most common measure of Naturalization Rates and the one we use is the annual naturalization flow rate. This is found by dividing the number of naturalizations that occur in a given country in a given year by the population of foreign citizens in that country at the beginning of that year.

Where:

R_Y = Naturalization Rate at time Y

N_Y = Total naturalized aliens in year Y

S_Y = Total migrant stock S calculated in year Y = Foreigners who are residents of Country 1 that are "at risk of naturalization." Not merely the foreign-born population because many foreign-born people have already naturalized, and because some foreign born are *jus sanguinis* citizens born abroad.

$$\text{Naturalization Rate } R_Y = \frac{N_Y}{S_Y} = \frac{\text{Total naturalized aliens in year } Y}{\text{Total migrant stock } S \text{ calculated in year } Y}$$

This measure of Naturalization Rates is a better reflection of current citizenship policy than stock rates alone (Reichel 2012: 3) and is used widely (Clarke et al. 1998; Bloemraad 2006; Howard 2009; Janoski 2010; Reichel 2012). In order to contextualize the *jus soli* adjustments made by Janoski, we compare with OECD (2012) data.

As explained in Chapter 6, in order to compare Janoski's adjusted Naturalization Rates to the raw OECD rates over time, we calculated the unadjusted rates for 2000–5 in countries with *jus soli* policies and found the ratio between the OECD data and the Janoski data. Our aim here was to ensure that Janoski's data did not differ substantially from the OECD data for countries without a *jus soli* policy, and to gain an intuition about the magnitude of the effect *jus soli* has in countries that use it. We were able to complete this calculation primarily using the OECD Naturalization Rates, but for Canada, Australia, and France, we were forced to make estimations based on national statistics office data. The process we used for obtaining that historical data is outlined below. After conducting these comparisons, we deemed Janoski's data credible and utilized them for the *jus soli* countries in our dataset. We also used these data in our record of historic Naturalization Rates.

Canada only collects data on its foreign citizen stock in its quinquennial census. We therefore used the 2001 and 2006 census data as reported in OECD (2013) to estimate foreign stock for 1999, 2000, and 2002–5, assuming linear growth over an annual period. Given that this population increased by 190,225 from 2001 to 2006 and 198,415 from 2006 to 2011 we believe that this is a reasonable approximation (OECD 2013). We then divided the OECD's raw citizenship acquisition data by the estimated foreign population in the prior year to obtain Naturalization Rates from 2000 to 2005, which we then averaged.

We used Australian census data from 2001 and 2006 to calculate the difference between the total population and Australian citizens, which we assume roughly corresponds to the number of foreigners. We then used the same method we applied to Canada to calculate estimated foreign stocks and Naturalization Rates from 2000 to 2005. The raw data come from the Australian Bureau of Statistics (2001; 2006).

Like Australia and Canada, France's rate is based on estimations of foreign stocks assuming linear growth. We used the foreign stock as reported in the OECD International Migration Outlook (2010) for 1999 and 2006 to interpolate foreign stocks for 2000 to 2004, which we used with the OECD's raw citizenship acquisition numbers to calculate estimated Naturalization Rates. Eurostat has published foreign stocks for France for January 1, 2003 and January 1, 2005, which we also used to calculate Naturalization Rates for 2003 and 2005. We did not use these stocks for 2004 and 2006, since that data was specifically presented on January 1, and therefore meets Reichel's (2012) requirement that foreign stock at the beginning of the year should serve as the denominator for Naturalization Rates (see note 1 in Chapter 6 for more detail). Using these Eurostat-based rates for 2003 and 2005 did not change the average rate from 4.3 percent, so we used our estimates based on OECD data for consistency. The raw data came from Eurostat (2016), "Population on 1 January by age group, sex, and citizenship," available online at: https://data.europa.eu/euodp/data/dataset/DyCiBSvR4z283JjDuwvdAQ.

After ensuring the validity of the Janoski adjustments, we assembled our Naturalization Rate dataset for inclusion in the k-means clustering algorithm. Our default source was 2011 data from OECD (2014). The following exceptions should be noted: Australia, Belgium, Canada, France, Germany, Ireland, New Zealand, United Kingdom, and United States Naturalization Rates are unpublished 2011 data from Tom Janoski (2016) containing *jus soli* adjustments.

For Brazil, Colombia, and Peru we used: OECD/IDB/OAS (2012), *International Migration in the Americas: Second Report of the Continuous Reporting System on International Migration in the Americas (SICREMI)*. These countries do not publish consistent foreign stock data, forcing us to use the UNPD (2015) foreign-born stock data as the denominator for Naturalization Rates in these countries. Like for Canada and Australia, we estimated the denominator in years without data assuming linear growth between available data points. We then divided the raw acquisition of citizenship data by the prior year's foreign-born stock estimate to get an estimate of the Naturalization Rate in these countries for that year.

For Bahrain, 2010 data are based on a qualitative estimate of 60,000 naturalizations between 2001 and 2011 (which we assumed occurred at a rate of 6,000 per year) and stock data from its national statistics office: see Baker (2011) for the qualitative estimate and stock data from GLMM (2014c), "Population estimates by nationality (Bahraini/Non-Bahraini) (mid-year estimates, 1981; 1990–2011)," available online at: http://gulfmigration.eu/population-estimates-by-nationality-bahraininon-bahraini-mid-year-estimates1981-1990–2011 in http://gulfmigration.eu. Originally from Central Informatics Organization, Manama, Bahrain.

For Kuwait, all naturalization data and foreign stock are drawn from: Kuwait Central Statistics Bureau (2007; 2010; 2012), *Annual Statistical Abstract*, available online at: www.csb.gov.kw/Socan_Statistic_EN.aspx?ID=18. In the 2010 and 2012 reports see tables 19 and 29. In the 2010 report, we referred to tables 19 and 30.

Data for China, Oman, Qatar, Saudi Arabia, Singapore, and the United Arab Emirates are all based on estimates of a 0 percent Naturalization Rate according to consultations with personnel from national statistics offices and news sources about policy standards. For China, the 2010 estimate is also based on government reporting on naturalized stock (National Bureau of Statistics of China 2010) and evidence that pathways to attaining Chinese citizenship are all but impossible, and attaining permanent residency is a special privilege of a select few (National Bureau of Statistics China 2010).

K-MEANS CLUSTERING ANALYSIS

For the k-means clustering analysis we standardized our variable data and used the kmeans() package in R to calculate the clusters. We use twenty-five random initial points as cluster centers and ran one-hundred iterations of the algorithm. Because the user needs to define the number of clusters, k, we ran the algorithm with two through nine clusters to analyze the results. There are a number of fit measures that can be analyzed to help choose clusters. First, we plotted the within-group sum of squares against number of clusters to look for an "elbow" where additional clusters do little to improve fit. This was largely unhelpful, as no clear elbow emerged.

We also used the NbClust() package in R, which provides thirty indexes to determine the optimal number of clusters in a dataset. Here we display two- to nine-cluster solutions.

We defend our selection of a seven (global cluster) and five (OECD) cluster solution in Chapter 7.

Accounting for Demand in the Regime Clusters

Some may argue that variation in immigration regime outcomes is a product not only of the independent variables that we identify, but also of broader demand factors that dictate migrant choices. To test for the possible role of such factors, we ran an independent algorithm that only considers cross-national variation using demand-based variables. These factors we select are among the most conventional drivers of migrant demand for admission. They include gross domestic product (GDP) per capita, unemployment rates, democracy scores, and the destination state's fragility index. These sources of these data are outlined below. Clustering solely on these desirability factors, we find demand taxonomies of little resemblance to our demographic data-driven solution. The substantial difference between clusters based on demographic data and demand factors undermine suggestions that demographic outcomes are simply expressions of pull factors (see Table A.3).

Sources for Demand Variables

The following data were used to assess demand factors:

To analyze GDP per capita as a possible pull factor for migrants, we used data from the United Nations (2016) in 2013 USD, from "GDP and its breakdown at current prices in US Dollars," United Nations Statistics, available online at: http://unstats.un.org/unsd/snaama/dnlList.asp

To assess the role of democratic status as a migrant pull factor, we employed Democracy Score of *The Economist* (2012) Intelligence Unit, "Democracy Index."

To analyze the role of political instability, we referred to Marshall and Cole (2013), "State Fragility Index and Matrix 2013," *Center*

TABLE A.I. *Global cluster solutions*

2 Clusters	3 Clusters	4 Clusters	5 Clusters	6 Clusters	7 Clusters	8 Clusters	9 Clusters
Australia	Brazil	Austria	Bahrain	Finland	Brazil	Brazil	Bahrain
Bahrain	Japan	Belgium	China	Sweden	Japan	South Korea	Kuwait
China	Mexico	Denmark	Kuwait	United States	Mexico	Finland	Oman
Kuwait	South Korea	France	Oman	Brazil	South Korea	Sweden	Saudi Arabia
New Zealand	Australia	Germany	Russia	Japan	Australia	United States	Brazil
Oman	Bahrain	Ireland	Saudi Arabia	Mexico	Canada	China	South Korea
Russia	China	Italy	Singapore	South Korea	New Zealand	Japan	Finland
Saudi Arabia	Kuwait	Netherlands	Austria	Bahrain	United Kingdom	Mexico	Sweden
Singapore	New Zealand	Norway	Denmark	China	Austria	Belgium	United States
Austria	Oman	Portugal	Germany	Kuwait	Denmark	France	Russia
Belgium	Russia	Spain	Norway	Oman	Germany	Ireland	Singapore
Brazil	Saudi Arabia	Switzerland	Switzerland	Russia	Netherlands	Italy	Australia
Canada	Singapore	Brazil	Australia	Saudi Arabia	Norway	Portugal	Canada
Denmark	Austria	Japan	Canada	Singapore	Switzerland	Spain	New Zealand
Finland	Belgium	Mexico	New Zealand	Australia	Belgium	Bahrain	United Kingdom
France	Canada	South Korea	United Kingdom	Canada	France	Kuwait	China
Germany	Denmark	Australia	Belgium	New Zealand	Ireland	Oman	Japan
Ireland	Finland	Canada	Finland	United Kingdom	Italy	Saudi Arabia	Mexico
Italy	France	Finland	France	Austria	Portugal	Australia	Belgium
Japan	Germany	New Zealand	Ireland	Denmark	Spain	Canada	France
Mexico	Ireland	Sweden	Italy	Germany	China	New Zealand	Ireland
Netherlands	Italy	United Kingdom	Netherlands	Netherlands	Russia	United Kingdom	Netherlands
Norway	Netherlands	United States	Portugal	Norway	Singapore	Russia	Norway
Portugal	Norway	Bahrain	Spain	Switzerland	Bahrain	Singapore	Austria
South Korea	Portugal	China	Sweden	Belgium	Kuwait	Austria	Denmark
Spain	Spain	Kuwait	United States	France	Oman	Denmark	Germany
Sweden	Sweden	Oman	Brazil	Ireland	Saudi Arabia	Germany	Switzerland
Switzerland	Switzerland	Russia	Japan	Italy	Finland	Netherlands	Italy
United Kingdom	United Kingdom	Saudi Arabia	Mexico	Portugal	Sweden	Norway	Portugal
United States	United States	Singapore	South Korea	Spain	United States	Switzerland	Spain

TABLE A.2. *OECD cluster solutions*

2 Clusters	3 Clusters	4 Clusters	5 Clusters	6 Clusters	7 Clusters	8 Clusters	9 Clusters
Australia	Japan	Belgium	Australia	Australia	France	Germany	Austria
Canada	Mexico	Finland	Canada	Canada	Ireland	Switzerland	Belgium
Denmark	South Korea	France	New Zealand	New Zealand	Italy	Japan	Netherlands
Germany	Austria	Ireland	United Kingdom	United Kingdom	Portugal	Mexico	Norway
Japan	Belgium	Italy	Austria	Finland	Australia	South Korea	Italy
Mexico	Denmark	Netherlands	Denmark	Sweden	Canada	France	Spain
New Zealand	France	Portugal	Germany	United States	New Zealand	Ireland	Japan
South Korea	Germany	Spain	Netherlands	Italy	United Kingdom	Portugal	Mexico
Switzerland	Ireland	Sweden	Norway	Portugal	Austria	Australia	South Korea
United Kingdom	Italy	United States	Switzerland	Spain	Belgium	Canada	Finland
Austria	Netherlands	Japan	Finland	Austria	Netherlands	New Zealand	Sweden
Belgium	Norway	Mexico	Sweden	Denmark	Norway	United Kingdom	United States
Finland	Portugal	South Korea	United States	Germany	Denmark	Finland	Germany
France	Spain	Austria	Belgium	Switzerland	Spain	Sweden	Switzerland
Ireland	Switzerland	Denmark	France	Japan	Germany	United States	Denmark
Italy	Australia	Germany	Ireland	Mexico	Switzerland	Italy	Australia
Netherlands	Canada	Norway	Italy	South Korea	Finland	Spain	New Zealand
Norway	Finland	Switzerland	Portugal	Belgium	Sweden	Denmark	France
Portugal	New Zealand	Australia	Spain	France	United States	Austria	Ireland
Spain	Sweden	Canada	Japan	Ireland	Japan	Belgium	Portugal
Sweden	United Kingdom	New Zealand	Mexico	Netherlands	Mexico	Netherlands	Canada
United States	United States	United Kingdom	South Korea	Norway	South Korea	Norway	United Kingdom

TABLE A.3. *Six-cluster solution for demand-related factors only*

2 Clusters	3 Clusters	4 Clusters	5 Clusters	6 Clusters	7 Clusters	8 Clusters	9 Clusters
Bahrain	Bahrain	Bahrain	Bahrain	Norway	Brazil	Italy	Austria
Brazil	Brazil	Brazil	Oman	Switzerland	China	New Zealand	Canada
China	China	China	Portugal	Austria	Mexico	Spain	Finland
Mexico	Mexico	Mexico	Saudi Arabia	Belgium	Russia	United Kingdom	Ireland
Oman	Oman	Oman	South Korea	Canada	Australia	Bahrain	Netherlands
Portugal	Portugal	Portugal	Spain	Finland	Denmark	Oman	Singapore
Russia	Russia	Russia	Australia	Germany	Sweden	Portugal	United States
Saudi Arabia	Saudi Arabia	Saudi Arabia	Austria	Ireland	Bahrain	Saudi Arabia	Norway
South Korea	South Korea	South Korea	Canada	Japan	Oman	South Korea	Brazil
Spain	Spain	Norway	Denmark	Kuwait	Portugal	Norway	China
Australia	Norway	Switzerland	Finland	Netherlands	Saudi Arabia	Switzerland	Mexico
Austria	Switzerland	France	Ireland	Singapore	South Korea	Brazil	Belgium
Belgium	Australia	Germany	Netherlands	United States	Belgium	China	France
Canada	Austria	Italy	Singapore	France	France	Mexico	Germany
Denmark	Belgium	Japan	Sweden	Italy	Germany	Russia	Japan
Finland	Canada	New Zealand	United States	New Zealand	Japan	Austria	Kuwait
France	Denmark	Spain	Belgium	Spain	Kuwait	Canada	Switzerland
Germany	Finland	United Kingdom	France	United Kingdom	Italy	Finland	Russia
Ireland	France	Australia	Germany	Australia	New Zealand	Ireland	Saudi Arabia
Italy	Germany	Austria	Italy	Denmark	Spain	Netherlands	Bahrain
Japan	Ireland	Belgium	Japan	Sweden	United Kingdom	Singapore	Oman
Kuwait	Italy	Canada	Kuwait	Bahrain	Austria	United States	Portugal
Netherlands	Japan	Denmark	New Zealand	Oman	Canada	Australia	South Korea
New Zealand	Kuwait	Finland	United Kingdom	Portugal	Finland	Denmark	Australia
Norway	Netherlands	Ireland	Norway	Saudi Arabia	Ireland	Sweden	Denmark
Singapore	New Zealand	Kuwait	Switzerland	South Korea	Netherlands	Belgium	Sweden
Sweden	Singapore	Netherlands	Brazil	Brazil	Singapore	France	Italy
Switzerland	Sweden	Singapore	China	China	United States	Germany	New Zealand
United Kingdom	United Kingdom	Sweden	Mexico	Mexico	Norway	Japan	Spain
United States	United States	United States	Russia	Russia	Switzerland	Kuwait	United Kingdom

for Systemic Peace, available online at: www.systemicpeace.org/inscr/
SFImatrix2013c.pdf.

To consider the role of unemployment rate as a pull factor for migrants,
we consulted the World Bank (2013c), "Unemployment, total (% of total
labor force)," available online at: http://data.worldbank.org/indicator/
SL.UEM.TOTL.ZS.

REASONS FOR REJECTING REGRESSION ANALYSIS TO UNDERSTAND REGIME CLUSTERING (CHAPTER 8)

As we argue in Chapter 8, it is not possible to undertake a regression
analysis for our small dataset of only thirty countries with complete data.
Here, we provide a detailed defense of our decision. Because of our small
dataset, Maximum Likelihood Estimates are highly unstable and often
unable to converge. An ideal approach would be to use a multinomial
logistic regression with cluster membership as the outcome variable that
we regress on our independent variable of interest.

One alternative approach is to use a linear probability model, which
is easier to estimate using ordinary least squares. Because the outcome
is dichotomous, our error terms will necessarily be heteroskedastic and
need to be adjusted. With this method, we dichotomize cluster membership as in cluster m_{i} (1) or not (0). Each cluster gets its own regression.
We then correct standard errors and combine regressions into a single
table. However, this approach raised concerns about omitted variable
bias due to our small sample size. For this reason, we elected to rely upon
bivariate analysis in our discussion in Chapter 8.

SOURCES FOR CORRELATIONAL VARIABLES IN CHAPTER 8

In order to examine correlations between regime cluster placement and
possible variables, we considered a series of correlations. The data sources
for each of these are set out below.

Colony–Colonizer Dataset

We used data from the Correlates of War Project, which documents states'
colonial status from 1816 to the present, to create a colony–colonizer
continuum for our countries.

We used: Correlates of War Project (2015), "Colonial/Dependency
Contiguity Data, 1816–2002," Version 3.0, available online at: www
.correlatesofwar.org/data-sets/colonial-dependency-contiguity.

In coding countries along a colony–colonizer continuum, we drew upon and extended previous work through the Correlates of War dataset (2015). Colony: Authors' index: 1 – major colonizer, 2 – minor colonizer, 3 – neither colonizer nor colonized, 4 – minor colonization, 5 – major colonization.

Our countries are categorized as a colony if part of their current integral territory (not including overseas regions or offshore islands) is listed as being a colony (not a protectorate or occupied territory or some other status) in the Correlates of War dataset. Likewise, countries that are listed as possessing colonies that were not minor islands are coded as colonizers. We excluded colonies that were contiguous with the current mainland territory from our analysis. A few countries both had their territory colonized and colonized other countries. We made the following subjective decisions in those cases based on which role colonization played in that nation's history:

- Australia – coded as colony
- New Zealand – coded as colony
- United States – coded as colony
- Denmark – coded as minor colonizer

The following countries are coded as neither on the basis that their colonies were too insignificant to make them behave like a colonizer:

- Russia (Alaska)
- Norway (Faeroe Islands)

Start Year

Under the Correlates of War dataset, the start year is 1816. However, setting this as the beginning of colonial empire is misleading as it ignores the period of colonization for many major colonies, including Australia (1788) and Mexico (1519). For this reason, we supplemented the Correlates of War starting years with web sources to recode to the true start date, where applicable, through internet sources. First priority was given to official government websites. Second priority was following citation links in Wikipedia. Third priority was given to third-party websites found through Google searches or Google books text searches. Sources for each country are available from the authors upon request.

End Year

The year (before 1993) when the last part of that nation's territory gained independence from a colonizer (for colonies) or when it ceded its last colony (for colonizers)

Total Time

End Year – Start Year

Categorization of Major/Minor

We found the median years that colonized countries were colonized and used that as a point to split the data. Every country that was colonized for more than the median was coded as a major colony and less than the median, a minor colony.

For colonizers, we adopted a different method that relied upon estimates of the maximum territory the colonizer held outside of its homeland at its peak size, even if this was before 1816. On the basis of this characterization, we divided the colonizers into two categories: (1) major colonizers and (2) minor colonizers. Major colonizers had a colonial land mass over three million square miles at the height of their colonial period. We employed this measure rather than a time dimension as it is possible that a colonizer could have been in control of a very small piece of land for a long period, which provides a misleading metric of the scope of colonial rule. Minor colonizers were those with less than three million square miles.

We then created a scale that differentiated between the following: (1) major colonizer; (2) minor colonizer; (3) neither; (4) short-term colony; (5) long-term colony. Long-term versus short-term colony was determined by calculating median years of colonization. Those countries to the right of the median were coded as long-term and those to the left as short-term. This coded scale was used as the independent variable in the analysis in Chapter 8.

Economic and Demographic Indices

To assess economic freedom, we used the Fraser Institute's (2013) "Economic Freedom of the World Index," available online at: http://efwdata.com/grid/WxRvYnU#/Grid.

In order to analyze the relationship between resource wealth and regime placement, we used the measurement of total natural resource rents (% of GDP): World Bank (2013b), "Total natural resource rents (% of GDP)," available online at: http://data.worldbank.org/indicator/ NY.GDP.TOTL.RT.ZS. We used the ten-year average from 2004 through to 2013.

To assess the role of welfare state provisions for OECD countries, we drew upon the Combined Generosity Welfare Index in the Comparative Welfare Entitlements Dataset 1970–2011 (Scruggs et al. 2014). We used the ten-year average from 2002 through to 2011.

To assess the role of partisanship of the governing party, we drew upon data on the Left–Right party balance (gov_party) measure from the CPDS III (Armingeon et al. 2013), average of 1990–2012. We used the ten-year average from 2003 through to 2012. This variable relies upon the so-called Schmidt Index to assess Cabinet partisan composition on a scale of 0 to 5 with 0 on the right and 5 on the social democratic left.

To analyze population aging, we took the population over 65 and above as a percentage of total population from World Bank (2013a), "Population 65 and above (% of total)," available online at: http://data .worldbank.org/indicator/SP.POP.65UP.TO.ZS.

References

Abel, Guy J., and Nicola Sander (2014). "Quantifying Global International Migration Flows." *Sciences* 343(6178), 1520–2.

Acemoglu, Daron, Simon Johnson, and James A. Robinson (2001). "The Colonial Origins of Comparative Development: An Empirical Investigation." *The American Economic Review* 91(5), 1369–401.

AHRC (2013). "Tell Me About: Temporary Protection Visas (Factsheet)." Australian Human Rights Commission, December. www.humanrights.gov .au/sites/default/files/document/publication/TPV_FactSheet.pdf.

Akkerman, Tjitske (2012). "Comparing Radical Right Parties in Government: Immigration and Integration Policies in Nine Countries." *West European Politics* 35(3), 511–29.

Akkerman, Tjitske, and Sarah L. de Lange (2012). "Radical Right Parties in Office: Incumbency Records and the Electoral Cost of Governing." *Government and Opposition* 47(4), 574–96.

Al-Arabiya (2013). "Breakthrough: Saudi Women Can Pass on Citizenship Rights to Their Children." *Al-Arabiya News*, February 16. www.alarabiya.net/ articles/2013/02/16/266668.html.

Alba, Richard, and Nancy Foner (2015). *Strangers No More: Immigration and the Challenges of Integration in North America and Western Europe.* Princeton: Princeton University Press.

Alboim, Naomi, and Karen Cohl (2013). *Shaping the Future: Canada's Rapidly Changing Immigration Policies.* Ottawa: Maytree Foundation.

Alho, Juha M. (2008). "Migration, Fertility, and Aging in Stable Populations." *Demography* 45(3), 641–50.

Ali, Syed (2010). *Dubai: Gilded Cage.* New Haven: Yale University Press.

Al-Qassemi, Sooud (2013). "Give Expats an Opportunity to Earn UAE Citizenship." *Gulf News*, September 22. http://gulfnews.com/opinion/thinkers/ give-expats-an-opportunity-to-earn-uae-citizenship-1.1234167.

American Immigration Council (2013a). "The Advantages of Family-Based Immigration." American Immigration Council, March 14. www.americanimmigrationcouncil.org/research/advantages-family-based-immigration.

(2013b). *A Guide to S.744: Understanding the 2013 Senate Immigration Bill.* Washington, DC: American Immigration Council. www.americanimmigration council.org/sites/default/files/research/guide_to_s744_corker_hoeven_final_ 12-02-13.pdf.

Andersen, Jørgen Goul (2007). "Restricting Access to Social Protection for Immigrants in the Danish Welfare State." *Benefits* 15(3), 257–69.

Angenendt, Steffen (2009). *Labor Migration Management in Time of Recession: Is Circular Migration a Solution?* Washington, DC: Transatlantic Academy Paper Series.

Angrist, Joshua D., and Jorn-Steffen Pischke (2009). *Mostly Harmless Econometrics: An Empiricist's Companion.* Princeton: Princeton University Press.

Anttonen, Anneli, and Gabrielle Meagher (2013). "Mapping Marketization: Concepts and Goals." In *Marketisation in Nordic Eldercare,* edited by Gabrielle Meagher and Marta Szebehely, 12–22. Stockholm: Stockholm University Department of Social Work.

Arango, Joaquin, and Maia Jachimowicz (2005). "Regularizing Immigration in Spain: A New Approach." Migration Policy Institute, September 1. www.migrationpolicy.org/article/regularizing-immigrants-spain-new-approach.

Armingeon, Klaus, Christian Isler, Laura Knöpfel, David Weisstanner, and Sarah Engler (2013). *Comparative Political Data Set (CPDSIII) 1960–2012.* Bern: Institute of Political Science, University of Bern.

Armstrong, Carolyn (2016). "The Limits of Communitarisation and the Legacy of Intergovernmentalism: EU Asylum Governance and the Evolution of the Dublin System." Ph.D. thesis, London School of Economics and Political Science. http://etheses.lse.ac.uk/3417/.

Arzheimer, Kai (2009). "Contextual Factors and the Extreme Right Vote in Western Europe, 1980–2002." *American Journal of Political Science* 53, 259–75.

Ashby, Nathan J. (2007). "Economic Freedom and Migration Flows Between U.S. States." *Southern Economic Journal* 73(3), 677–97.

(2010). "Freedom and International Migration." *Southern Economic Journal* 77(1), 49–62.

Australian Bureau of Statistics (2001). *2001 Census.* Canberra: Australian Bureau of Statistics QuickStats. www.abs.gov.au/websitedbs/censushome.nsf/home/ quickstats.

(2006). *2006 Census.* Canberra: Australian Bureau of Statistics QuickStats. www.abs.gov.au/websitedbs/censushome.nsf/home/quickstats.

Australian Productivity Commission (2015). *Migrant Intake into Australia: Draft Report.* Canberra: Australian Productivity Commission. www.pc.gov.au/ inquiries/completed/migrant-intake/draft/migrant-intake-draft.pdf.

Auwal, Mohammad A. (2010). "Ending the Exploitation of Migrant Workers in the Gulf." *Fletcher Forum of World Affairs* 34(2), 87–108.

Bader, Veit (2007). "The Governance of Islam in Europe: The Perils of Modelling." *Journal of Ethnic and Migration Studies* 33(6), 871–86.

Bahn, Susanne (2013). "Workers on 457 Visas: Evidence from the Western Australian Resources Sector." *Australian Bulletin of Labour* 39(2), 34–58.

Baker, Aryn (2011). "What Lies Beneath: Bahrain's 'New Citizens' Fuel Unrest." *Time*, March 11.

Baker, Bryan C. (2007). *Trends in Naturalization Rates*. Washington, DC: Department of Homeland Security Office of Immigration Statistics.

Baldwin-Edwards, Martin (2007). "Illegal Migration in the Mediterranean." In *Fifth International Seminar on Security and Defence in the Mediterranean: Multi-Dimensional Security*, 115–24. Barcelona: Barcelona Centre for International Affairs (CIDOB).

  (2011). *Labour Immigration and Labour Markets in the GCC Countries: National Patterns and Trends*. London: London School of Economics and Political Science Kuwait Programme on Development, Governance and Globalisation in the Gulf States.

Banting, Keith (2000). "Looking in Three Directions: Migration and the European Welfare State in Comparative Perspective." In *Immigration and Welfare: Challenging the Borders of the Welfare State*, edited by Michael Bommes and Andrew Geddes, 12–33. London: Routledge.

  (2005). "The Multicultural Welfare State: International Experience and North American Narratives." *Social Policy & Administration* 39(2), 98–115.

  (2014). "Transatlantic Convergence? The Archaeology of Immigrant Integration in Canada and Europe." *International Journal* 69(1), 66–84.

Banting, Keith, and Will Kymlicka, eds. (2006). *Multiculturalism and the Welfare State: Recognition and Redistribution in Contemporary Democracies*. Oxford: Oxford University Press.

Banting, Keith, Richard Johnston, Will Kymlicka, and Stuart Soroka (2011). "Are Diversity and Solidarity Incompatible?" *Inroads* 28, 36–49.

Barrett, Alan, and Bertrand Maître (2011). *Immigrant Welfare Receipt Across Europe: Discussion Paper No. 5515*. Bonn: IZA Institute of Labor Economics.

Barslund, Mikkel, and Matthias Busse (2014). "Labour Mobility in the EU: Dynamics, Patterns and Policies." *Intereconomics* 49(3), 116–58.

Bartram, David (2006). *International Labor Migration: Foreign Workers and Public Policy*. New York: Palgrave Macmillan.

Batalova, Jean, and B. Lindsay Powell (2006). "'The Best and the Brightest': Immigrant Professionals in the U.S." In *The Human Face of Global Mobility: International Highly Skilled Migration in Europe, North America and the Asia-Pacific*, edited by Michael Peter Smith and Adrian Favell, 81–102. New Brunswick: Transaction Publishers.

Bauböck, Rainer (1992). *Immigration and the Boundaries of Citizenship*. Warwick: Centre for Research in Ethnic Relations.

Bauböck, Rainer, Eva Ersbøll, Kees Groenendijk, and Harald Waldrauch, eds. (2006). *Policies and Trends in 15 European States*. Vol. 1 of *Acquisition and Loss of Nationality*. Amsterdam: Amsterdam University Press.

Bay, Ann-Helén, and Axel West Pedersen (2006). "The Limits of Social Solidarity: Basic Income, Immigration and the Legitimacy of the Universal Welfare State." *Acta Sociologica* 49(4), 419–36.

Bearce, David H., and Jennifer A. Laks Hutnick (2011). "Toward an Alternative Explanation for the Resource Curse: Natural Resources, Immigration and Democratization." *Comparative Political Studies* 44(6), 689–718.

Becker, Ulrich (2004). "The Challenge of Migration to the Welfare State." In *The Welfare State, Globalization, and International Law*, edited by Eyal Benvenisti and Georg Nolte, 1–31. Heidelberg: Spring-Verlag.

Beetsma, Roel, Massimo Giuliodori, Mark Walschot, and Peter Wierts (2013). "Fifty Years of Fiscal Planning and Implementation in the Netherlands." *European Journal of Political Economy* 31, 119–38.

Beine, Michel, Anna Boucher, Brian Burgoon, Mary Crock, Justin Gest, Michael Hiscox, Patrick McGovern, Hillel Rapoport, Joep Schaper, and Eiko Thielemann (2015). "Comparing Immigration Policies: An Overview from the Impala Database." *International Migration Review* 50(4), 827–63.

Beneria, Lourdes, Carmen Diana Deere, and Naila Kabeer (2012). "Gender and International Migration: Globalization, Development, and Governance." *Feminist Economics* 18(2), 1–33.

Berg, Laurie (2016). *Migrant Rights and Work: Law's Precariousness at the Intersection of Immigration and Labor*. London: Routledge.

Berg, Linda, and Andrea Spehar (2013). "Swimming Against the Tide: Why Sweden Supports Increased Labour Mobility Within and from Outside the EU." *Policy Studies* 34(2), 142–61.

Bermingham, John R. (2001). "Immigration: Not a Solution to Problems of Population Decline and Aging." *Population and Environment* 22(4), 355–63.

Billari, Francesco C., and Gianpiero Dalla-Zuanna (2011). "Is Replacement Migration Actually Taking Place in Low Fertility Countries?" *Genus* 67(3), 105–23.

Bloch, Alice (2002). *The Migration and Settlement of Refugees in Britain*. Basingstoke: Palgrave Macmillan.

Block, Laura (2015). "Regulating Membership: Explaining Restriction and Stratification of Family Migration in Europe." *Journal of Family Issues* 36(11), 1433–52.

Block, Laura, and Saskia Bonjour (2013). "Fortress Europe or Europe of Rights? The Europeanisation of Family Migration Policies in France, Germany and the Netherlands." *European Journal of Migration and Law* 15(2), 203–24.

Bloemraad, Irene (2006). *Becoming a Citizen: Incorporating Immigrants and Refugees in the United States*. Berkeley: University of California Press.

Boeri, Tito, Herbet Brücker, Frédéric Docquier, and Hillel Rapoport, eds. (2012). *Brain Drain and Brain Gain: The Global Competition to Attract High-Skilled Migrants*. Oxford: Oxford University Press.

Bolin, Niklas, Gustav Lidén, and Jon Nyhlén (2014). "Do Anti-Immigration Parties Matter? The Case of the Sweden Democrats and Local Refugee Policy." *Scandinavian Political Studies* 37(3), 323–43.

References 211

Bolzendahl, Catherine (2010). "Directions of Decommodification: Gender and Generosity in 12 OECD Nations." *European Sociological Review* 26(2), 125–41.

Bommes, Michael (2000). "National Welfare State, Biography and Migration: Labour Migrants, Ethnic Germans and the Re-Ascription of Welfare State Membership." In *Immigration and Welfare: Challenging the Borders of the Welfare State*, edited by Michael Bommes and Andrew Geddes, 90–108. London: Routledge.

Bond, Melissa, and Noel Gaston (2011). "The Impact of Immigration on Australian-Born Workers: An Assessment Using the National Labour Market Approach." *Economic Record* 30(3), 400–13.

Bonjour, Saskia (2014). "The Transfer of Pre-Departure Integration Requirements for Family Migrants Among Member States of the European Union." *Comparative Migration Studies* 2(2), 203–26.

Borjas, George J. (1989). "Economic Theory and International Migration." *International Migration Review* 23(3), 457–85.

(1999). *Heaven's Door: Immigration Policy and the American Economy*. Princeton: Princeton University Press.

(1993). "Immigration Policy, National Origin, and Immigrant Skills: A Comparison of Canada and the United States." In *Small Differences That Matter: Labor Markets and Income Maintenance in Canada and the United States*, edited by David Card and Richard B. Freeman, 21–44. Chicago: University of Chicago Press.

(2001). "Welfare Reform and Immigration." In *The New World of Welfare*, edited by Rebecca M. Blank and Ron Haskins, 369–90. Washington, DC: Brookings Institute Press.

Boswell, Christina (2008). "UK Labour Migration Policy: Permanent Revolution?" Working paper, Centro Studi de Politica Internazionale, Rome.

Boucher, Anna (2009). "Canada and Gender-Based Analysis of Immigration Law and Policy." In *Human Rights and Social Policy: A Comparative Analysis of Values and Citizenship in OECD Countries*, edited by Ann Nevile, 174–200. Northampton, MA: Edward Elgar.

(2014). "Familialism and Migrant Welfare Policy: Restrictions on Social Security Provision for Newly-Arrived Immigrants." *Policy and Politics* 42(3), 367–84.

(2016). *Gender, Migration and the Global Race for Talent*. Manchester: Manchester University Press.

(2007). "Skill, Migration and Gender in Australia and Canada: The Case of Gender-Based Analysis." *Australian Journal of Political Science* 42(3), 383–401.

Boyd, Monica (1994). "Gender Concealed, Gender Revealed: The Demography of Canada's Refugee Flows." Centre for the Study of Population Working Paper Series 94–122, Florida State University, Tallahassee, Florida.

(1999). "Gender, Refugee Status and Permanent Settlement." *Gender Issues* 17(1), 5–25.

(2014). "Recruiting High Skill Labour in North America: Policies Outcomes and Futures." *International Migration* 52(3), 40–54.

Boyd, Monica, and Deanna Pikkov (2004). *Gendering Migration, Livelihood and Entitlements: Migration Women in Canada and the United States.* Geneva: United Nations Research Institute for Social Development.

Breunig, Christian, Xun Cao, and Adam Luedtke (2012). "Global Migration and Political Regime Type: A Democratic Disadvantage." *British Journal of Political Science* 42(4), 825–54.

Brick, Kate (2011). *Regularizations in the European Union: The Contentious Policy Tool.* Washington, DC: Migration Policy Institute.

Brochmann, Grete (2002). "Citizenship and Inclusion in European Welfare States: The EU Dimension." In *Migration and the Externalities of European Integration*, edited by Sandra Lavenex and Emek M. Uçarer, 179–94. Oxford: Lexington Books.

Brubaker, Rogers (1992). *Citizenship and Nationhood in France and Germany.* Cambridge, MA: Harvard University Press.

Brücker, Herbet, Gil S. Epstein, Barry McCormick, Gilles Saint-Paul, Alessandra Venturini, and Claus Zimermann (2002). "Managing Migration in the European Welfare State." In *Immigration Policy and the Welfare System*, edited by Tito Boeri, Gordon Hanson, and Barry McCormick, 1–167. Oxford: Oxford University Press.

Bruni, Michele (2013). "China between Economic Growth and Mass Immigration." *China & World Economy* 21(2), 56–77.

Büchel, Felix, and Joachim R. Frick (2005). "Immigrants' Economic Performance Across Europe: Does Immigration Policy Matter?" *Population Research and Policy Review* 25(2), 175–212.

Bucken-Knapp, Gregg, Jonas Hinnfors, Andrea Spehar, and Pia Levin (2014). "No Nordic Model: Understanding Differences in the Labour Migration Policy Preferences of Mainstream Finnish and Swedish Political Parties." *Comparative European Politics* 12(6), 584–602.

Budlender, Deborah (2013). *MiWORC Report N°2. Improving the Quality of Available Statistics on Foreign Labour in South Africa: Existing Data-Sets.* Johannesburg: African Centre for Migration and Society, University of the Witwatersrand.

Bureau of Entry and Exit Administration of the Ministry of Public Security (2011). "2009 Statistics of Main Exit and Entry." Ministry of Public Security. www.mps.gov.cn/n16/n84147/n84211/n84424/2478762.html.

Cangiano, Alessio, and Salvatore Strozza (2008). "Foreign Immigration in Southern European Receiving Countries: New Evidence from National Data Sources." In *International Migration in Europe: New Trends and New Methods of Analysis*, edited by Corrado Bonifazi, Marek Oklóski, Jeannette Schoorl, and Patrick Simon, 153–78. Amsterdam: Amsterdam University Press.

Careja, Romana, and Patrick Emmenegger (2009). "The Politics of Public Spending in Post-Communist Countries." *East European Politics and Societies* 23(2), 165–84.

Carrera, Sergio, Anaïs Faure Atger, Elspeth Guild, and Dora Kostakopoulou (2011). *CEPS Policy Brief No. 240. Labour Immigration Policy in the EU: A Renewed Agenda for Europe 2020.* Brussels: Centre for European Policy Studies.

Castles, Francis, and Deborah Mitchell (1992). "Identifying Welfare State Regimes: The Links Between Politics, Instruments and Outcomes." *Governance* 5(1), 1–26.

Castles, Stephen (2006). "Guestworkers in Europe: A Resurrection?" *International Migration Review* 40(4), 741–66.

Castles, Stephen, and Godula Kosack (1973). *Immigrant Workers and Class Structure in Western Europe*. London: Oxford University Press.

Castles, Stephen, and Mark J. Miller (2009). *The Age of Migration: International Population Movements in the Modern World*. Basingstoke: Palgrave Macmillan.

Caviedes, Alexander (2016). "European Integration and Governance of Migration." *Journal of Contemporary European Research* 12(1), 533–66.

(2010). *Prying Open Fortress Europe: The Turn to Sectoral Labor Migration*. New York: Lexington Books.

Cebula, Richard J. (2014). "The Impact of Economic Freedom and Personal Freedom on Net In-Migration in the U.S.: A State-Level Empirical Analysis, 2000 to 2010." *Journal of Labor Research* 35(1), 88–103.

Cebula, Richard J., and Jeff R. Clark (2011). "Migration, Economic Freedom, and Personal Freedom: An Empirical Analysis." *Journal of Private Enterprise* 27(1), 43–62.

Cebula, Richard J., Maggie Foley, and Joshua C. Hall (2015). "Freedom and Gross In-Migration: An Empirical Study of the Post-Great Recession Experience." *Journal of Economics and Finance* 40(2), 402–20.

Cerna, Lucie (2010). "The EU Blue Card: A Bridge Too Far?" Paper prepared for the Fifth Pan-European Conference on EU Politics, Porto, Portugal, June 23–26.

(2013). "Understanding the Diversity of EU Migration Policy in Practice: The Implementation of the Blue Card Initiative." *Policy Studies* 34(2), 180–200.

Cetin, Elif (2015). "The Italian Left and Italy's (Evolving) Foreign Policy of Immigration Controls." *Journal of Modern Italian Studies* 20(3), 377–97.

Chalcraft, John (2010). *Monarchy, Migration and Hegemony in the Arabian Peninsula*. London: London School of Economics and Political Science Kuwait Programme on Development, Governance and Globalisation in the Gulf States.

Chaloff, Jonathan, and Georges Lemaître (2009). "Managing Highly-Skilled Labour Migration: A Comparative Analysis of Migration Policies and Challenges in OECD Countries." OECD Social, Employment and Migration Working Papers No. 79, Organisation for Economic Cooperation and Development (OECD), Paris.

Chan, Stephanie, Jon E. Fox, Denis Kim, and John D. Skrentny (2007). "Defining Nations in Asia and Europe: A Comparative Analysis of Ethnic Return Migration Policy." *International Migration Review* 41, 793–825.

Charsley, Katharine, Brooke Storer-Church, Michaela Benson, and Nicholas van Hear (2012). "Marriage-Related Migration to the UK." *International Migration Review* 46(4), 861–90.

Chin, Rita (2009). *The Guestworker Question in Postwar Germany*. Cambridge: Cambridge University Press.

Chou, Meng-Hsuan, and Nicolas Baygert (2007). "The 2006 French Immigration and Integration Law: Europeanisation or Nicolas Sarkozy's Presidential Keystone?" Working Paper No. 45, ESRC Centre on Migration, Policy and Society, University of Oxford, Oxford.

Chryssogelos, Angelos (2015). "Refugees: The EU's Crisis Within a Crisis." Chatham House, November 25. www.chathamhouse.org/expert/comment/refugees-eus-crisis-within-crisis.

CIA (2010). "The World Factbook." Central Intelligence Agency. Last modified January 12, 2012. www.cia.gov/library/publications/download/download-2010.

Cigagna, Claudia, and Giovanni Sulis (2015). *On the Potential Interaction Between Labour Market Institutions and Immigration Policies: IZA Discussion Paper No. 9016.* Bonn: IZA Institute of Labor Economics. http://ftp.iza.org/dp9016.pdf.

Citizenship and Immigration Canada (1994). "The Relative Performance of Selected Independents and Family Class Immigrants in the Labour Market." Draft paper, Economic and Demographic Research and Analysis Division, Strategic Research and Analysis Branch, Policy Sector, Ottawa-Hull.

Clarke, James, Elsbeth van Dam, and Liz Gooster (1998). "New Europeans: Naturalisation and Citizenship in Europe." *Citizenship Studies* 2(1), 43–67.

Cobb-Clark, Deborah A., and Siew-Ean Khoo, eds. (2006). *Public Policy and Immigrant Settlement.* Northampton, MA: Edward Elgar.

Cohen, Robin (2010). *The Cambridge Survey of World Migration.* Cambridge: Cambridge University Press.

Collier, David, Jody LaPorte, and Jason Seawright (2012). "Putting Typologies to Work: Concept Formation, Measurement, and Analytic Rigor." *Political Research Quarterly* 65(1), 217–32.

Consterdine, Erica (2015). "Managed Migration under Labour: Organised Public, Party Ideology and Policy Change." *Journal of Ethnic and Migration Studies* 41(9), 1433–52.

Cook-Martín, David, and David Scott FitzGerald (2014). *Culling the Masses: The Democratic Origins of Racist Immigration Policy in the Americas.* Cambridge, MA: Harvard University Press.

Cornelius, Wayne A., and Takeyuki Tsuda (2004). "Controlling Immigration: The Limits of Government Intervention." In *Controlling Immigration*, 2nd edn, edited by Wayne A. Cornelius, Takeyuki Tsuda, Philip L. Martin, and James F. Hollifield, 3–48. Stanford: Stanford University Press.

Cornelius, Wayne A., Takeyuki Tsuda, Philip L. Martin, and James F. Hollifield, eds. (2004). *Controlling Immigration: A Global Perspective*, 2nd edn. Stanford: Stanford University Press.

Correlates of War Project (2015). *Colonial Contiguity Data, 1816–2016.* Version 3.0. www.correlatesofwar.org/data-sets/colonial-dependency-contiguity.

Cort, David A. (2012). "Spurred to Action or Retreat? The Effects of Reception Contexts on Naturalization Decisions in Los Angeles." *International Migration Review* 46(2), 483–516.

Craig, Richard B. (2014). *The Bracero Program: Interest Groups and Foreign Policy*. Austin: University of Texas Press.

Crock, Mary, and Daniel Ghezelbash (2010). "Do Loose Lips Bring Ships? The Role of Policy, Politics and Human Rights in Managing Unauthorised Boat Arrivals." *Griffith Law Review* 19(2), 238–87.

Crock, Mary, Ben Saul, and Azadeh Dastyari (2006). *Future Seekers II: Refugees and Irregular Migration in Australia*. Sydney: Federation Press.

Crush, Jonathan (2011). *Complex Movements, Confused Responses: Labour Migration in South Africa. Policy Brief No. 25*. Waterloo, ON: South African Migration Programme.

Czaika, Matthias, and Hein de Haas (2014). "The Globalization of Migration: Has the World Become More Migratory?" *International Migration Review* 48(2), 283–323.

Dauvergne, Catherine (2000). "Gendering Permanent Residency Statistics." *Melbourne University Law Review* 24(2), 280–309.

(2016). *The New Politics of Immigration and the End of Settler Societies*. New York: Cambridge University Press.

Dearden, Lizzie (2016). "Germany Follows Switzerland and Denmark to Seize Cash and Valuables from Arriving Refugees." *Independent*, January 23. www .independent.co.uk/news/world/europe/germany-follows-switzerland-and- denmark-to-seize-cash-and-valuables-from-arriving-refugees-a6828821 .html.

DeLaet, Debra L. (1999). "Introduction: The Invisibility of Women in Scholarship on International Migration." In *Gender and Migration*, edited by Gregory A. Kelson and Debra L. DeLaet, 1–17. New York: New York University Press.

Devitt, Camilla (2011). "Varieties of Capitalism, Variation in Labour Immigration." *Journal of Ethnic and Migration Studies* 37(4), 579–96.

Devlin, Ciaran, Olivia Bolt, Dhiren Patel, David Harding, and Ishtiaq Hussain (2014). *Impacts of Migration on UK Native Employment: An Analytical Review of the Evidence*. London: Home Office and Department for Business Innovation and Skills.

DeWaard, Jack, Keuntae Kim, and James Raymer (2012). "Migration Systems in Europe: Evidence from Harmonized Flow Data." *Demography* 49(4), 1307–33.

Diehl, Claudia, and Michael Blohm (2003). "Rights or Identity? Naturalization Processes Among 'Labor Migrants' in Germany." *International Migration Review* 37(1), 133–62.

Djelic, Marie-Laure (2006). "Marketization: From Intellectual Agenda to Global Policy Making." In *Transnational Governance: Institutional Dynamics of Regulation*, edited by Marie-Laure Djelic and Kerstin Sahlin-Andersson, 53– 73. Cambridge: Cambridge University Press.

Dobrowolsky, Alexandra (2007). "(In)Security and Citizenship: Security, Im/ migration and Shrinking Citizenship Regimes." *Theoretical Inquiries in Law* 8(2), 629–61.

Docquier, Frédéric, B. Lindsay Lowell, and Abdeslam Marfouk (2009). "A Gendered Assessment of Highly Skilled Emigration." *Population and Development Review* 35(2), 297–321.

Donato, Katharine M., and Andrea Tyree (1986). "Family Reunification, Health Professionals, and the Sex Composition of Immigrants to the United States." *Social Science Review* 70(3), 226–30.

Donato, Katharine M., Joseph T. Alexander, Donna R. Gabbacia, and Johanna Leinonen (2012). "Variations in the Gender Composition of Immigrant Populations: How They Matter." *International Migration Review* 45(3), 495–526.

Dongdong, Zhang (2012). "Who Benefit [*sic*] Most as China Lowers Threshold for 'Green Card'?" *People's Daily*, December 20. http://en.people.cn/90882/8064510.html.

Doomernik, Jeroen, Rey Koslowski, Jonathan Laurence, Rahsaan Maxwell, Ines Michalowski, and Dietrich Thränhardt (2009). *No Shortcuts: Selective Migration and Integration*. Washington, DC: Transatlantic Academy.

Dronkers, Jaap, and Maarten Peter Vink (2012). "Explaining Access to Citizenship in Europe: How Citizenship Policies Affect Naturalization Rates." *European Union Politics* 13(3), 390–412.

Dumbravă, Costică (2007). "Citizenship Regulation in Eastern Europe: Acquisition of Citizenship at Birth and Through Regular Naturalisation in Sixteen Postcommunist Countries." *CEU Political Science Journal* 2(4), 450–72.

Duncan, Fraser (2010). "Immigration and Integration Policy and the Austrian Radical Right in Office: The FPÖ/BZÖ, 2000–2006." *Contemporary Politics* 16(4), 337–54.

Dustmann, Christian, Francesca Fabbri, and Ian Preston (2005). "The Impact of Immigration on the British Labour Market." *Economic Journal* 115, F324–41.

Easterlin, Richard (2013). "Happiness Growth and Public Policy." *Economic Inquiry* 51(1), 1–15.

Economist, The (2012). "Democracy Index." *The Economist* Intelligence Unit.
  (2013). "Deported Yemeni Migrant Workers: Down and Out." *The Economist*, December 10. www.economist.com/blogs/pomegranate/2013/12/deported-yemeni-migrant-workers.

Ellerman, David (2005). "Labour Migration: A Developmental Path or a Low-Level Trap?" *Development in Practice* 15(5), 617–30.

Ellermann, Antje (2015). "Do Policy Legacies Matter? Past and Present Guest Worker Recruitment in Germany." *Journal of Ethnic and Migration Studies* 41(8), 1235–53.

Ersts, Peter J. (2013). *Geographic Distance Matrix Generator (Version 1.2.3)*. American Museum of Natural History, Center for Biodiversity and Conservation. http://biodiversityinformatics.amnh.org/open_source/gdmg.

Esping-Andersen, Gøsta (1990). *The Three Worlds of Welfare Capitalism*. Princeton: Princeton University Press.

European Commission (2011). "European Union Democracy Observatory on Citizenship (EUDO)." http://eudo-citizenship.eu/.

Eurostat (2016). "Population on 1 January by Group, Sex, and Citizenship." *European Union Open Data Portal*. Last modified May 12, 2017. https://data.europa.eu/euodp/data/dataset/DyCiBSvR4z283JjDuwvdAQ.

Fackler, Martin (2010). "New Dissent in Japan Is Loudly Anti-Foreign." *New York Times*, August 28. www.nytimes.com/2010/08/29/world/asia/29japan .html.

Fahrmeir, Andreas (2007). *Citizenship: The Rise and Fall of a Modern Concept*. New Haven: Yale University Press.

Falcó-Gimeno, Albert, and Ignacio Jurado (2011). "Minority Governments and Budget Deficits: The Role of the Opposition." *European Journal of Political Economy* 27(3), 554–65.

Fargues, Philippe (2011). "Immigration Without Inclusion: Non-Nationals in Nation-Building in the Gulf States." *Asian and Pacific Migration Journal* 20(3–4), 273–92.

Favell, Adrian (2008). "The New Face of East-West Migration in Europe." *Journal of Ethnic and Migration Studies* 34(5), 701–16.

Fawcett, James T. (1989). "Networks, Linkages, and Migration Systems." *International Migration Review* 23(3), 671–80.

Ferwerda, Jeremy, and Nicholas L. Miller (2014). "Political Devolution and Resistance to Foreign Rule: A Natural Experiment." *American Political Science Review* 108(3), 642–60.

Fielding, Anthony (1993). "Migrations, Institutions and Politics: The Evolution of European Migration Policies." In *Mass Migration in Europe: The Legacy and the Future*, edited by Russell King, 40–61. London: Belhaven Press.

Finotelli, Claudia, and Ines Michalowski (2012). "The Heuristic Potential of Models of Citizenship and Immigrant Integration Reviewed." *Journal of Immigrant and Refugee Studies* 10(3), 231–40.

Fisher, Stephen (2007). "(Change in) Turnout and (Change in) the Left Share of the Vote." *Electoral Studies* 26(3), 598–611.

Fitzgerald, Jennifer, David Leblang, and Jessica C. Teets (2014). "Defying the Law of Gravity: The Political Economy of International Migration." *World Politics* 66(3), 406–45.

Fong, Pang Eng (2006). "Foreign Talent and Development in Singapore." In *Competing for Global Talent*, edited by Christiane Kuptsch and Pang Eng Fong, 155–68. Geneva: International Labour Office.

Foster, Jason, and Bob Barnetson (2015). "Exporting Oil, Importing Labour, and Weakening Democracy: The Use of Foreign Migrant Workers in Alberta." In *Alberta Oil and the Decline of Democracy in Canada*, edited by Meenal Shrivastava and Lorna Stefanick, 249–74. Edmonton: Athabasca University Press.

Foster, Jason, and Alison Taylor (2013). "In the Shadows: Exploring the Notion of 'Community' for Temporary Foreign Workers in Boomtown." *Canadian Journal of Sociology* 38(2), 167–90.

Fouad, Daad (1999). "Demographic Indicators and Family Social Security: Effects and Consequences." Police Studies, Dubai Police General Headquarters Research and Studies Centre, No. 92, August.

Fraser Institute (2013). *Economic Freedom of the World Index*. http://efwdata .com/grid/WxRvYnU#/Grid

Freeman, Gary P. (1994). "Can Liberal States Control Unwanted Migration?" *Annals of the American Academy of Political and Social Science* 534, 17–30.

(2011). "Comparative Analysis of Immigration Politics: A Retrospective." *American Behavioral Scientist* 55(12), 1541–60.

(1995). "Modes of Immigration Policies in Liberal Democratic States." *International Migration Review* 29(4), 881–902.

(2006). "National Models, Policy Types and the Politics of Immigration in Liberal Democracies." *West European Politics* 29(2), 227–47.

Freeman, Gary P., and David K. Hill (2006). "Disaggregating Immigration Policy: The Politics of Skilled Labor Recruitment in the U.S." In *The Human Face of Global Mobility: International Highly Skilled Migration in Europe, North America and the Asia-Pacific*, edited by Michael Peter Smith and Adrian Favell, 103–29. New Brunswick: Transaction Publishers.

Freier, Luisa Freier, and Diego Acosta Arcarazo (2015). "Beyond Smoke and Mirrors? Discursive Gaps in the Liberalisation of South American Immigration Law." In *A Liberal Tide? Immigration and Asylum Law and Policy in Latin America*, edited by David J. Cantor, Luisa F. Freier, and Jean-Pierre Gauci, 33–56. London: Institute of Latin American Studies, University of London.

Friberg, Jon Horgen (2012). "The 'Guestworker Syndrome' Revisited? Migration and Unemployment Among Polish Workers in Oslo." *Nordic Journal of Migration Research* 2(4), 316–24.

Fron, Pauline, Georges Lemaitre, Thomas Liebig, and Cécile Thoreau (2008). *Standardised Statistics on Immigrant Inflows: Results, Sources and Methods*. Paris: OECD.

(2011). *Standardised Statistics on Immigrant Inflows: Results, Sources and Methods*. Paris: OECD.

Gamlen, Alan (2010). *International Migration Data and the Study of Super-Diversity*. Göttingen: Max Planck Institute for the Study of Religious and Ethnic Diversity.

Gardner, Andrew M. (2010). *City of Strangers: Gulf Migration and the Indian Community in Bahrain*. Cornell: Cornell University Press.

Garip, Filiz (2012). "Discovering Diverse Mechanisms of Migration: The Mexico-U.S. Stream from 1970 to 2000." *Population and Development Review* 38(3), 393–433.

Geddes, Andrew (2000). "Denying Access: Asylum Seekers and Welfare Benefits in the UK." In *Immigration and Welfare: Challenging the Borders of the Welfare State*, edited by Michael Bommes and Andrew Geddes, 134–47. London: Routledge.

George, Alexander L., and Andrew Bennett (2005). *Case Study and Theory Development in the Social Sciences*. Cambridge, MA: MIT Press.

Gest, Justin (2010). *Apart: Alienated and Engaged Muslims in the West*. New York and London: Oxford University Press/Hurst and Company.

(2016). *The New Minority: White Working Class Politics in an Age of Immigration and Inequality*. New York: Oxford University Press.

Gest, Justin, and Sean Gray (2016). *Silent Citizenship: The Politics of Marginality in Unequal Democracies*. New York: Routledge.

Gest, Justin, Anna Boucher, Suzanna Challen, Brian Burgoon, Eiko Thielemann, Michel Beine, Patrick McGovern, Mary Crock, Hillel Rapoport, and

Michael Hiscox (2014). "Measuring and Comparing Immigration, Asylum and Naturalization Policies Across Countries: Challenges and Solutions." *Global Policy* 5(3), 261–74.

Givens, Terri, and Adam Luedtke (2005). "European Immigration Policies in Comparative Perspective: Issue Salience, Partisanship and Immigrant Rights." *Comparative European Politics* 3(1), 1–22.

GLMM (2014a). "Bahrain: New Visas, Renewals, and Terminations by Type of Visa (Q3 2008 – Q1 2014)." Manama, Bahrain: Labour Market Regulatory Authority. http://gulfmigration.eu/bahrain-new-visas-renewals-and-terminations-by-type-of-visa-q3-2008-q1-2014.

(2014b). "Oman: Residence Permits by Type of Permit (Employment/Family Reunion/Domestic Labour (2007–2013)." Muscat, Oman: Royal Oman Police. http://gulfmigration.eu/oman-residence-permits-by-type-of-permit-employment-family-reuniondomestic-labour-2007–2013.

(2013a). "Permits Issued by Type (Residence/Work) (Saudi Arabia, 1984–2011)." Riyadh, Saudi Arabia: Ministry of Interior. http://gulfmigration.eu/permits-issued-by-type-residence-work-saudi-arabia-1984–2011.

(2014c). "Population Estimates by Nationality (Bahraini/Non-Bahraini), (Mid-year Estimates, 1981; 1990–2011)." Central Informatics Organization, Manama, Bahrain. http://gulfmigration.eu/population-estimates-by-nationality-bahraininon-bahraini-mid-year-estimates1981-1990–2011.

(2013b). "Residence Permits by Type/Purpose of Permit and Sex of Holder (Kuwait) (2009; 2011; 2012)." Kuwait City, Kuwait: Ministry of Interior. http://gulfmigration.eu/residence-permits-by-type-purpose-of-permit-and-sex-of-holder-2009-2011-2012.

(2013c). "Residence Permits Issued by Purpose of Entry (Saudi Arabia 1984–2011)." Riyadh, Saudi Arabia: Ministry of Interior. http://gulfmigration.eu/permits-issued-by-type-residence-work-saudi-arabia-1984–2011/.

Global Forum on Migration and Development (2012). *Background Paper for RT 2.2: Addressing South-South Migration and Development Policies.* Geneva: Global Forum on Migration and Development.

Goldring, Luin, and Patricia Landolt (2013). "Conceptualising Precarious Non-Citizenship in Canada." In *Producing and Negotiating Non-Citizenship: Precarious Legal Status in Canada*, edited by Luin Goldring and Patricia Landolt, 3–28. Toronto: Toronto University Press.

Gonzalez-Barrera, Ana, and Jens Manuel Krogstad (2014). "U.S. Deportations of Immigrants Reach Record High in 2013." Pew Research Center, October 2. www.pewresearch.org/fact-tank/2014/10/02/u-s-deportations-of-immigrants-reach-record-high-in-2013/.

Goodman, Sara Wallace (2012). "Fortifying Citizenship: Policy Strategies for Civic Integration in Western Europe." *World Politics* 64(4), 659–98.

(2010). "Integration Requirements for Integration's Sake? Identifying, Categorising and Comparing Civic Integration Policies." *Journal of Ethnic and Migration Studies* 36(5), 753–72.

Goto, Junichi (2007). "Latin Americans of Japanese Origin (Nikkeijin) Working in Japan: A Survey." World Bank Policy Research Working Paper 4203,

Research Institute for Economics and Business Administration, Kobe University Japan, April.

Government of Singapore (2014). "Visitor Whose Spouse is a Singapore Citizen (SC) or Singapore Permanent Resident (SPR)." Immigration and Checkpoints Authority. Last modified November 11, 2016. www.ica.gov.sg/page.aspx?pageid=175.

Graham, Otis L., Jr. (2004). *Unguarded Gates: A History of America's Immigration Crisis*. Lanham: Rowman & Littlefield.

Green, Alan G., and David Green (1995). "Canadian Immigration Policy: The Effectiveness of the Points System and Other Instruments." *Canadian Journal of Economics* 28(4b), 1006–41.

  (2004). "The Goals of Canada's Immigration Policy: A Historical Perspective." *Canadian Journal of Urban Research* 13(1), 102–39.

Green, David (2017). "As Its Population Ages, Japan Quietly Turns to Immigration." Migration Policy Institute, March 28. www.migrationpolicy.org/article/its-population-ages-japan-quietly-turns-immigration.

Green-Pedersen, Christoffer, and Pontus Odmalm (2008). "Going Different Ways? Right-Wing Parties and Immigrant Issue in Denmark and Sweden." *Journal of European Public Policy* 15(3), 367–81.

Greer, Ian and Virginia Doellgast (2013). "Marketization, Inequality, and Institutional Change." Working paper, No WERU 5, University of Greenwich, London.

Grimmer, Justin, and Gary King (2011). "General Purpose Computer-Assisted Clustering and Conceptualization." *Proceedings of the National Academy of Sciences of the United States of America* 108(7), 2643–50.

Gudbrandsen, Frøy (2010). "Partisan Influence on Immigration: The Case of Norway." *Scandinavian Political Studies* 33(3), 248–70.

Guellec, Dominique, and Mario Cervantes (2001). *International Mobility of Highly Skilled Workers: From Statistical Analysis to Policy Formulation*. Paris: OECD.

Guiraudon, Virginie (1997). "Policy Change Behind Gilded Doors: Examining the Evolution of Aliens' Rights in Contemporary Western Europe 1974–1994." Ph.D. thesis, Harvard University Department of Government.

Guiraudon, Virginie, and Christian Joppke (2001). *Controlling a New Migration World*. London: Routledge.

Gurowitz, Amy (1999). "Mobilizing International Norms: Domestic Actors, Immigrants, and the Japanese State." *World Politics* 51(3), 413–45.

Gwartney, James, Robert Lawson, and Joshua Hall (2015). "Economic Freedom Dataset." In *Economic Freedom of the World: 2015 Annual Report*. Vancouver: Fraser Institute. www.freetheworld.com/datasets_efw.html.

Habboush, Mahmoud (2013). "Call to Naturalise Some Expats Stirs Anxiety in the UAE." *Reuters*, October 10. http://uk.reuters.com/article/2013/10/10/uk-emirates-citizenship-feature-idUKBRE99904J20131010.

Hainmueller, Jens, and Dominik Hangartner (2013). "Who Gets a Swiss Passport? A Natural Experiment in Immigrant Discrimination." *American Political Science Review* 107(1), 159–87.

Hamilton, Nora, and Norma Stoltz Chinchilla (1991). "Central American Migration: A Framework for Analysis." *Latin American Research Review* 26(1), 75–110.

Hamlin, Rebecca (2012). "Illegal Refugees: Competing Policy Ideas and the Rise of the Regime of Deterrence in American Asylum Politics." *Refugee Survey Quarterly* 31(2), 33–53.

(2014). *Let Me Be a Refugee: Administrative Justice and the Politics of Asylum in the United States, Canada, and Australia*. New York: Oxford University Press.

Hammar, Tomas (1985). "Introduction." In *European Immigration Policy: A Comparative Case Study*, edited by Tomas Hammar, 1–13. Cambridge: Cambridge University Press.

(1990). *Democracy and the Nation-State: Aliens, Denizens, and Citizens in a World of International Migration*. Avebury: Ashgate.

Han, Kyung Joon (2015). "The Impact of Radical Right-Wing Parties on the Positions of Mainstream Parties Regarding Multiculturalism." *West European Politics* 38(3), 557–76.

Hansen, Randall (2000). *Citizenship and Immigration in Post-War Britain: The Institutional Origins of a Multicultural Nation*. Oxford: Oxford University Press.

Hanson, Gordon, Kenneth F. Scheve, Matthew J. Slaughter, and Antonio Spilimbergo (2002). "Immigration and the US Economy: Labour-Market Impacts, Illegal Entry, and Policy Choices." In *Immigration Policy and the Welfare System*, edited by Tito Boeri, Gordon Hanson, and Barry McCormick, 169–285. Oxford: Oxford University Press.

Harper, Marjory, and Stephen Constantine (2010). *Migration and Empire*. Oxford: Oxford University Press.

Harrison, Ryan (2014). "GCC Citizenship Debate: A Place to Call Home." *Gulf Business*, January 5. http://gulfbusiness.com/2014/01/gcc-citizenship-debate-a-place-to-call-home/#.VUDiXmTBzG.

Harzig, Christiane, and Dirk Hoerder (2009). *What is Migration History?* Cambridge: Polity Press.

Hastie, Trevor, Robert Tibshirani, and Jerome Friedman (2009). *The Elements of Statistical Learning: Data Mining, Inference, and Prediction*, 2nd edn. New York: Springer-Verlag.

Hatton, Timothy J., and Jeffrey G. Williamson (2008). *Global Migration and the World Economy: Two Centuries of Policy and Performance*. Cambridge, MA: MIT Press.

Hawkins, Freda (1988). *Canada and Immigration: Public Policy and Public Concern*, 2nd edn. Montreal: McGill-Queen's University Press.

(1991). *Critical Years in Immigration: Canada and Australia Compared*. Kingston, ON: McGill-Queen's University Press.

Hawthorne, Lesleyanne (2010). "Demography, Migration and Demand for International Students." In *Globalisation and Tertiary Education in the Asia-Pacific: The Changing Nature of a Dynamic Market*, edited by Christopher Findlay and William G. Tierney, 91–120. Singapore: World Scientific Publishing Co.

(2008). *The Impact of Economic Selection Policy on Labour Market Outcomes for Degree-Qualified Migrants in Canada and Australia*. Montreal: Institute for Research on Public Policy.

Heater, Derek (2004). *A Brief History of Citizenship*. Edinburgh: Edinburgh University Press.

Helbling, Marc, Liv Bjerre, Friederike Römer, and Malisa Zobel (2017). "Measuring Immigration Policies: The IMPIC Database." *European Political Science* 16(1), 79–98.

Hennebry, Jenna L., and Kerry Prebisch (2012). "A Model for Managed Migration? Re-Examining Best Practices in Canada's Seasonal Agricultural Worker Program." *International Migration* 50(s1), e19–e40.

Hill, Laura E., and Joseph M. Hayes (2011). "How Would Selecting for Skill Change Flows of Immigrants to the United States? A Simulation of Three Merit-Based Point Systems." *Review of Economics of the Household* 9(1), 1–23.

Hinnfors, Jonas, Andrea Spehar, and Gregg Bucken-Knapp (2012). "The Missing Factor: Why Social Democracy Can Lead to Restrictive Immigration Policy." *Journal of European Public Policy* 19(4), 585–603.

Hirota, Hidetaka (2017). *Expelling the Poor*. New York: Oxford University Press.

Hirschman, Albert O. (1964). "The Paternity of an Index." *American Economic Review* 54(5), 761.

Hochschild, Jennifer L., and John Mollenkopf (2009). "The Complexities of Immigration: Why Western Countries Struggle with Immigration Politics and Policies." In *Delivering Citizenship*, edited by Bertelsmann Stiftung, European Policy Centre, Migration Policy Institute, 3–15. Berlin: Verlag Bertelsmann Stiftung.

Hollifield, James F. (1992). *Immigrants, Markets and States: The Political Economy of Postwar Europe*. Cambridge, MA: Harvard University Press.

(2000). "The Politics of International Migration: How Can We 'Bring the State Back In'?" In *Migration Theory: Talking across Disciplines*, edited by Caroline B. Brettell and James F. Hollifield, 137–86. London: Routledge.

Hollifield, James F., Philip L. Martin, and Pia M. Orrenius, eds. (2014). *Controlling Immigration: A Global Perspective*, 3rd edn. Stanford: Stanford University Press.

Honaker, James (2011). "Learning Vectors for Case Study Analysis." Working paper, Meetings of the Society for Political Methodology, Princeton University, July.

Hooghe, Marc, Ann Trappers, Bart Meuleman, and Tim Reeskens (2008). "Migration to European Countries: A Structural Explanation of Patterns." *International Migration Review* 42(2), 476–504.

Hort, Sven Olsson, and Stein Kuhnle (2000). "The Coming of East and South-East Asian Welfare States." *Journal of European Social Policy* 10(2), 162–84.

Houstoun, Marion F., Roger G. Kramer, and Joan Mackin Barrett (1984). "Female Predominance of Immigration to the United States Since 1930: A First Look." *International Migration Review* 18, 908–63.

Howard, Marc Morjé (2006). "Comparative Citizenship: An Agenda for Cross-National Research." *Perspectives on Politics* 4(3), 443–55.

(2010). "The Impact of the Far Right on Citizenship Policy in Europe: Explaining Continuity and Change." *Journal of Ethnic and Migration Studies* 36(5), 735–51.

(2009). *The Politics of Citizenship in Europe.* New York: Cambridge University Press.

Hugo, Graeme (2009). "Best Practice in Temporary Labour Migration for Development: A Perspective from Asia and the Pacific." *International Migration* 47(5), 23–74.

(2006). "Temporary Migration and the Labour Market in Australia." *Australian Geographer* 37(2), 211–31.

Human Rights Watch (2016). *Closed Doors: Mexico's Failure to Protect Central American Refugee and Migrant Children.* New York: Human Rights Watch.

(2014). "Kuwait: UPR Submission." Human Rights Watch, June. www.hrw .org/news/2015/01/11/kuwait-upr-submission-2014.

Immigration and Customs Enforcement (2015). "FY 2015 ICE Immigration Removals." U.S. Department of Homeland Security. www.ice.gov/ removal-statistics.

International Migrants Bill of Rights (2017). Georgetown University Law Center, imbr.info.

International Migration Policy and Law Analysis Database (IMPALA) (2015). "The International Migration Policy and Law Analysis Database, Project Description." www.impaladatabase.org.

IOM (2008). *World Migration 2008: Managing Labour Mobility in the Evolving Global Economy.* Geneva: International Organization for Migration. https:// publications.iom.int/system/files/pdf/wmr_1.pdf.

Ireland, Patrick (2004). *Becoming Europe: Immigration, Integration, and the Welfare State.* Pittsburgh: University of Pittsburgh Press.

Ivanov, Sergey (2012). "International Migration in Russia." *Problems of Economic Transition* 55(5), 3–25.

Izzak, B. 2016. "Assembly to Pass Key Law Today 110,000 Granted Citizenship Since 2012." *The Kuwait Times,* December 20. http://news.kuwaittimes.net/website/ assembly-pass-key-laws-today-110000-granted-citizenship-since-2012.

Jacobson, David (1996). *Rights Across Borders: Immigration and the Decline of Citizenship.* Baltimore: Johns Hopkins Press.

Janoski, Thomas (2010). *The Ironies of Citizenship: Naturalization and Integration in Industrialized Countries.* Cambridge: Cambridge University Press.

(2011). "What We Need Citizenship Indicators For Depends On Who Are 'We.'" In "Which Indicators Are Most Useful For Comparing Citizenship Policies?", edited by Rainer Bauböck and Marc Helbling, 19–21. EUI Working Papers, Robert Schuman Centre for Advanced Studies, Florence, Italy.

Jasso, Guillermina, and Mark Rosenzweig (1995). "Do Immigrants Screened For Skills Do Better Than Family-Reunification Immigrants?" *International Migration Review* 29(1), 85–111.

Jing, Song (2007). "Vietnamese Refugees Well Settled in China, Await Citizenship." UNHCR, May 10. www.unhcr.org/464302994.html.

Jones-Correa, Michael (2005). "Bringing Outsiders In." In *The Politics of Democratic Inclusion*, edited by Christina Wolbrecht and Rodney E. Hero, 75–102. Philadelphia: Temple University Press.

(2001). "Under Two Flags: Dual Nationality in Latin America and Its Consequences for Naturalization in the United States." *International Migration Review* 35(4), 997–1029.

Joppke, Christian (2010). *Citizenship and Immigration*. Cambridge: Polity Press.

(2005a). "Exclusion in the Liberal State." *European Journal of Social Theory* 8(1), 43–61.

(1999). *Immigration and the Nation-State: The United States, Germany and Great Britain*. Oxford: Oxford University Press.

(2005b). *Selecting by Origin: Ethnic Migration in the Liberal State*. Cambridge, MA: Harvard University Press.

(1998). "Why Liberal States Accept Unwanted Immigration." *World Politics* 50(2), 266–93.

Kalicki, Konrad (2016). "Security Fears and Bureaucratic Rivalry: The Politics of Foreign Labor Admission in Japan and Taiwan." Working paper, Emerging Immigration Scholars Conference, Los Angeles, February 26–27.

Kapiszewski, Andrzej (2006). "Arab Versus Asian Migrant Workers in the GCC Countries." Working paper, United Nations Expert Group Meeting on International Migration and Development in the Arab Region, Beirut, Lebanon.

Karlson, Stephen H., and Eliakim Katz (2010). "Immigration Amnesties." *Applied Economics* 42(18), 2299–315.

Kelley, Ninette, and Michael J. Trebilcock (1998). *The Making of the Mosaic: A History of Canadian Immigration Policy*. Toronto: University of Toronto Press.

Kenny, Mary Anne, and Nicholas Procter (2014). "'Fast Track' Asylum Processing Risks Fairness for Efficiency." *The Conversation*, December 8. https://theconversation.com/fast-track-asylum-processing-risks-fairness-for-efficiency-35146.

Kerwin, Donald, Kate Brick, and Rebecca Kilberg (2012). "Unauthorized Immigrants in the United States and Europe: The Use of Legalization/ Regularization as a Policy Tool." *Migration Policy Institute*, May 9. www.migrationpolicy.org/article/unauthorized-immigrants-united-states-and-europe-use-legalizationregularization-policy-tool.

Khaleej Times (2012). "Over 930 Children To Get UAE Citizenship." *Khaleej Times*, April 7. www.khaleejtimes.com/article/20120407/ARTICLE/304079896/1002.

Khan, Azfar, and Hélène Harroff-Tavel (2010). "Reforming the *Kafala*: Challenges and Opportunities in Moving Forward." *Asian and Pacific Migration Journal* 20(3–4), 293–313.

King, Russell (1993). "European International Migration 1945–90: A Statistical and Geographical Overview." In *Mass Migration in Europe: The Legacy and the Future*, edited by Russell King, 20–39. London: Belhaven Press.

(2012). "Theories and Typologies of Migration: An Overview and a Primer." Willy Brandt Series of Working Papers in International Migration and Ethnic

Relations 3/12, Malmö Institute for Studies of Migration, Diversity and Welfare (MIM), Malmö University, Sweden.

Klotz, Audie (2013). *Migration and National Identity in South Africa, 1860–2010*. New York: Cambridge University Press.

Kofman, Eleonore, and Veena Meetoo (2008). "Family Migration." In *World Migration Report 2008*, edited by Gervais Appave and Ryszard Cholewinski, 151–72. Geneva: International Organization for Migration.

Kofman, Eleonore, and Parvati Raghuram (2006). "Gender and Global Labour Migration: Incorporating Skilled Workers." *Antipode* 38(2), 282–303.

Koopmans, Ruud (2004). "Migrant Mobilisation and Political Opportunities: Variation Among German Cities and a Comparison with the United Kingdom and the Netherlands." *Journal of Ethnic and Migration Studies* 30(3), 449–70.

Koopmans, Ruud, Ines Michalowski, and Stine Waibel (2012). "Citizenship Rights for Immigrants: National Political Processes and Cross-National Convergence in Western Europe, 1980–2008." *American Journal of Sociology* 117(4), 1202–45.

Koopmans, Ruud, Paul Statham, Marco Giugni, and Florence Passy (2005). *Contested Citizenship: Immigration and Cultural Diversity in Europe*. Minneapolis: University of Minnesota Press.

Koser, Khalid (2009). "Study of Employment and Residence Permits for Migrant Workers in Major Countries of Destination." Working paper, International Migration Papers No. 95, International Migration Programme, International Labour Organization, Geneva.

Koslowski, Rey (2014). "Selective Migration Policy Models and Changing Realities of Implementation." *International Migration* 52(3), 26–39.

Kovacheva, Vesela, and Dita Vogel (2009). "The Size of the Irregular Foreign Resident Population in the European Union in 2002, 2005 and 2008: Aggregated Estimates." Annex 3 to Working Paper No. 4, Hamburg Institute of International Economics, Hamburg.

Kovessy, Peter (2014). "The (Narrow) Path to Qatari Citizenship." *Doha News*, October 9. http://dohanews.co/path-qatari-citizenship.

Krasner, Stephen D. (1982). "Structural Causes and Regime Consequences: Regimes as Intervening Variables." *International Organization* 36(2), 185–205.

Kratochwil, Friedrich, and John Gerard Ruggie (1997). "International Organization: The State of the Art." In *The Politics of Global Governance: International Organizations in an Independent World*, edited by Paul F. Diehl, 29–39. Boulder: Lynne Rienner.

Kretsedemas, Philip, and Ana Aparicio (2004). *Immigrants, Welfare Reform, and the Poverty of Policy*. Westpoint: Greenwood.

Kritz, Mary M., Lin Lean Lim, and Hania Zlotnik, eds. (1992). *International Migration Systems: A Global Approach*. Oxford: Clarendon Press.

Krogstad, Jens Manuel, and Jeffrey S. Passel (2015). "5 Facts About Illegal Immigration in the U.S." Pew Research Center, July 24. www.pewresearch.org/fact-tank/2015/07/24/5-facts-about-illegal-immigration-in-the-u-s.

Kruyt, Arrien, and Jan Niessen (1997). "Integration." In *Immigration Policy for a Multicultural Society: A Comparative Study of Integration, Language and Religious Policy in Five Western European Countries*, edited by Hans Vermeulen, 15–56. Brussels: Migration Policy Group.

Kupiszewska, Dorota, and Marek Kupiszewski (2011). "Harmonization of International Migration Data." Working paper, Consortium for Applied Research on International Migration (CARIM), Methodological Workshop, Warsaw, Poland, October 27–28.

Kuwait Central Statistics Bureau (2007). *Annual Statistical Abstract*. www.csb.gov.kw/Socan_Statistic_EN.aspx?ID=18.

    (2010). *Annual Statistical Abstract*. www.csb.gov.kw/Socan_Statistic_EN.aspx?ID=18.

    (2012). *Annual Statistical Abstract*. www.csb.gov.kw/Socan_Statistic_EN.aspx?ID=18.

Lahav, Gallya (2004). *Immigration and Politics in the New Europe: Reinventing Elite*. Cambridge: Cambridge University Press.

Lake, Marilyn, and Henry Reynolds (2008). *Drawing the Global Colour Line: White Men's Countries and the Question of Racial Equality*. Melbourne: Melbourne University Press.

Latham, A. J. H. (1986). "Southeast Asia: A Preliminary Survey, 1800–1914." In *Migration Across Time and Nations: Population Mobility in Historical Contexts*, edited by Ira A. Glazier and Luigi De Rosa, 11–29. New York: Holmes and Meier.

Laurence, Jonathan (2003). "Immigrant Integration Through Religious Community: Jews and Muslims in the New Germany." Talk, CES-Berlin Dialogues, WZB Berlin Social Science Centre, Berlin, February.

    (2006). "(Re)constructing Community in Berlin: Turks, Jews, and German Responsibility." In *Transformations of the New Germany*, edited by Ruth A. Starkman, 199–232. Basingstoke: Palgrave Macmillan.

Lee, Sang-Hyop, and Andrew Mason (2011). "International Migration, Population Age Structure and Economic Growth in Asia." *Asian and Pacific Migration Journal* 20(2), 195–213.

LeMay, Michael (1987). *From Open Door to Dutch Door: An Analysis of U.S. Immigration Policy Since 1820*. New York: Praeger.

Lenard, Patti Tamara (2012). "How Does Canada Fare? Canadian Temporary Labour Migration in Comparative Perspective." In *Legislated Inequality: Temporary Labour Migration in Canada*, edited by Patti Tamara Lenard and Christine Straehle, 272–96. Quebec: McGill-Queen's University Press.

Longva, Anh Nga (1999). "Keeping Migrant Workers in Check: The Kafala System in the Gulf." *Middle East Report* 211, 20–2.

Lori, Noora (2008). "National Security and the Management of Labor: A Case Study of the United Arab Emirates." *Asian and Pacific Migration Journal* 20(3–4), 315–37.

Lowell, B. Lindsay (2011). "Growing Modern American Guestworkers: The Increasing Supply of Temporary H-2A Agricultural Workers." Working paper, 8th IZA institute of Labor Economics Annual Migration Meeting. Washington, DC, May 12–15.

Lowell, B. Lindsay, and Johanna Avato (2014). "The Wages of Skilled Temporary Migrants: Effects of Visa Pathways and Job Portability." *International Migration* 52(3), 85–98.

Lu, Hui (2012). "721 Foreigners Get 'Green Cards' in Beijing." *Xinhua*, May 28. http://news.xinhuanet.com/english/china/2012-05/28/c_131615516.htm.

Lucassen, Leo (2005). *The Immigrant Threat: The Integration of Old and New Migrants in Western Europe Since 1850*. Urbana: University of Illinois Press.

Lucchino, Paolo, Chiara Rosazza-Bondibene, and Jonathan Portes (2012). *Examining the Relationship Between Immigration and Unemployment Using National Insurance Number Registration Data*. London: National Institute of Economic and Social Research.

Mafukidze, Jonathan (2006). "A Discussion of Migration and Migration Patterns and Flows in Africa." In *Views on Migration in Sub-Saharan Africa*, edited by Catherine Cross, Derik Gelderlom, Niel Roux, and Jonathan Mafukidze, 103–29. Cape Town: HSRC Press.

Mahdavi, Pardis (2015). "Children of the Emir: Perverse Integration and Incorporation in the Gulf." In *Migrant Encounters: Intimate Labor, the State, and Mobility Across Asia*, edited by Sara L. Friedman and Pardis Mahdavi, 71–91. Philadelphia: University of Pennsylvania Press.

Mansouri, Fethi, Michael Leach, and Amy Nethery (2009). "Temporary Protection and the Refugee Convention in Australia, Denmark and Germany." *Refuge* 26(1), 135–47.

Marshall, Monty G., and Benjamin R. Cole (2013). "State Fragility Index and Matrix 2013." Centre for Systemic Peace. www.systemicpeace.org/inscr/SFImatrix2013c.pdf.

Martin, John P. (2011). "Migration in the Post-Crisis World." In *International Migration Outlook 2011*, edited by OECD, 29–31. Paris: OECD Publishing.

Martin, Philip L. (2004). "Germany: Managing Migration in the Twenty-First Century." In *Controlling Immigration: A Global Perspective*, 2nd edn, edited by Wayne A. Cornelius, Takeyuki Tsuda, Philip L. Martin, and James F. Hollifield, 221–53. Stanford: Stanford University Press.

Massey, Douglas S. (2007). "Understanding America's Immigration 'Crisis.'" *Proceedings of the American Philosophical Society* 151(3), 309–27.

(1999). "Why Does Immigration Occur? A Theoretical Synthesis." In *The Handbook of International Migration: The American Experience*, edited by Charles Hirschman, Philip Kasinitz, and Josh DeWind, 34–52. New York: Russell Sage Foundation.

Massey, Douglas S., and Chiara Capoferro (2004). "Measuring Undocumented Migration." *International Migration Review* 38(3), 1075–102.

Massey, Douglas S., Joaquin Arango, Graeme Hugo, Ali Kouaouci, Adela Pelligrino, and J. Edward Taylor (1998). *Worlds in Motion: Understanding International Migration at the End of the Millennium, International Studies in Demography*. Oxford/New York: Clarendon Press/Oxford University Press.

Mau, Steffen, Heike Brabandt, Lena Laube, and Christof Roos (2012). *Liberal States and the Freedom of Movement: Selective Borders, Unequal Mobility*. London: Palgrave Macmillan.

Mazzolari, Francesca (2009). "Dual Citizenship Rights: Do They Make More and Richer Citizens?" *Demography* 46(1), 169–91.

McCabe, Kristen, Serena Yi-Ying Lin, Hiroyuki Tanaka, and Piotr Plewa (2009). "Pay to Go: Countries Offer Cash to Immigrants Willing to Pack Their Bags." Migration Policy Institute, November 5. www.migrationpolicy.org/article/pay-go-countries-offer-cash-immigrants-willing-pack-their-bags/.

McDowell, Linda (2009). "Old and New European Economic Migrants: Whiteness and Managed Migration Policies." *Journal of Ethnic and Migration Studies* 35(1), 19–36.

McGill, Jenny (2013). "International Student Migration: Outcomes and Implications." *Journal of International Students* 3(2), 167–81.

McKeown, Adam (2004). "Global Migration, 1846–1940." *Journal of World History* 15(2), 155–89.

McLaughlin, Janet (2010). "Classifying the 'Ideal Migrant Worker': Mexican and Jamaican Transnational Farmworkers in Canada." *Focaal* 57, 79–94.

McLaughlin, Janet, and Jenna Hennebry (2013). "Pathways to Precarity: Structural Vulnerabilities and Lived Consequences for Migrant Farmworkers in Canada." In *Producing and Negotiating Non-Citizenship: Precarious Legal Status in Canada*, edited by Luin Goldring and Patricia Landolt, 175–94. Toronto: Toronto University Press.

McLeod, Keith, and David Maré (2013). *The Rise of Temporary Migration in New Zealand and Its Impact on the Labour Market.* Wellington: Ministry of Business, Innovation and Employment.

Meagher, Gabrielle and Susan Goodwin (2015). "Introduction: Capturing Marketisation in Australian Social Policy." In *Markets, Rights and Power in Australian Social Policy*, edited by Gabrielle Meagher and Susan Goodwin, 1–27. Sydney: Sydney University Press.

Menz, Georg (2009). *The Political Economy of Managed Migration: Nonstate Actors, Europeanization, and the Politics of Designing Migration Policies.* Oxford/New York: Oxford University Press.

Menzel, Annie (2013). "Birthright Citizenship and the Racial Contract." *Du Bois Review: Social Science Research on Race* 10(1), 29–58.

Messina, Anthony M. (2007). *The Logics and Politics of Post-WWII Migration to Western Europe.* New York: Cambridge University Press.
   (1996). "The Not So Silent Revolution: Postwar Migration to Western Europe." *World Politics* 49(1), 130–54.

Meyers, Eytan (2004). *International Immigration Policy: A Theoretical and Comparative Analysis.* New York: Palgrave.

Migration Advisory Committee (2012). *Analysis of the Impacts of Migration.* London: Home Office.

Migration Policy Group (2006/2011). "Migration Integration Policy Index (MIPEX)." www.mipex.eu/.

Ministry of Manpower Singapore (2012). "Extension of Maximum Period of Employment for Unskilled Work Permit Holders." www.mom.gov.sg/~/media/mom/documents/press-releases/2012/faqs%20on%20extension%20of%20maximum%20poe.pdf.

(2015). "Foreign Workforce Numbers." www.mom.gov.sg/statistics-publications/others/statistics/Pages/ForeignWorkforceNumbers.aspx.

Mirilovic, Nikola (2010). "The Politics of Immigration: Dictatorship, Development, and Defense." *Comparative Politics* 42(3), 273–92.

Money, Jeanette (1999). *Fences and Neighbours: The Political Geography of Immigration Control in Advanced Market Economy Countries.* Ithaca, NY: Cornell University Press.

Money, Jeanette, and Dana Zartner Falstrom (2006). "Interests and Institutions in Skilled Migration: Comparing Flows into the IT and Nursing Sectors in the US." In *The Human Face of Global Mobility: International Highly Skilled Migration in Europe, North America and the Asia-Pacific*, edited by Michael Peter Smith and Adrian Favell, 131–56. New Brunswick: Transaction Press.

Morales, Laura, Jean-Benoit Pilet, and Didier Ruedin (2015). "The Gap between Public Preferences and Policies on Immigration: A Comparative Examination of the Effect of Politicisation on Policy Congruence." *Journal of Ethnic and Migration Studies* 41(9), 1495–516.

Nagy, Sharon (2010). "Families and Bachelors: Visa Status, Family Lives, and Community Structure among Bahrain's Foreign Residents." In *Viewpoints: Migration and the Gulf*, 58–62. Washington, DC: Middle East Initiative. See www.voltairenet.org/IMG/pdf/Migration_and_the_Gulf.pdf.

Nakache, Delphine, and Paula J. Kinoshita (2010). *The Canadian Temporary Foreign Worker Program: Do Short-Term Economic Needs Prevail Over Human Rights Concerns?* Montreal: Institute for Research on Public Policy (IRPP).

National Bureau of Statistics of China (2010). *2010 Population Census of the People's Republic of China.* www.stats.gov.cn/english/newsandcomingevents/t20110428_402722244.htm.

Nelson, Moira, and Nathalie Giger (2011). "The Electoral Consequences of Welfare State Retrenchment: Blame Avoidance or Credit Claiming in the Era of Permanent Austerity?" *European Journal of Political Research* 50(1), 1–23.

Neumayer, Eric (2005). "Asylum Recognition Rates in Western Europe: Their Determinants, Variation, and Lack of Convergence." *Journal of Conflict Resolution* 49(1), 43–66.

Oakley, Sharon (2007). "Accelerated Procedures for Asylum in the European Union: Fairness Versus Efficiency." Sussex Migration Working Paper No. 43, Sussex Centre for Migration Research, University of Sussex, April.

OECD (2008). *International Migration Outlook 2008.* Paris: OECD.

(2009). *International Migration Outlook 2009.* Paris: OECD.

(2010). *International Migration Outlook 2010.* Paris: OECD.

(2012). *International Migration Outlook 2012.* Paris: OECD.

(2013). *International Migration Outlook 2013.* Paris: OECD.

(2014a). *International Migration Outlook 2014.* Paris: OECD.

(2014b). "Is Migration Good for the Economy?" *Migration Policy Debates*, May. www.oecd.org/migration/OECD%20Migration%20Policy%20Debates%20Numero%202.pdf.

(2006). *Trends in International Migration: Continuous Reporting System on Migration.* Paris: OECD.

OECD/IDB/OAS (2012). *International Migration in the Americas: Second Report of the Continuous Reporting System on International Migration in the Americas (SICREMI)*. Washington, DC: Organization of American States.

Oishi, Nana (2012). "The Limits of Immigration Policies: The Challenges of Highly Skilled Migration in Japan." *American Behavioral Scientist* 56(8), 1080–100.

Okólski, Marek (2004). "The Effects of Political and Economic Transition on International Migration in Central and Eastern Europe." In *International Migration: Prospects and Policies in a Global Market*, edited by Douglas S. Massey and J. Edward Taylor, 35–58. Oxford: Oxford University Press.

Özden, Caglar, Christopher Parsons, Maurice Schiff, and Terrie Walmsley (2009). "The Evolution of Global Bilateral Migration 1960–2000." Paper presented at International Conference on Migration and Development, Washington, DC, September 10.

Palley, Thomas I. (2004). "From Keynesianism to Neoliberalism: Shifting Paradigms in Economics." In *Neoliberalism: A Critical Reader*, edited by Deborah Johnston and Alfredo Saad-Filho, 20–9. London: Pluto Press.

Palmunen, Aili (2005). "Learning from the Mistakes of the Past: An Analysis of Past and Current Temporary Worker Policies and Their Implications for a Twenty-First Century Guest Worker Program." *Kennedy School Review* 6, 47.

Papademetriou, Demetrios G. (2002). "A Grand Bargain: Balancing the National Security, Economic, and Immigration Interests of the U.S. and Mexico." Working paper, Washington, DC, Migration Policy Institute, April.

Papadopoulos, Theodoros (2011). "Immigration and the Variety of Migrant Integration Regimes in the European Union." In *Migration and Welfare in the "New" Europe: Social Protection and the Challenges of Integration*, edited by Emma Carmel, Alfio Cerami, and Theodoros Papadopoulos, 23–47. Bristol: Policy Press.

Parkes, Roderick, and Steffen Angenendt (2010). "After the Blue Card: EU Policy on Highly Qualified Migration." Discussion paper, Heinrich Böll Foundation, Berlin, February.

Paul, Kathleen (1995). "'British Subjects' and 'British Stock': Labour's Postwar Imperialism." *Journal of British Studies* 34, 233–76.

Paul, Regine (2013). "Strategic Contextualisation: Free Movement, Labour Migration Policies and the Governance of Foreign Workers in Europe." *Policy Studies* 34(2), 122–41.

Penninx, Rinus (2005). "Integration of Migrants: Economic, Social, Cultural and Political Dimensions." In *The New Demographic Regime: Population Challenges and Policy Responses*, edited by Miroslav Macura, Alphonse L. MacDonald, and Werner Haug, 137–52. New York: United Nations Population Fund.

Peters, Margaret E (2017). *Trading Barriers: Immigration and the Remaking of Globalization*. Princeton: Princeton University Press.

Piper, Nicola (2005). *Migrant Labor in Southeast Asia: Country Study: Singapore*. Singapore: Asian Research Institute Friedrich Ebert Stiftung (FES) Project on Migrant Labor in South East Asia.

Piper, Nicola, and Keiko Yamanaka (2008). "Feminised Migration in East and Southeast Asia and the Securing of Livelihoods." In *New Perspectives on Gender and Migration: Livelihoods, Rights and Entitlements*, edited by Nicola Piper, 159–88. London: Routledge.

Plewa, Piotr (2013). "The Politics of Seasonal Labour Migration in Switzerland, France and Spain." *International Migration* 51(6), 101–17.

(2009). "Voluntary Return Programmes: Could They Assuage the Effects of the Economic Crisis?" Working Paper No. 75, Centre on Migration, Policy and Society, University of Oxford.

Portes, Alejandro (1997). "Immigration Theory for a New Century: Some Problems and Opportunities." *International Migration Review* 31, 799–825.

Portes, Alejandro, and Ruben G. Rumbaut (1996). *Immigrant America: A Portrait*. Berkeley: University of California Press.

Razin, Assaf, and Jackline Wahba (2011). "Migration Policy and the Generosity of the Welfare State in Europe." *DICE Report* 9(4), 28–31.

Reichel, David (2012). "Regulating Political Incorporation of Immigrants: Naturalisation Rates in Europe." Working paper, International Centre for Migration Policy Development, Vienna, Austria, December.

(2011). "We Need Different Indicators for Different Research Questions." In *Which Indicators Are Most Useful For Comparing Citizenship Policies?* edited by Rainer Bauböck and Marc Helbling, 7–9. EUI Working Papers, Robert Schuman Centre for Advanced Studies, Florence, Italy.

Rhys, Jane Bristol (2010). "A Lexicon of Migrants in the United Arab Emirates (UAE)." In *Viewpoints: Migration and the Gulf*, 24–6. Washington, DC: Middle East Initiative. See http://www.voltairenet.org/IMG/pdf/Migration_and_the_Gulf.pdf.

Richardson, Sue (1999). *Reshaping the Labour Market: Regulation, Efficiency and Equality in Australia*. Cambridge: Cambridge University Press.

Richardson, Sue, Sue Stack, Megan Moskos, Laurence Lester, Josh Healy, Lauren Miller-Lewis, Diana Ilsley, and John Horrocks (2004). *The Changing Labour Force Experience of New Migrants: Inter-Wave Comparisons for Cohort 1 and 2 of the LSIA*. Canberra: Department of Immigration and Multicultural and Indigenous Affairs.

Roberts, Molly, and Kara Ross Camarena (2012). "It's the Journey, not the Destination: Estimating Refugee Flows from Stock Data." Unpublished working paper. Harvard University.

Rodriguez, Francisco, and Dani Rodrik (2000). "Trade Policy and Economic Growth: A Skeptic's Guide to Cross-National Evidence." In *NBER Macroeconomics Annual 2000*, edited by Benjamin S. Bernake and Kenneth S. Rogoff, 261–338. Cambridge, MA: MIT Press.

Rosenblum, Marc R. (2011). *US Immigration Policy Since 9/11: Understanding the Stalemate over Comprehensive Immigration Reform*. Washington, DC: Migration Policy Institute, and Woodrow Wilson International Center for Scholars.

Rosewarne, Stuart (2010). "Globalisation and the Commodification of Labour: Temporary Labour Migration." *The Economic and Labour Relations Review* 20(2), 99–110.

(2012). "Temporary International Labor Migration and Development in South and Southeast Asia." *Feminist Economics* 18(2), 63–90.

Rothstein, Bo (2011). *The Quality of Government: Corruption, Social Trust and Inequality in International Perspective*. Chicago: University of Chicago Press.

Roylance, Tyler (2015). "Singapore and the Limits of Authoritarian Prosperity." *Freedom House – Freedom at Issue Blog*, March 26. https://freedomhouse.org/blog/singapore-and-limits-authoritarian-prosperity.

Ruhs, Martin (2009). *Migrants Rights, Immigration Policy and Human Development*. Human Development Research Paper 2009/23, United Nations Development Programme, New York, April.

(2010). "Migrant Rights, Immigration Policy and Human Development." *Journal of Human Development and Capabilities* 11(2), 259–79.

(2013). *The Price of Rights: Regulating International Labor Migration*. Princeton: Princeton University Press.

Ruhs, Martin, and Philip Martin (2008). "Numbers Vs. Rights: Trade-Offs and Guest Worker Programs." *The International Migration Review* 42(1), 249–65.

Ruhs, Martin, and Carlos Vargas-Silvia (2015). "The Labour Market Effects of Immigration." Migration Observatory briefing, COMPAS, University of Oxford, May.

Russell, Sharon S. (1989). "Politics and Ideology in Migration Policy Formulation: The Case of Kuwait." *International Migration Review* 23(1), 24–47.

Sahoo, Ajaya K., Dave Sangha, and Melissa Kelly (2010). "From 'Temporary Migrants' to 'Permanent Residents': Indian H-1B Visa Holders in the United States." *Asian Ethnicity* 11(3), 293–309.

Salt, John (1989). "A Comparative Overview of International Trends and Types, 1950–80." *International Migration Review* 23(3), 431–56.

Salt, John, and Janet Dobson (2013). "Cutting Net Migration to the Tens of Thousands: What Exactly Does That Mean?" MRU Discussion Paper, Migration Research Unit, Department of Geography, University College London, London, November.

Sang-Hun, Choe (2009). "South Koreans Struggle with Race." *New York Times*, November 1. www.nytimes.com/2009/11/02/world/asia/02race.html.

SBS (2016). "There Are Now 24 Million Australians." *SBS*, February 16. www.sbs.com.au/news/article/2016/02/16/there-are-now-24-million-australians.

Schain, Martin (2006). "The Extreme-Right and Immigration Policy-Making: Measuring Direct and Indirect Effects." *West European Politics* 29(2), 270–89.

(2012). "On Models and Politics." *Comparative European Politics* 10, 369–76.

(2008). *The Politics of Immigration in France, Britain, and the United States: A Comparative Study, Perspectives in Comparative Politics*. New York: Palgrave Macmillan.

Schneider, Jan, and Axel Kreienbrink (2010). "Return Assistance in Germany: Programmes and Strategies Fostering Return to and Reintegration in Third Countries." Working Paper 21, European Migration Network and Federal Office for Migration and Refugees, Nuremberg.

Schönwälder, Karen, and Triadafilos Triadafilopoulos (2012). "A Bridge or Barrier to Incorporation? Germany's 1999 Citizenship Reform in Critical Perspective." *German Politics & Society* 30(1), 52–70.

Scruggs, Lyle (2014). "Social Welfare Generosity Scores in CWED 2: A Methodological Genealogy." Comparative Welfare Entitlements Dataset Working Paper 01, February.

Scruggs, Lyle, Detlef Jahn, and Kati Kuitto (2014). *Comparative Welfare Entitlements Data Set 1970–2011.* http://cwed2.org/.

Segal, Uma A., Doreen Elliott, and Nazneen S. Mayadas (2010). *Immigration Worldwide: Policies, Practices and Trends.* Oxford: Oxford University Press.

Seol, Dong-Hoon (2012). "The Citizenship of Foreign Workers in South Korea." *Citizenship Studies* 16(1), 119–33.

(2005). "Global Dimensions in Mapping the Foreign Labor Policies of Korea: A Comparative and Functional Analysis." *Development and Society* 34(1), 25–124.

Seol, Dong-Hoon, and John D. Skrentny (2004). "South Korea: Importing Undocumented Workers." In *Controlling Immigration: A Global Perspective,* 2nd edn, edited by Wayne A. Cornelius, Takeyuki Tsuda, Philip L. Martin, and James F. Hollifield, 481–513. Stanford: Stanford University Press.

Shachar, Ayelet (2006). "The Race for Talent: Highly Skilled Migrants and Competitive Immigration Regimes." *New York University Law Review* 81(1), 148–206.

Shah, Nasra M. (2011). "Kuwait's Revised Labor Laws: Implications for National and Foreign Workers." *Asian and Pacific Migration Journal* 20(3–4), 339–63.

(2009). "The Management of Irregular Migration and its Consequences for Development: GCC." Working Paper 19, Asia Regional Programme on Governance of Labour Migration, Bangkok.

(2006). "Restrictive Labour Immigration Policies in the Oil-Rich Gulf: Effectiveness and Implications for Sending Asian Countries." Paper presented at the UN Expert Group Meeting on International Migration and Development in the Arab Region: Challenges and Opportunities, Beirut, Lebanon, May 15–17.

Shah, Nasra, Makhdoom Shah, and Zoran Radovanovic (1998). "Patterns of Desired Fertility and Contraceptive Use in Kuwait." *International Family Planning Perspectives* 24(3), 133–8.

Shaham, Dahlia (2008). "Foreign Labor in the Arab Gulf: Challenges to Nationalization." *al Nakhlah* (Fall), 1–14.

Sharma, Nandita (2006). *Home Economics: Nationalism and the Making of "Migrant Workers" in Canada.* Toronto: University of Toronto Press.

Shu, Jing, and Lesleyanne Hawthorne (1995). "Asian Female Students in Australia: Temporary Movements and Student Migration." *Journal of the Australian Population Association* 12(2), 113–30.

Singapore Department of Statistics (2007). *Population Trends 2007.* Singapore: Department of Statistics, Ministry of Trade & Industry. http://unpan1.un.org/intradoc/groups/public/documents/apcity/unpan030879.pdf.

(2008). *Population in Brief 2008*. Singapore: National Department of Statistics, Ministry of Trade & Industry. www.nptd.gov.sg/PORTALS/o/HOMEPAGE/ HIGHLIGHTS/population-in-brief-2008.pdf.

(2009). *Population in Brief 2009*. Singapore: National Department of Statistics, Ministry of Trade & Industry. www.nptd.gov.sg/content/NPTD/news/_jcr_ content/par_content/download_o/file.res/Population%20in%20Brief%20 2009.pdf.

(2010). *Population in Brief 2010*. Singapore: National Department of Statistics, Ministry of Trade & Industry. www.nptd.gov.sg/content/NPTD/news/_jcr_ content/par_content/download_31/file.res/Population%20in%20Brief%20 2010.pdf.

(2011). *Population in Brief 2011*. Singapore: National Department of Statistics, Ministry of Trade & Industry. http://app.msf.gov.sg/Portals/o/Files/SPRD/ Population%20in%20Brief%202011.pdf.

Singapore Parliament (2011). "Written Answers to Questions: Applications for Permanent Residence." *Singapore Parliament Reports (Hansard)*. Parliament 12, Session 1, Volume 88, Sitting 6. October 21.

Singapore Prime Minister's Office (2012). *Our Population Our Future*. Singapore: National Population and Talent Division.

Skeldon, Ronald (2006). "Interlinkages Between Internal and International Migration in the Asian Region." *Population, Space and Place* 12(1), 15–30.

(2007). "Migration and Labor Markets in Asia and Europe." *Asian and Pacific Migration Journal* 16(3), 425–41.

Smith, Christopher L. (2012). "The Impact of Low-Skilled Immigration on the Youth Labor Market." *Journal of Labor Economics* 30(1), 55–89.

Solimano, André. (2010). *International Migration in the Age of Crisis and Globalization: Historical and Recent Experiences*. Cambridge: Cambridge University Press.

Soysal, Yasemin Nuhoglu (1994). *Limits of Citizenship*. Chicago: University of Chicago Press.

Statistics South Africa (2012). *Documented Immigrants in South Africa*. Pretoria: Statistics South Africa.

Swedish Migration Agency [Migrationsverket] (2015). "Migration and Asylum 2005–2015." Last modified January 20, 2017. www.migrationsverket .se/English/About-the-Migration-Agency/Facts-and-statistics-/Statistics/ Overview-and-time-series.html.

Tan, Soo Kee (2012). "Foreign Workers' Policies and Issues in South Korea." In *Asian Migration Policy: South, Southeast and East Asia*, edited by Mizanur Rahman and Ahshan Ullah, 41–56. New York: Nova Science Publishers, Inc.

Tattolo, Giovanna (2004). "Arab Labor Migration to the GCC States." Working paper, Jean Monnet Observatory on Trans-Mediterranean Relations, Rome.

Tham, Joo-Cheon, and Iain Campbell (2011). "Temporary Migrant Labour in Australia: The Visa Scheme and Challenges for Labour Regulation." Working paper, Centre for Employment and Labour Relations Law, University of Melbourne, March.

Tham, Joo-Cheong, Iain Campbell, and Martina Boese (2016). "Why is Labour Protection for Temporary Migrant Workers So Fraught? An Australian Perspective." In *Temporary Labour Migration in the Global Era: Regulatory Challenges*, edited by Joanna Howe and Rosemary Owens, Chapter 8. London: Hart.

Thielemann, Eiko R. (2006). "The Effectiveness of Governments' Attempts to Control Unwanted Migration." In *Immigration and the Transformation of Europe*, edited by Craig A. Parsons and Timothy M. Smeeding, 442–72. Cambridge: Cambridge University Press.

Thielemann, Eiko, Richard Williams, and Christina Boswell (2010). *What System of Burden-Sharing Between Member States for the Reception of Asylum Seekers?* Brussels: European Parliament.

Thiollet, Helene (2011). "Migration as Diplomacy: Labor Migrants, Refugees, and Arab Regional Politics, in the Oil-Rich Countries." *International Labor and Working-Class History* 79(Special Issue 01), 103–21.

Tichenor, D. (2002). *Dividing Lines: The Politics of Immigration Control in America*. Princeton: Princeton University Press.

Toshkov, Dimiter Doychinov (2014). "The Dynamic Relationship Between Asylum Applications and Recognition Rates in Europe (1987–2010)." *European Union Politics* 15(2), 192–214.

TRAC Immigration (2014). "Ice Deportations: Gender, Age and Country of Citizenship." Last modified April 9, 2014. http://trac.syr.edu/immigration/reports/350/.

Triadafilopoulos, Triadafilos, and Karen Schönwälder (2006). "How the Federal Republic Became an Immigration Country: Norms, Politics and the Failure of West Germany's Guest Worker System." *German Politics and Society* 24(3), 1–19.

Trujillo-Pagán, Nicole (2014). "Emphasizing the 'Complex' in the 'Immigration Industrial Complex.'" *Critical Sociology* 40(1), 29–46.

Tsuda, Takeyuki (1999). "The Permanence of 'Temporary' Migration: The 'Structural Embeddedness' of Japanese-Brazilian Immigrant Workers in Japan." *The Journal of Asian Studies* 58(3), 687–722.

Tsuda, Takeyuki, and Wayne A. Cornelius (2004). "Japan: Government Policy, Immigrant Reality." In *Controlling Immigration: A Global Perspective*, 2nd edn, edited by Wayne A. Cornelius, Takeyuki Tsuda, Philip L. Martin, and James F. Hollifield, 439–76. Stanford: Stanford University Press.

Tuomioja, Erkki (2004). "Migration on the Increase: Is Finland Ready for It?" Tuomioja.org, July 5. http://tuomioja.org/puheet/2004/01/migration-on-the-increase-is-finland-ready-for-it-kulttuurikeskus-caisa-helsinki-7-5-2004/.

United Nations (Department of Economic and Social Affairs) (2009). World Population Aging Population Division, ESA/P/WP/212, December.

United Nations (UN) (2016). "GDP and Its Breakdown at Current Prices in US Dollars." UN Stats. Last modified December 2016. http://unstats.un.org/unsd/snaama/dnlList.asp.

United Nations (UN) (2013). *International Migration Report*. New York: United Nations.

United Nations (UN) (1994). *The Migration of Women: Methodological Issues in the Measurement and Analysis of Internal and International Migration.* Santo Domingo, Dominican Republic: United Nations International Research and Training Institute for the Advancement of Women (INSTRAW).

United Nations (UN) (2006). *State of World Populations: A Passage to Hope, Women and International Migration.* New York: United Nations Population Fund.

United Nations Economic Commission for Europe (UNECE) (2011). *Statistics on International Migration: A Practical Guide for Countries of Eastern Europe and Central Asia.* Geneva: United Nations.

United Nations Population Division (UNPD) (1998). *International Migration Policies.* New York: UN Department of Economic and Social Affairs.

United Nations Population Division (UNPD) (2008). *International Migration Flows To and From Selected Countries: The 2008 Revision.* New York: UN Department of Economic and Social Affairs. CD-ROM.

United Nations Population Division (UNPD) (2012). "Migrants by Origin and Destination: The Role of South-South Migration." *Population Facts,* June. www.un.org/esa/population/publications/popfacts/popfacts_2012-3_South-South_migration.pdf.

United Nations Population Division (UNPD). (2013). *Trends in International Migration Stock: Migrants by Destination and Origin.* New York: United Nations Department of Economic and Social Affairs. United Nations database, POP/DB/MIG/Stock/Rev.2013.

United Nations Population Division (UNPD) (2015). *Trends in International Migration Stock: The 2015 Revision.* New York: United Nations Department of Economic and Social Affairs.

United Nations Development Program Kuwait (UNDP Kuwait) (2011). "UNDP Jobs–24608- Consultant to Develop a National Youth Strategy for the State of Kuwait." United Nations Development Program Jobs. https://jobs.undp.org/cj_view_job.cfm?cur_job_id=24608.

USCIS (2015). "USCIS Expands Efforts to Highlight Citizenship and Immigrant Integration." U.S. Citizenship and Immigration Services, September 17. www.uscis.gov/news/news-releases/uscis-expands-efforts-highlight-citizenship-and-immigrant-integration.

Van Amersfoort, Hans, and Rinus Penninx (1994). "Regulating Migration in Europe: The Dutch Experience, 1960–92." *The Annals of the American Academy of Political Science* 534, 133–46.

Van Oers, Ricky (2013). *Deserving Citizenship: Citizenship Tests in Germany, the Netherlands and the United Kingdom.* Leiden: Brill.

Van Riemsdijk, Micheline (2011). "Rescaling Governance of Skilled Migration in the European Union: The European Blue Card." *Population, Space and Place* 18(3), 344–58.

Van Spanje, Joost (2010). "Contagious Politics." *Party Politics* 16(5), 563–86.

Vertovec, Steven (2007). "Circular Migration: The Way Forward in Global Policy?" International Migration Institute Working Papers, International Migration Institute, University of Oxford, Oxford.

Vieira, Ricardo, and José Trindade (2008). "Migration, Culture and Identity in Portugal." *Language and Intercultural Communication* 8(1), 36–49.

Vink, Maarten (2005). *The Limits of European Citizenship*. New York: Palgrave Macmillan.

(2011). "Naturalisation Rates and Rejection Rates Measure Different Phenomena, and Have Different Problems." In *Which Indicators Are Most Useful For Comparing Citizenship Policies?* edited by Rainer Bauböck and Marc Helbling, 11–13. EUI Working Papers, Robert Schuman Centre for Advanced Studies, Florence, Italy.

Vink, Maarten, and Rainer Bauböck (2013). "Citizenship Configurations: Analysing the Multiple Purposes of Citizenship Regimes in Europe." *Comparative European Politics* 11(5), 621–48.

Vis, Barbara (2010). *The Politics of Risk-Taking*. Amsterdam: Amsterdam University Press.

Wanner, Richard A. (2003). "Entry Class and the Earnings Attainments of Immigrants to Canada, 1980–1995." *Canadian Public Policy* 29(1), 53–71.

Watkins, Tate, and Bruce Yandle (2010). "Can Freedom and Knowledge Economy Indexes Explain Go-Getter Migration Patterns?" *Journal of Regional Analysis and Policy* 40(2), 104–15.

Wickramasekara, Piyasiri (2013). "Circular and Temporary Migration Regimes and Their Implications for Families." QScience Proceedings, Family, Migration and Dignity Special Issue. See www.qscience.com/doi/pdf/10.5339/qproc.2013.fm.

Wimmer, Andreas, and Nina Glick Schiller (2002). "Methodological Nationalism and Beyond: Nation-State Building, Migration and the Social Sciences." *Global Networks* 2(4), 301–34.

Wooldridge, Jeffrey M. (2013). *Introductory Econometrics: A Modern Approach*. Boston: Cengage Learning.

World Bank (2013a). "Population 65 and Above (% of total)." World Bank. http://data.worldbank.org/indicator/SP.POP.65UP.TO.ZS.

(2013b). "Total Resource Rents (% of GDP)." World Bank. http://data.worldbank.org/indicator/NY.GDP.TOTL.RT.ZS.

(2013c). "Unemployment, Total (% of total labor force)." World Bank. http://data.worldbank.org/indicator/SL.UEM.TOTL.ZS.

Wray, Helena, Agnes Agoston, and Jocelyn Hutton (2014). "A Family Resemblance? The Regulation of Marriage Migration in Europe." *European Journal of Migration and Law* 16(2), 209–47.

Wright, Chris F. (2014). "How Do States Implement Liberal Immigration Policies? Control Signals and Skilled Immigration Reform in Australia." *Governance* 27(3), 397–421.

Xu, Qingwen (2007). "Globalization, Immigration and the Welfare State: A Cross-National Comparison." *Journal of Sociology and Social Welfare* 34(2), 87–106.

Yakovlev, Pavel, and Tanner Steinkopf (2014). "Can Economic Freedom Cure Medical Brain Drain?" *Journal of Private Enterprise* 29(3), 97–117.

Yap, Mui Teng (1999). "The Singapore State's Responses to Migration." *SOJOURN* 14(1), 198–211.

Yeoh, Brenda S. A., and Weiqiang Lin (2012). *Rapid Growth in Singapore's Immigrant Population Brings Policy Challenges.* Washington, DC: Migration Policy Institute.

Zaslove, Andrej (2004). "Closing the Door? The Ideology and Impact of Radical Right Populism on Immigration Policy in Austria and Italy." *Journal of Political Ideologies* 9(1), 99–118.

Zavis, Alexandra (2016). "Haitians, Africans, Asians: The Sharp Rise in Non-Latin American Migrants Trying to Cross into the Us from Mexico." *LA Times,* December 22. www.latimes.com/projects/la-fg-immigration-trek-america-tijuana/.

Zhang, Xiang (2011). "NW China's Gansu Province Grants 'Green Cards' to Foreigners." *Xinhua,* July 21. http://news.xinhuanet.com/english2010/china/2011-07/21/c_131000923.htm.

Zimmermann, Klaus F. (2005). *European Migration: What Do We Know?* Oxford: Oxford University Press.

Zlotnik, Hania (1992). "Empirical Identification of International Migration Systems." In *International Migration Systems: A Global Approach,* edited by Mary M. Kritz, Lin Lean Lim, and Hania Zlotnik, 19–40. Oxford: Clarendon Press.

   (1998). "International Migration 1965–96: An Overview." *Population and Development Review* 24(3), 429–68.

Zou, Le (2012). "Fears Grow That Hard Green Card Rules Turning Foreigners Away from China." *The Global Times,* May 3. www.globaltimes.cn/NEWS/tabid/99/ID/707519/Fears-grow-that-hard-green-card-rules-turning-foreigners-away-from-China.aspx.

Zulean, Marian, and Irina Roventa (2012). "Romania: Where Europe Ends." In *Opening the Door: Immigration and Integration in the European Union,* edited by Vit Novotny, 92. Brussels: Centre for European Studies.

Index

3/19/20
3